YOUR BILLS IMMEDIATELY?

You don't really need to pay your bills on time. Not unless you especially enjoy granting your creditors interest-free loans, paying them service charges, and helping them to reap windfalls through debt leverage. In detail that will enrage you, and language that will make you laugh out loud, "YOUR CHECK IS IN THE MAIL" prepares you to do battle against the credit establishment with their own weapons.

- Use their computer to help you delay payment.
- Outfox the collectors who threaten you with counterploys of your own.
- Pay a little at the right time and you may escape paying any more at all.
- Wipe out your debts completely, with perfect legality and have thousands of dollars in cash assets left.

Give everyone a run for his money by using yours longer. "YOUR CHECK IS IN THE MAIL" can prove to you that you can buy an awful lot now—and pay for it an awful lot later.

"YOUR CHECK IS IN THE MAIL"

How to Stay Legally and Profitably in Debt

Bruce Goldman
Robert Franklin
Kenneth Pepper, Esquire

WARNER BOOKS

A Warner Communications Company

To
John Maynard Keynes
the father of deficit spending

Contents

Introduction

In late April, 1974, the publisher of the hardbound version of this book sent the manuscript to the printer.

In June, 1974, with a lot of hustling and a little luck, the publisher should put the book on sale.

But, if he follows accepted trade practices, he probably won't get around to paying the printer until, at the earliest, August. That's because the bookseller won't get around to paying *him* until September or October.

The majority of people who buy this book, however, will pay cash on the barrelhead. While the bookstores, the publisher, and the printer who get this cash will use it as two- to four-month interest-free loans before relinquishing a share of it to the companies that they owe money to. And the publishing industry is not some kind of weird exception to the way that business is generally done with the consuming public; rather, it's a perfectly typical example of the general rule.

There's a huge inverted pyramid of interest-free loans

to business made in this manner, and its point rests squarely between your shoulder blades.

Unfortunately, if you're like most consumers, your efforts to ease the burden only make it heavier. Because the method of "relief" that most people turn to is interest-bearing credit, and rising prices have made more Americans turn to it than ever before.

In 1973, more than $13.8 billion worth of goods, services, and cash advances were charged to bank credit cards, up $3.3 billion from the year before. And at the end of the year, more than one-third of that money—$5.6 billion, to be specific—was still owing. And that's just for bank cards. People also owed $6.5 billion to retail store charges and a mere $1.8 million to travel-and-entertainment and gasoline cards.*

In the event that numbers that big seem somewhat meaningless, one woman in New Orleans described what this means on a personal level. "I'm forever running out of cash," she told a New York *Times* reporter. "One trip to the grocery store shoots the whole wad, so . . . I use my credit cards every chance I get. That way you can stall paying a while."†

And that is precisely what this book is all about. For too long, there's been a double standard of bill payment in this country, where your creditors take as long as they want to pay up on their obligations, while you must either pay cash or pay interest, or both. After reading the book, you should be able to make your own individual contribution to redressing the balance.

Of course, the book also offers more tangible benefits. For example, it can save you from signing away your rights, protections, and bargaining power for the dubious privilege of getting into the wrong kind of debt.

It can show you how to save hundreds of dollars a year by circumventing interest and "service" charges. (On bank cards alone, assuming the lower of the two interest rates charged—12 percent annually for cash advances—

*John H. Allan, "As Prices Soar, Bank-Card Use Jumps," New York *Times*, April 22, 1974.
†Allan, "As Prices Soar, Bank-Card Use Jumps."

this works out to just under $1.7 billion per year nationally.)

It can show you how to use credit to protect yourself against unscrupulous merchants and purveyors of shoddy goods and services.

It can show you how to manipulate "customer service" bureaucracies—seemingly composed of the deaf, the illiterate, and the criminally insane—for quick action, and how to use the bureaucracies' own strong points against them when you want interest-free delay.

Finally, it can let you use credit to improve your standard of living by practicing your creditors' technique of living on other people's money.

But before you can use credit to do any of these things, you have to be able to get it.

The New Orleans woman quoted before and her husband are an upper-middle-class couple and, as such, have a lot of credit sources available. The wife has a wallet stuffed with BankAmericard, Master Charge, Sears card, J.C. Penney card, Woolco card, Nieman-Marcus card, New Orleans shopper's card, four local charge-account cards, and an assortment of gasoline cards.

Her husband has *two* wallets full of plastic—one for each hip pocket. In addition to all the cards his wife lugs around, he has an American Express card, Playboy card, Hertz card, American International Rentacar card, Fairmont Hotel card, and a card of instruction on what to do if all the other cards are lost or stolen.

Your ability to get credit cards will, of course, vary with your income. But other factors—like how long you've worked at the same job, how long you've lived at the same address, how many dependents you have, and whether you rent or own your home—also figure into it (see charts).

Diners Club will consider applications from people earning a minimum of $10,000 a year. For Carte Blanche, applicants must earn $10,000 a year, be currently employed, and have a checking or savings account. One airline, on the other hand, will give credit cards to people who have lived and worked at the same place for a year and earn as little as $5,000.

11

In New York City, welfare recipients demonstrated to get credit cards from Sears and Korvette's (a discount chain), and these demonstrations met with some success, which, in a perverse way, they should have. At this time, in particular, welfare recipients have a steadier source of income than many highly skilled, highly paid people who work for their money. Also, believe it or not, many welfare families enjoy better real incomes than some blue-collar working families. The Joint Subcommittee on Fiscal Policy of the House of Representatives Joint Economic Committee conducted a nationwide sampling of 1,059 poverty families in six low-income areas in representative parts of the country and found that many so-called poverty families were receiving cash and in-kind benefits from a wide variety of welfare programs (food stamps, day care, medicaid, etc.), and that after computing the cash value of in-kind welfare, the income levels of a sizable percentage exceeded the take-home pay of people who work for a living. About 20 percent of the welfare families were enrolled in five or more federal aid programs, and their monthly incomes ranged from $306 to $676 (this works out to $3,672 to $8,112 per year, *before taxes*). "These tax-free benefits," the Subcommittee reported, "exceed the median wage levels for full-time workingmen, which range from $303 to $502 [per month] in the five urban areas . . . The sizable average benefits going to these [welfare] households indicate that many of them are better off now than they would be if they derived all of their income from wages, given the wage level at which their members would find employment and the social security and income taxes that would have to be paid from those wages.*

Once you get credit, certain other factors will help you make easier use of it. Like living in or near a big city. Just as banks are where the money is, cities are where most of the sources of credit are. Also, living in a city or big suburb gives you the kind of anonymity that protects deadbeats from ostracism—or even discovery. In

*Anthony Dolan, "What Ever Happened to the Welfare Crisis?" *National Review*, February 1, 1974.

12

These are forms that have appeared in bank loan advertising, to encourage people to apply for loans and do the preliminary screening themselves (which saves the loan department the time and money spent on weeding out obvious rejects). Although they're not official and binding loan-rating charts, they do indicate what creditors' values are, and some of these value judgments are surprising. For example, in the left-hand chart (line D), one would assume that because his expenses would be lower, a person living with parents would be a better risk than one living in a furnished apartment, who in turn would be a better risk than one renting an unfurnished apartment, who in turn would be less chancy than one grappling with a home mortgage. However, this is just opposite from the bank's scale of values. Another interesting item on this chart is that the applicant must have lived at a previous address at least six years to get as many points as for living at his present address for three years. It is also interesting to compare the different values pertaining to marital status on the two rating charts. To the loan department using the left-hand chart a single person is just as bad a risk as a separated, divorced, or widowed person, even though separation or divorce may impose a back-breaking alimony burden on the potential borrower. The bank using the right-hand chart seems to have a more realistic view of things, as it does with living facilities. One pleasant surprise from both charts is the relatively low income required for a top rating in the income category. The left-hand bank gives top score for monthly incomes as low as $801 after taxes. This works out to $9612 net annual income, or, with the addition of 25 percent for taxes, $12,015 per year gross income. This is only a few hundred dollars higher than the U.S. median annual household income. The right-hand bank gives top score to $1500 monthly income (gross, we presume), which works out to $18,000 per year and, again, is not as high as you might have expected. Finally, note the last line on the right-hand chart, which shows some additional factors that improve your desirability as a potential borrower.

DIRECTIONS

"Circle the one number on each line that most closely describes you, and enter it in the code box to the right. If you have scored 18 points or more you are eligible for a loan for any worthwhile purpose or for an increase in your line of credit. Just refold, seal and mail today".*

CODE BOX

SAMPLE LINE	18-21 **1**	22-25 **2**	26-40 **2**	41-64 **2**	65 & OVER **1**

AGE

A	18-21 **1**	22-25 **2**	26-40 **2**	41-64 **2**	65 & OVER **1**

MARITAL STATUS

B	SINGLE **1**	SEPARATED **1**	DIVORCED **1**	WIDOWED **1**	MARRIED **2**

DEPENDENTS

C	ONE **2**	TWO **2**	THREE **2**	FOUR **2**	5 OR MORE **1**

LIVING FACILITIES

D	WITH PARENTS **1**	RENT FURN **2**	RENT UNFURN **3**	OWN MTG **5**	OWN NO MTG **6**

YEARS AT PRESENT ADDRESS

E	UNDER 1 YR **1**	1-2 YRS **1**	3-5 YRS **2**	6-10 YRS **3**	OVER 10 YRS **3**

YEARS AT PREVIOUS ADDRESS

F	UNDER 1 YR. **1**	1-2 YRS **1**	3-5 YRS **1**	6-10 YRS **2**	OVER 10 YRS **2**

TOTAL MONTHLY INCOME (take home)

G	UNDER $400 **1**	$400-$600 **2**	$601-$800 **3**	$801-$1000 **5**	OVER $1000 **5**

YEARS WITH PRESENT EMPLOYER

H	UNDER 1 YR **1**	1-3 YRS **2**	4-6 YRS **3**	7-10 YRS. **4**	OVER 10 YRS **5**

MO. RENT OR MORTGAGE PYMT.

I	UNDER $100 **2**	$100-$135 **2**	$136-$175 **2**	$176-$200 **2**	OVER $200 **2**

TOTAL MO. OBLIGATIONS (exclude rent or mtg. pymt.)

J	UNDER $75 **3**	$201-$300 **2**	$126-$200 **2**	$75-$125 **2**	OVER $300 **1**

OCCUPATION

K	PART-TIME **1.**	UNSKILLED **2**	SKILLED **3**	EXEC SUPER **3**	PROFESS. **3**

© MOTIVATIONAL SYSTEMS, INC , NEW YORK, N. Y. 1972

TOTAL

Reminder: If you score 18 points or more — mail today! Less than 18 points? Let's talk!

*The right of final approval is reserved by the bank.

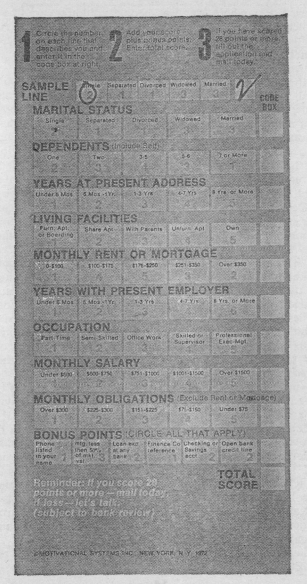

1 Circle the number on each line that describes you and enter it in the code box at right.

2 Add your score plus bonus points. Enter total score.

3 If you have scored 28 points or more, fill out the application and mail today.

SAMPLE LINE	Single	Separated	Divorced	Widowed	Married	✓	CODE BOX
	(2)	1	1	3	3		

MARITAL STATUS

Single	Separated	Divorced	Widowed	Married
?	1	1	3	3

DEPENDENTS (Include Self)

One	Two	3-5	5-6	7 or More
2	3	4	3	1

YEARS AT PRESENT ADDRESS

Under 6 Mos.	6 Mos.-1 Yr.	1-3 Yrs.	4-7 Yrs.	8 Yrs. or More
1	2	3	4	5

LIVING FACILITIES

Furn. Apt. or Boarding	Share Apt.	With Parents	Unfurn. Apt.	Own
1	2	3	4	5

MONTHLY RENT OR MORTGAGE

0-$100	$100-$175	$176-$250	$251-$350	Over $350
1	4	?	?	2

YEARS WITH PRESENT EMPLOYER

Under 6 Mos.	6 Mos.-1 Yr.	1-3 Yrs.	4-7 Yrs.	8 Yrs. or More
1	2	3	?	6

OCCUPATION

Part-Time	Semi-Skilled	Office Work	Skilled or Supervisor	Professional Exec-Mgt.
1	2	3	?	?

MONTHLY SALARY

Under $600	$600-$750	$751-$1000	$1001-$1500	Over $1500
			4	

MONTHLY OBLIGATIONS (Exclude Rent or Mortgage)

Over $300	$225-$300	$151-$225	$75-$150	Under $75
1	2	3	4	5

BONUS POINTS (CIRCLE ALL THAT APPLY)

Phone listed in your name	mtg. less then 50% of mkt. val.	Loan exp at any bank	Finance Co reference	Checking or Savings acct	Open bank credit line
1	3	2		2	2

Reminder: If you score 28 points or more — mail today, if less — let's talk. (subject to bank review)

TOTAL SCORE

New York, where we live, people couldn't care less if someone were being murdered on their doorsteps. And people who don't react to cold-blooded murder certainly aren't going to get worked up about somebody else's unpaid bills.

If you live in a small town, it would behoove you to deal with national or big-city creditors (this is what's known as not fouling your own nest), or else be known as a member of two categories of people who are virtually immune to small-town moral restrictions: (1) people with old money, who therefore can do no wrong, or (2) artists, musicians, advertising flakes, and other long-haired-Communist-hippie-punk-weirdos, who can do no right, regardless of whether they pay their bills or not.

Occupationally, it helps to work in an office, because you enjoy access to the telephones, typewriters, and duplicating machines that help you deal with creditors on their own level and during normal working hours. But if you do, it's better not to work for a large, paternalistic organization unless you hold down an important enough position in the hierarchy to be exempt from the company's restrictive outlook on its employees' private lives. Companies which have no compunctions about senior vice-presidents sitting down with competitors and conspiring to fix prices or bribe politicians tend to get self-righteous and uptight about junior clerks who get behind on their personal bills.

Nothing suggested in this book is illegal. Nothing is the least bit less moral than what your creditors do in paying *their* bills. And everything is highly effective.

One of the authors used these techniques to finance the renovation of a Manhattan brownstone, which is no minor undertaking. Another uses them to protect himself from, and avenge himself on, those companies abounding in today's throwaway society who are far more interested in collecting money than providing value in return for it.

Naturally, not everyone can derive equal benefit from a book like this, no more than everybody can have equal heights, weights, and incomes.

Generally speaking, the benefit you derive from this book will vary with the amount of time you can spare to

16

apply its principles. The time involved is a few hours a week, either during business hours or on your own time. If you're married, and your wife isn't petrified by a stranger's voice on the phone, her time and resourcefulness will be an asset. How much time and energy you expend will depend on how far into debt you are and how long you want to stay that way, but in any event, it's far less time than most Americans devote to far less profitable pursuits.

Finally, you'll need a certain amount of emotional stamina. Delay, obfuscation, inefficiency, and stupidity are demoralizing, even when the final outcome is in your favor. You'll need the patience to go through weeks, if not months, of what lawyers call building a case.

But in return, you'll get the inner knowledge that you no longer have to be intimidated by a system that owes its success exclusively to the consent of its victims.

CHAPTER ONE

Calvin Died in 1564.
Unfortunately, His Ethic Didn't

IN BIBLICAL TIMES, the lending of money, goods, or services was considered an act of charity; and lending at interest, a sin (Exodus 22:24). In the years since then, mankind has made a tremendous moral progress—to the point where usury is considered a virtue and only inability to pay a sin. This didn't all happen overnight.

The books of Exodus and Deuteronomy contain many commandments concerning debt, all of which favor the person who needs the money most. For example, people who employed day-laborers were required to pay each day's wages in cash before nightfall. But creditors who had taken a debtor's blanket as security for a loan were required to return that security blanket each night. Borrowers were released by law from unpaid debts at the end of every sixth year, and creditors were forbidden to withhold credit simply because the year of release was coming up. Even business loans were required to be interest-free, although in post-Biblical times a creditor could go to the Sancadrin (rabbinical court), obtain a business permit, and transform himself into, in effect, a stockholder in his debtor's venture, assuming a share of the profits or losses.

Charging of interest was permitted on loans to nonresident aliens, the theory being that most strangers passing through were itinerant merchants using the money to make money. Also, with communications so primitive as to make skip-tracing impossible, a certain amount of extra risk was incurred by the lender.

When compared to Judaism, Christianity is a religion more concerned with faith than with laws, but here, too, there is an official attitude that favors the debtor: "Forgive us our debts as we forgive our debtors." (This is from the Lord's Prayer.)

In imperial Rome, under the law of the Twelve Tables, a debtor got a thirty-day grace period after his loan fell due. If he still didn't pay, the creditor could put him in chains, parade him around Rome, and humiliate him publicly as an object lesson to other would-be defaulters; but for the next sixty days, the creditor was prohibited by law from taking drastic action. Drastic action consisted of selling the debtor into slavery, putting him to death, or in case of multiple debt, dividing his body among the creditors (with a sword or some other sharp instrument) in proportion to the respective balances outstanding.

In thirteenth-century Italy, Thomas Aquinas declared that lending money at interest was permissible on loans for the purpose of production. Three centuries later, in England, Henry VIII gave his royal approval to lending at interest for the purpose of consumption.

At about the same time, in Geneva, John Calvin promulgated ideas that at first glance seem irrelevant to the entire subject of credit: that hard work was intrinsically virtuous and leisure intrinsically sinful, that a strong correlation existed between heavenly grace and temporal wealth and power, that obedience to established authority was therefore a sacred duty, and as a corollary, that paying bills (along with such other moral imperatives as not kissing your wife in public and not playing cards on Sunday) was at least as important as fearing God.

In our own time, the permissiveness of Thomas Aquinas and Henry Tudor has been combined with the barbarity of the law of the Twelve Tables and the sanctimonious puritanism of the Calvinist ethic to produce a system that oppreses credit purchasers in a country that wasn't born until more than two centuries after Calvin died: the United States of America.

It's highly ironic that in America—the America brought forth upon this continent by heretics, felons, indentured servants, inmates of debtors' prisons, and other assorted ne'er-do-wells; the America of black liberation, women's liberation, and gay liberation—there is no such thing as debtors' liberation. In 1972, Americans made $127,332,000,000* (that's 127 *billion* dollars) worth of installment-credit purchases, which, estimating our population at 200 million, works out to $636.66 of debt for every man, woman, and child in the United States. (The country's total debts—including those racked up by businesses and big government—exceed $2.8 *trillion,* with each citizen's share of that debt exceeding $13,000.)† Yet, we Americans are still in such thrall to the ethic of a man dead and buried for over four centuries that 99 percent of us pay our bills, and 95 percent of us pay them on time. To look at these figures another way, only 4 percent of American bill payers pay late, and only 1 percent fail to pay at all.‡

But perhaps the greatest irony is that many countries which got their Calvinism firsthand cling to it far less tenaciously than we do. In France, for example, tax

---

*This figure breaks down as follows:

Automobile loans	$44,122,000,000
Repair and modernization loans	6,201,000,000
Personal loans	36,922,000,000
Credit for consumer goods (including charge accounts and credit cards)	40,080,000,000

The last figure, which covers the kind of debt this book is talking about, represents almost a third of the total.

†Of this, corporations owe $1 trillion, governments about $1 trillion, and mortgagees $600 million, which makes the $200 million consumer debt look like peanuts by comparison.

‡Figures from "Privacy, The Horror Side of Credit," *Modern Living, Time,* December 20, 1968.

evasion and double sets of books (one for real, one for the tax man) are not only socially acceptable but popular practices. In England, banks honor checking customers' overdrafts as a matter of course, and paying a bespoke tailor the full amount due for a bill is tantamount to giving him his walking papers.

Perhaps the reason for our country's singular attitude toward bill paying is the result of its singular technological-business progress. Along with the blessings of inflation, pollution, over-production, and radical chic, this progress has made us the beneficiaries of systematic, scientific techniques for persuading us to buy more than we can afford and then for making us suffer the consequences. First, we are told to buy what we want now, regardless of whether we can afford it with cash on hand or in savings. Then, we're encouraged to buy now and pay (a lot more) later by signing up for credit at interest rates exceeding what the laws define as usury.* And finally, we're subjected to defamation, fraud, insult, invasion of privacy, and extortion as creditors bear down, on the debtors that they themselves have overburdened, to enforce the Calvinist ethic.

Enforce it, that is, for everyone but themselves.

The New York Telephone Company, for example, receives a minimum of $70 million per month in interest-free loans through the simple expedient of wording their monthly phone bills in such a way that the charge for one month's service in advance appears to be a charge for the past month's service.

Until the state attorney general's office made them cut it out, the Waldorf-Astoria Hotel was not above inflating each guest's bill with a two-dollar-a-day charge for "sundries," regardless of whether or not such sundries were used or whether, in fact, they even existed.

In full-page, national magazine advertisements ad-

---

*New York State's Usury Law, for example, defines rates above 8 percent as usurious. However, there's also a Revolving Credit Law, put on the books as the result of pressure from banks, department stores, and other revolving-credit lenders, which permits interest as high as 18 percent per year—when charged by banks, department stores, and other revolving-credit lenders.

dressed to financial officers of companies doing large credit business, the cash management division of First National Bank in St. Louis stated, "Fast coming in. Slow going out. In effective cash management, isn't that what it's all about?" Unfortunately, the ad made no mention of whether that attitude carries over to the bank's own loan customers.

Lennen & Newell was one of the 25 largest advertising agencies in the country, and their annual billings exceeded the national budgets of many smaller nations. Combined. Yet in early 1973, Lennen & Newell declared bankruptcy and later went out of business because several of its clients—including blue-chip corporations listed in *Fortune*'s 500—couldn't be bothered with paying several million dollars' worth of bills for television time, which the agency had to shell out itself to the networks.

Of course, if Lennen & Newell followed standard advertising agency practice for payment of bills, they were merely hoist, albeit on a larger scale, on their own petard. Contracts between advertising agencies and unions representing actors appearing in commercials stipulate that actors must be paid a studio fee within ten days after a shooting session. Yet, when one actress played a role in a commercial, more than a month went by before the accounting department of Young & Rubicam, the third-largest advertising agency in the country, exhausted its catalogue of excuses and coughed up the money she'd earned, was entitled to, and in fact, needed to live on.

Movie theaters are so behind in paying studios for film rentals that in March, 1970, two studios—Universal and 20th Century-Fox—started assessing 1½ percent per month late fees. Of course, all that time the movie theaters were getting away with late payments without interest, you paid promptly at the box office whenever you went to see a movie.

In today's economic squeeze, slow bill paying coupled with fast bill collection is a trick that many of your creditors use to take money out of not only your pocket but the pockets of *their* creditors as well.

According to Dun & Bradstreet, some 918 companies went out of business in 1972, apparently because they

22

couldn't collect on their receivables. In most cases, these receivables were owed by other companies they were doing business with, as evidenced by the fact that the failure rate for manufacturers and wholesalers was four to five times as high as the rate for retailers.*

In the second quarter of 1969, a National Association of Credit Management survey of 447 manufacturers' past-due bills (note: manufacturers generally sell to middle-man businesses and rarely, if ever, to the consuming public) showed that uncollected bills equaled 41.3 days' sales, an all time high since the survey was first instituted.

Wall Street Journal interviews with executives of thirty manufacturing and service companies selling primarily if not completely to other companies revealed the following:†

80 percent complained of marked increases in uncollected bills.

Almost all admitted—off the record, of course—that their companies were coping by slowing down their own bill payments. "Sure our customers have slowed their bill paying, but so have we," admitted the financial vice-president of an office equipment manufacturer.

Big, prosperous companies were no faster in paying their bills than small, hungry outfits. According to an officer of a small electronics company, "I'd have to bite my tongue to keep from saying what I'm tempted to say about some of our so-called triple A, blue-chip customers who are slow paying their bills."

At the company's 1974 stockholders' meeting, David Ogilvy, chairman of Ogilvy & Mather International, advertising, reported that while billing rose 13 percent, uncollected receivables rose 43 percent, or more than

---

The Business Failure Record 1972, Business Economics Department, Dun & Bradstreet, Inc.

†Harlan S. Byrne, "Tardy Bill Payers—Many Firms Conserve Their Cash by Delays in Settling Accounts," *Wall Street Journal*, October 21, 1969.

three times as much as billings. If the corporations his agency did business with paid on time, Ogilvy estimated his company would have had an extra $20 million to invest or use to pay off bank loans.*

In short, there is a double standard. Many companies constantly hound you to pay your bills quickly, but quick payment of bills is something they'd rather preach than practice. This being the case, there's nothing morally wrong with treating your creditors the way they treat theirs.

There's also nothing very hard about it. When one company stiffs another, it doesn't come right out and say, "We're not paying our bills." Instead, it resorts to one of a number of subterfuges, which creditors often see through but have to put up with if they're not going to destroy all hope of repeat business.

According to the same *Wall Street Journal* survey, the favorite ploy is to blame delays on computer malfunctions. "I could retire if I had a dollar for every time I've heard that one," said a vice-president of a business forms company. Another tactic is prolonged complaint about the quantity or quality of the goods received or the arithmetic in the bill, which can delay payment for about a year and often produce a discount from the original price as well.

Still another gambit is a deliberate slowdown in the accounting department. "Credit men say that many of the late-payment checks they have been getting are dated two or even three months earlier. They say this means that the check went through the usual processing steps only to be waylaid while passing through the customer's treasurer for signing and mailing."†

Late payment of bills is relatively easy for the individual credit customer to get away with. You may recall that 5 percent of the people pay bills either late or not at all. But in a country of more than 200 million, that's 10 million people.

*Philip H. Dougherty, "Advertising: Late-Paying Clients," *New York Times,* May 14, 1974.
†Byrne, "Tardy Bill Payers."

Treating your creditors the way they treat theirs also has a number of practical advantages. For example, about the only time most creditors will listen to complaints about goods, services, or billing practices is when they have to in order to get paid. This, incidentally, is a matter of practice, not of theory. The theory is that you pay for your purchases like a good little sheep, and then, if something goes wrong, you approach the creditor, hat in hand, for your money back. When this fails, you take him to court, where you're forced to stand alone against a corporate legal staff hired to delay, postpone, or complicate the matter until you either give up in disgust or settle out of court for less than you're entitled to.

But when you withhold payment in the first place, and defects are discovered later, the creditor must sue you. Which gives you an excellent defense in court and, with the proper strategy, places all the advantages of court delay and the resulting pressures to abandon the case on your side. As you'll see later on, this usually gets you off free or at the worst, gets you off at a discount.

But even if you lose in court, you're far from lost. Contrary to what they'd have you believe, creditors can't put you in prison for nonpayment of money you owe them (exceptions: the Internal Revenue Service and divorced wives who haven't gotten their alimony). The worst they can do is repossess the merchandise (after you've had free use of it), or if they go into court, persevere, and win, they can make you pay the amount you originally owed in the first place, plus interest.

Keeping the disputed money in a savings account can offset the cost of interest charged by the court,* but even

* Interest on a judgment is not the 18 percent per year you'd have had to pay if you'd gone through normal credit channels, but a considerably lower rate set by state law. This varies with prevailing interest rates and in the last few years in New York State has ranged from 5½ percent to 7½ percent. So by putting the unpaid money into a 5¾ percent savings account, you could come out on the wrong side of a lawsuit, yet not too far behind.

If you made the mistake of getting into an 18 percent a year interest account, the 5½ to 7½ percent interest charged by law will be computed on the 18 percent interest as well as on the

25

if you spent the money instead, you'd still profit. You see, one of the most expensive things that money can buy these days is money.

Mortgage interest rates are so high, for example, that in June, 1973, Wright Patman, chairman of the House Banking and Currency Committee, called for the creation of a federal agency to make loans to home buyers who couldn't afford the banks' rates.

"Executive credit," bank credit cards, and revolving charge accounts cost 18 percent a year on purchases and 12 percent on cash advances (which means you can save 6 percent by drawing cash advances to pay for purchases). Even bank loans, the cheapest form of credit available to consumers, run as high as 7 to 8 percent discounted in advance, which works out to an *effective* interest rate of 14 to 16 percent.†

Interest rates being what they are, most people who need money today can't afford to pay for it. And unfortunately, all too many people need money.

In December, 1968, *Life* magazine showed how six typical families were making—or, as it turned out, failing to make—ends meet on incomes ranging from $19,000 to $24,000 a year. And mind you, that was in 1968 when $20,000 was still worth the paper it was printed on and before government price controls "reduced" inflation from 3.8 percent to 9 percent a year.

One family habitually took out bank loans of $3,500 to $5,000 each year for eight years. Another charged 75 percent of its purchases, saved absolutely nothing, and wondered where its $20,000 a year went. (A home mortgage and a car loan were outstanding, and "it is customary for neither [husband nor wife] to carry more than a

---

purchase price. But if you have a halfway decent defense (an ignored complaint, for example), you could end up with the 18 percent interest not being included in the amount of the judgement.

† Let's say you borrow $1,000 for one year. The bank gives you $920 and keeps $80 for interest. At the beginning of the year, you owe $1,000; at the end of the year, zero. This gives you an average balance of $500, of which $80 is 16 percent.

single dollar bill, although both have wallets bulging with charge-a-plates."*)

A third family paid cash for everything, in the somewhat misguided belief that doing so would keep them "out of trouble," a state of being that in their case consisted of wearing homemade tennis clothes, giving their son do-it-yourself haircuts, depending on their own garden as their sole source of fresh vegetables, and having a savings account balance of zero.

Now if this family, earning $20,000 a year before taxes and probably about $17,000 after and spending every penny of it, bought everything on credit instead of in cash, they could have substantially increased their effective gross income by making their creditors' money available to themselves. (This is the acceptable business practice called *leverage*.) They could have profited by investing their money. They could have come out ahead by avoiding creditors' finance charges. And they could have made a killing on inflation. Regardless of how terrible inflation is, it does have one important advantage: It invariably tends to favor the debtors. As prices go up, the value of the money that pays those prices goes down. The dollars paid back later are actually worth less in terms of real purchasing power than the same dollars paid back earlier. And this results in a cash discount for the late-paying debtor.

With the 1973 inflation rate, this nets out to a discount of about 9 percent.

In terms of actual price increases, buying early and paying late can save considerably more than that. Taking the period from May, 1972, to April, 1973, as an example, the Consumer Price Index † shows that meats, poultry, and fish were 24.7 percent more expensive, fresh fruits up 113.8 percent, onions 171.4 percent. Compared to those figures, a 10.9 percent rise in the cost of men's work shoes, a 10.1 percent increase in the cost of women's

*"Almost All of Them End Up in the Red," *Life*, December 20, 1968.
† Compiled by the U.S. Bureau of Labor Statistics, Washington, D.C.

27

haircuts, a 9.8 percent boost to the price of used cars, and the fact that operating room expenses went up by 6.7 percent almost look like big savings. Of course, all those figures were compiled for the year ending April, 1973, and therefore take no account of the recent rise of approximately 50 percent in the price of a gallon of gasoline, when you can get it, and the 30 percent cost increase in mailing a letter after midnight, December 28, 1975.

For the fourth quarter of 1974, the inflation rate was 14.4 percent.

Steady inflation even favors debtors paying off loans, on time, and with interest. Figures compiled by *Money* magazine show that steady 5 percent inflation can reduce the 10 percent interest on a three-year auto loan to an effective 3 percent and the 9 percent interest on a twenty-five-year mortgage to practically nothing (see charts). And those figures were based on 5 percent inflation, which is less than one-half the rate of inflation rate that we have now.

At the inflation rate of the fourth quarter of 1974, even someone making overdrafts on his bank card or line-of-credit checking account and paying interest at the rate of 12 percent per year stands to make a 2.4 percent annual profit.

In fact, according to Dr. Ernest J Oppenheimer, financial consultant and authority on inflation, the big losers are not the people who go into debt, not the people who spend their money, but the people who indulge in the traditional Calvinist virtues of thrift and prompt bill payment. "A rate of inflation of one percent," he writes, "will reduce the purchasing power of savers in the aggregate by $25 billion. At the same time, it will give all borrowers a windfall of the same amount . . . It involves the repayment of debts with sharply depreciated currencies . . . In the aggregate, savers are losing an estimated $200 billion in purchasing power in 1974 alone. If one applies this analysis to the past few years, one would find that savers have lost many hundreds of billions of dollars to inflation, making them by far the greatest victims of this scourge . . . In effect, frugal people have been subsidizing those who have lived beyond their means (the most notable of whom is the federal government, followed closely by the government of the city of New York) . . . Viewed from this vantage point, inflation can be readily understood. It enables borrowers to pursue their spending spree without worrying about ever having to meet their obligations in full."*

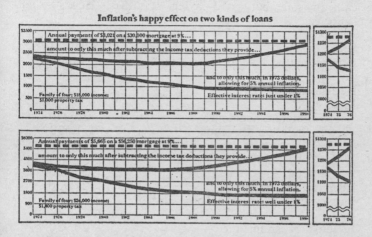

Inflation's happy effect on two kinds of loans

Twenty-five-year mortgages at 9% and three-year auto loans of $3,300 at 10% (right) demonstrate a beneficial aspect of inflation. The effective interest rate on the auto loans will be slightly under 3% for the $18,000 family, just over 2% for the family with $24,000 income. The graphs assume a property tax increase of 5% a year and salary increases of 8% (historically, wages have risen about 3% faster than inflation); state income tax is based on New Mexico's, which is roughly average.

REPRINTED FROM PAGE 44 OF THE NOVEMBER 1973 ISSUE OF MONEY MAGAZINE BY SPECIAL PERMISSION; © 1973, TIME INC. GRAPHS BY DONALD CREWS.

*Ernest J. Oppenheimer, " 'Disguised Bankruptcy' That's What Inflation Really Adds Up To" *Barron's* October 28, 1974.

What this all means is that debtors who pay late profit in two ways: They buy now, before prices get still higher; and they pay later, with dollars whose value is even lower.

Here's how everything works out in concrete terms. Let's take a family of four with a household income of $20,000 per year. Assume that this family buys everything on credit, stalls creditors for a year, and invests the cash in safe but good-paying securities. Here's what happens:

Gross income	$20,000
Less estimated federal income tax*	3,000
Net income	17,000
Plus:	
12% interest avoidance	$2,040
9% inflation discount†	1,530
8% investment income	1,360
Subtotal	4,930
Effective net income	21,930
Plus estimated federal income tax*	5,000
Effective gross income	26,930
Less initial gross income	20,000
Effective raise	$ 6,930

In short, we're not talking about peanuts here. We're talking about a raise of almost $7,000 a year. This raise works out to $133.27 a week. On the basis of a five-day, thirty-five hour week, that's $26.65 per day or $3.81 per

* Based on married wage-earner, four exemptions, standard deduction. In order to keep things simple and uniform, these estimates ignore social security withholding as well as state and city income taxes, state disability and unemployment insurance withholding where applicable, and voluntary deductions like health insurance, union dues, bond-a-month plan, etc.

†With today's inflation rates, this is a highly conservative estimate.

hour. Which means that every minute you delay a creditor (assuming you earn $20,000 and have a family of four) is $.06 in your pocket. And all on only three or four hours of your time, at most, per week.

Unless you're so kindly disposed toward your creditors that you enjoy granting them interest-free loans, paying them interest, and helping them reap windfalls through debt leverage, there's much to be said for buying an awful lot now and paying for it an awful lot later.

You will please note, however, that paying later is not the same as not paying at all. There's nothing moral about outright theft. And besides, that you *can* be put in jail for.

Slow payment, on the other hand, is neither immoral nor illegal. You can be sued for it, but you can't be put in jail. It has the seal of approval of American commerce (in practice, if not in pronouncement) and of the United States government itself, which, since 1933, has been spending money it didn't have and calling the technique *deficit spending*. (Money paid out for social security in the 1930s, for example, came from money that the Social Security Administration didn't expect to receive until the 1950s.) "Ever since the New Deal," Dr. Oppenheimer writes, "the U.S. economy has been rigged in favor of spenders and against savers."*

Of course, since people can't get away with as much as governments can, you may fear that you won't be able to get away with deficit spending for as long as the government has. You may fear that long-term deficit spending will catch up with you in the long run, just as it's now starting to catch up with the government. But one or two years of stalling is hardly the long run. Besides, as John Maynard Keynes, the father of deficit spending, wrote: "In the long run, we shall be dead."

*Ernest J. Oppenheimer, op. cit.

CHAPTER TWO

Choose Your Creditors as Carefully as They Choose You

ORDINARILY, WHEN PEOPLE consider debt (which is what credit is), they ask two questions: "Should I get into debt?" And, if yes: "How much debt should I get into?"

If you bought this book and are still reading it, the answer to question one is obviously yes. The answer to question two must come from your expert, intimate, up-to-date knowledge of your own finances.

Unfortunately, two other, more important questions generally go unanswered, largely because they almost invariably go unasked by people who should know better: "What *kind* of debt should I get into?" And: "To whom?"

Although creditors will generally open accounts for as many suckers as are available, they do exercise some selectivity, and it would behoove you to exercise at least as much as they do before you go charging off all over town. All debts are not created equal.

For example, types of debts that credit establishments encourage you to get into are almost always less advantageous to you than the kinds of debt they shut up about.

Especially when they talk about replacing one kind of debt with another. In debt-consolidation loans, finance companies encourage you to replace all your relatively low-interest or no-interest monthly payments with one "smaller" monthly payment. True, the payment is lower, but considerably more of it goes for interest (i.e., to the finance company as profit). Also, they go on longer, so the smaller monthly payments add up to a considerably larger amount than the sum of the payments they replaced, once you eventually finish paying them out (you should live so long).

Another example: Come late March, the banks come out with ads saying, "Who [sic] would you rather owe—the government or, us?"—the implication being that if you can't pay your income taxes on time, the bank would be a more benign creditor than the Internal Revenue Service and its state counterparts. In fact, the opposite is true.

At the time the ad quoted ran, owing the bank cost 8 percent per year discounted in advance, which (as explained in Chapter 1) is a real interest rate of 16 percent. Owing the government entailed interest of 6 percent on the outstanding balance, a saving of almost two-thirds. Moreover, the procedure for getting a 6 percent loan from the government was far simpler than that for obtaining a 16 percent loan from the bank, and the government, being a government, is far more lax in collecting.

Still another form of debt that creditors encourage and that you should avoid (for reasons to be discussed shortly) is the highly advertised bank "credit card"—Master Charge, BankAmericard, and the gold American Express card*—that banks were so anxious to get into the wallets of potential debtors that they mailed them out unsolicited until various state attorneys general and the Feds made them stop.

But these are specifics, and a general rule is probably more useful. It just so happens there is one: "Borrowing" goods and services is much better than borrowing money. You have more rights and safeguards.

*Remember: the *gold* American Express card is a bank credit card. You have to apply for it through a bank, and a list of participating banks is included with the application form.

When you borrow goods and services directly from the seller or manufacturer (without the services of a bank, bank credit card, or finance company), you have certain protections against defects in what you borrow. Among these are your right to actually receive what you'll eventually be paying for and to have any resemblance between your purchases and their advertised descriptions be more than coincidental.

In addition, there are implied warranties that your purchase will be suitable for the purpose you bought it for (e.g., that an iron will actually iron clothes), and there are often express warranties made by the seller or manufacturer that you can require either one to live up to.

You also have these rights when you buy goods and services by borrowing money, but they're considerably harder to exercise simply because your protections help you against the seller of the goods, not against the lender of the money. Unless a cash loan has been given to you in counterfeit money or a rubber cashier's check, you can't complain that the money you've borrowed is defective. Nor can you return it and get your money back.

Actually, once your signature is at the bottom of a promissory note (the term is used here to denote any contract for the borrowing of money), your options for avoiding payment are severely limited. You can file for bankruptcy (not recommended except as a last resort). If the lender has engaged in unfair collection practices, and you can prove it, and you live in the right jurisdiction (Texas, for example), you can sue for relief from debt and for civil damages resulting from those unfair practices. Other than those two courses, your only defense against collection under a promissory note is that your signature has been forged, which you'll have a hard time proving if it hasn't been.

"Aha!" you say, "All I have to do is stick to borrowing merchandise and stay away from borrowing money." Sorry to disappoint you, but in actual practice it's not as simple as that. Loans of money are often designed by creditors to masquerade as loans of goods and services.

When you buy a car on credit, for example, there's no question that you're taking out a loan to pay for it. In other words, you're borrowing money from a bank, finance company, or manufacturer's credit subsidiary, and this money is given to the dealer. The resulting triangular relationship works out fine for the dealer and fine for the lender but not so hot for the borrower. The dealer gets his money from the bank. The bank gets a security interest in the car which gives it the right to repossess if you don't pay. And the borrower gets the opportunity to pay, no matter what subsequently happens to the car.

The engine can self-destruct in ten seconds, the wheels can fall off, the whole car can even be stolen, but the borrower still has to pay for it. The reasoning is that the bank has lent money and expects to be repaid. As far as it's concerned, the car is just security; and any problems you have with it are between you and the dealer, who already has his money for it. While you and he fight it out, you continue paying the bank under penalty of repossession of the car and forfeiture of all the payments you've made on it to date.

With smaller purchases, however, the nature of your debt isn't so obvious, because of the creditor's desire to lull the debtor into a false sense of security about payment, this state of mind being conducive to making purchases that, on cooler reflection, the debtor would see he couldn't afford.

The mechanics of the loan differ slightly from a car loan, but the result is the same. The purchaser signs a retail installment agreement instead of a loan form, and the lender is usually the store instead of a bank. But whether you sign a loan agreement or a retail installment agreement, the document with your signature on the dotted line is a promissory note. A promissory note is a negotiable instrument. It can be bought and sold, and your obligation under it can be transferred from the seller of the merchandise to the buyer of your note.

When this happens, you end up in the same three-cornered relationship as you'd be in had you bought a car and financed it with a bank loan. In fact, you'd be in worse shape because companies in the retail installment business, being far less regulated than banks, are generally far less scrupulous.

Promissory notes can be sold, and many retail installment merchants make a point of selling them to a third party (usually a finance company), known legally as a *holder in due course*. A holder in due course is immune from making good on defects, nondelivery, fraud, and the like on the part of the seller. He can sit back, watch you fight it out with the seller (who's already been paid), and go to court, if necessary, to get his money from you.

This legal concept has created an entire industry that profits from preying on debtors and rendering them defenseless, particularly those debtors too poor or too ignorant to have got into some other kind of debt in the first place.

The customers are almost exclusively those black or Spanish-speaking people who live at or slightly above the welfare level. The merchandise is usually shoddy, fails to live up to the claims made for it, and sometimes is never delivered. The prices for this junk usually rival those for good merchandise at the better department stores downtown (where lower-class nonwhites fear to tread), and are set so that the first two or three installment payments will take care of the actual cost and markup of the merchandise, with any additional payments being pure gravy. Finally, the retail installment agreements are invariably sold to a holder in due course, usually as soon as the ink on the purchaser's signature has dried. While the merchants and the holder-in-due course finance companies are working hand in glove to soak the poor, the common-law theory is that the finance company just bought a promissory note, knows nothing about the nature of the lender's business, and therefore should not be held responsible for its abuses.

According to Philip G. Schrag, attorney in charge of consumer litigation for the NAACP Legal Defense Fund, and quoted by Craig Karpel in *New York* magazine, "If Greedy Merchant gets Ernest Black to sign a [retail installment] contract for a 'new color television' and the set turns out to be an old, battered black-and-white instrument, or *even if Merchant never delivers any set at all* [emphasis in original], Merchant can sell Black's contract to Ghetto Finance, Inc., for a lump sum, and Black is out

36

of luck. Ghetto has a right to payment in full from Black, and Black has no right to tell a court that he's been robbed."*

Needless to say, the legal fiction that the holder in due course knows nothing about the affairs of the merchant is precisely that—a fiction. One example given by Karpel is that of Tremont-Webster Furniture Corp., at 412 East Tremont Avenue, Bronx, and Argent Industrial Corp., which buys Tremont-Webster's promissory notes and is located next door, at 410. ("No doubt it is a convenience for a holder in due course to have the store about whose affairs it knows nothing right next door." †)

For a debtor caught in this kind of squeeze, there's really only one hope. The Coburn Corporation of America, which "has made skillful use of the holder-in-due-course principle to protect itself against the charges that the merchants it finances engage in fraudulent or unconscionable practices," ‡ and is big enough to be listed on the American Stock Exchange, reported that of $50 million in retail installment finance business, $5.1 million —more than 10 percent—had to be written off as uncollectible.

This is more than an interesting but irrelevant digression, because even if you're not black, even if your first language is English, not Spanish, and even if you don't live in a neighborhood like the Central Ward, Watts, or Bedford-Stuyvesant, you may be a victim of the same racket as the people who do.

Admittedly, it's a white-collar, genteel version of the same racket. The differences are largely superficial, and there are four of them. First of all, you'll be able to purchase from many merchants on this kind of credit instead of being limited to one or two at a time. Second, the holder in due course is a bank instead of a finance company. Third, because banks' debtors are more middle class and therefore more subject to the bourgeois need for respectability than, say, Coburn Corporation's debtors,

* Craig Karpel, "Ghetto Fraud on the Installment Plan," *New York*, May 21, June 2, 1969.
† Karpel, "Ghetto Fraud on the Installment Plan."
‡ Karpel, "Ghetto Fraud on the Installment Plan."

the banks' collection rate is probably higher than Coburn's 89 percent plus. And fourth, to mislead you about the whole nature of your debt, you have a wallet-size plastic card to identify you as a sucker.

It's called a Master Charge card, or a BankAmericard, or an American Express card (the gold one, not the green one); and generally every effort is made in the promotion of these cards to convince you that they're plain, ordinary charge cards or travel and entertainment cards. These cards give you all the consumer protection enjoyed by a $5,000-a-year, non-English-speaking Cuban who was forced by economic necessity to drop out of school in the fourth grade.

Instead of being charge cards, these pieces of charge-card-like plastic entitle you to automatic cash loans of varying amounts at 12 to 18 percent interest per year.* As you make purchases and "charge" them to your card, you are borrowing money from the bank. This money is credited directly to the merchant or merchants you buy from, and if you have any problems with your merchandise, the bank can legally sit back and say, "You two go and fight it out." Should you fail to keep up your payments while the battle rages, the bank can confiscate money in your savings or checking account.

There are, however, some words of encouragement:

If you live in Massachusetts, you should know that the state bankers' association went on record before the legislature as having instituted provisions for charging off

---

* This is what makes American Express' attempts to switch customers from green to gold cards particularly pernicious. Apparently, the $15 per year for each of about 2 million cards, plus a 2¾ to 6 percent cut of the bill from every merchant who accepts any charge is not enough for American Express; they want to add 18 percent interest per year without doing anything extra to earn it. And don't be taken in by claims that if you pay in the first thirty days, you'll get off without interest. According to Life magazine, sending out bills of this nature as many as twenty-one days after the billing date is common practice. And according to Fortune, only 30 percent of active accounts in this type of system get off free of interest. (Paul O'Neil, "A Little Gift from Your Friendly Banker, Life, March 27, 1970. Irwin Ross, "The Credit Card's Painful Coming of Age," Fortune, October, 1971.)

to the seller any debts that go unpaid because of a dispute between the seller and the card-carrying buyer.

In 1970, New York State enacted a law which prohibits banks and finance companies from hiding behind the holder-in-due-course relationship and, in the words of then Governor Nelson Rockefeller, will put an end to the "interlocking relationship" between finance company and seller that strips consumers of their normal legal defenses. Ten other states—California, Delaware, Michigan, Missouri, New Mexico, Oregon, Pennsylvania, Texas, Vermont, and Massachusetts—have similar laws on the books, and the F.T.C. has proposed a regulation of this kind to cover all fifty states. Now for the bad news: The New York law is great for reliefers but not so hot for middle-class working people, because it specifically fails to cover credit-card transactions, automobile purchases, or services like home repairs that could entail a promissory note.

In April, 1973, a bill was passed by the U.S. Senate prohibiting banks from charging savings and checking deposits for bank-card debt without first obtaining the depositor's consent. As of this writing, the bill is waiting for members of the House of Representatives to divert some time from Watergate and their own re-election campaigns and schedule the bill for hearings. You might ask your congressman about this when he comes around asking for your vote.

Finally, there's federal legislation which took effect in 1975 that makes the first steps towards eliminating the whole problem on a national level. One piece follows New York's lead in eliminating holder-in-due-course relationships for retail promissory notes. Another gives the bank card holder a legal leg to stand on in dealing with disputes over shoddy goods and services.

This legislation became effective on October 28, 1975, states that when you have a complaint about a purchase of more than $50 made within 100 miles of your place of residence, charged to a bank card, and if you can prove you've attempted to obtain satisfaction, you are then legally entitled to withhold payment not only from the seller of the merchandise, but from the bank as well. This may sound very confusing, but it really isn't. You have to have charged a purchase on your bank card. If you have a complaint about what you bought, you must have voiced that complaint to the seller and be able to prove you did. (A carbon copy of a letter of complaint should constitute reasonable proof.) And that's about it—you don't have to pay the bank until you get satisfaction. There are, of course, two little loopholes to watch out for—you're not covered if the purchase was too small or you made it too far from home. If you took advantage of a $49.95 special, you're out of luck. And if you charged things on your trip to Hawaii, you're also out of luck (unless you happen to live there). As you can see, the law is far from perfect, but it is a first, albeit equivocal, step in the right direction.

The moral of this story is that just because it's plastic, that doesn't automatically make it an open-account charge card. Before you sign up for a card (unless you're getting it not to use, but to keep a zero balance on for a good credit reference [see next chapter]), find out precisely what it is that you're signing up for.

One guide is advertising. BankAmericard, in an uncharacteristic burst of honesty, tells prospects to "think of it as money," which is precisely what it is. Another ad says it's "more than a credit card" (it is—more grief for you). If you spot this kind of wording, steer clear. To give you an idea of how prevalent these "credit" cards are, 55 million of the 275 million credit cards in use are bank cards.

But more important than the wording in the advertising is the wording of the contract you have to sign to get the card. Sometimes the card *is* the contract, with the terms printed on the back in six-point (one-twelfth-inch-high) flyspeck type and your signature on the front.

Two dead giveaways are the word *loan* and a stipulation of a maximum credit limit in dollars. Another is the expression *line of credit*, if anyone at the bank should be indiscreet enough to use it. Any credit card issued by a bank falls into this category, as do some from department stores. When in doubt, bring the forms to a lawyer for translation before you sign them. If your company doesn't have a lawyer on salary who's friendly enough to advise you, then spending a few dollars for a consultation with a lawyer could prove a good investment.

The kind of plastic you do want to get includes thirty-day open-balance charge accounts from department stores, gasoline credit cards, and travel and entertainment cards like Carte Blanche, Diners Club, and American Express green. If you have a business of your own, standard thirty-day credit accounts from business suppliers will do fine in addition.

When and if you default on charge debts (as opposed to loans), your creditors can turn them over to bill collectors or lawyers; but these people are merely agents of the creditor, not holders in due course, and your basic protections against defects and misrepresentations always apply. You can go to court claiming that your goods and services were defective, not as advertised, the wrong size, damaged in delivery, or not delivered at all, secure in the knowledge that such objections are relevant and material. With bank cards or negotiable promissory notes, you can't.

Now that you know what kind of debt to get into, you ought to be discouraged from getting into it with just anybody. Take as much care in selecting the companies whose credit you'll accept as they take in selecting the people they offer it to. The rule of thumb is: If you want to win, pick on a bully. The reasons are both ethical and practical.

First, a large corporation is more likely to do credit business as a matter of course, with the credit organization organized as a profit center. A mom-and-pop operation is more likely to be strictly cash.

Second, a large corporation needs your money much less than the corner grocery store. After all, you represent maybe a ten-millionth of a large company's business, and they have large cash reserves to subsist on. For example, a gasoline company like Exxon or Texaco does billions of dollars of business annually; in 1972, the average motorist spent about $250 a year on gas, part of it in cash. Once a motorist gets away from the neighborhood gas station, brand preference is more a function of which brand is nearest when the gas gauge edges down toward "empty" than of any deep-seated loyalty. As a result, an average motorist holding credit cards from every major gasoline company would have made at most $50 a year in credit purchases from each one. A large gasoline company probably spends more than that per minute on paper clips.

To a neighborhood store, however, you represent a considerably larger share of the total business. And with far smaller cash reserves, the business is far less able to do without your money.

Two more reasons why business with local establishments should be done on a cash basis: (1) The more a person needs your money, the more active and determined (and therefore troublesome) he is at collecting it, and (2) it just isn't right to improve your standard of living at the expense of someone's livelihood.

In a way, it's fortunate that large corporations can, indeed, flourish without your money because their very size extends the amount of time required to complete even the simplest, most routine processes for collecting it. This is explained by Parkinson's law, which states that in life in general and bureaucracies in particular, work expands to occupy the time, personnel, and other resources allocated for its completion. The reason for this is that the easiest way for executives to gain status is through the multiplication of subordinates, and the more subordinates there are, the more time is diverted into personnel problems, interoffice correspondence, intramural power struggles, fouled-up communication, and the like; lost through mankind's innate propensity for boondoggling, procrastination, and coffee breaks; and wasted because of large organizations' ability to create a comfortable environment in which fools can prosper undetected. All of which is to say that with a large corporation, any transaction takes longer, including those involving credit complaints and collection of unpaid bills. As a debtor, this fact is in your favor.

Because bill collecting takes up more time and people in a large corporation, it also consumes more money. For the local butcher, tracking down a recalcitrant debtor involves no investment more major than taking his thumb off the scale long enough to make a one-message-unit phone call or take a one- or two-block walk. For a large corporation, the investment includes salaries, rent, electricity, secretaries, filing space and materials, office equipment, WATS lines, depreciation, computer time and programming, stationery, business forms, postage, and mail-room, supervisory, executive, and auditing time.

It is interesting to note that although general-purpose credit cards of the type most large companies honor were originally supposed to drastically reduce, if not totally eliminate, the paperwork arising from many separate bills, they've actually done just the opposite. "Credit Card Use in the U.S.," a study compiled by the University of Michigan Institute for Social Research, shows that general-purpose credit cards have caused paperwork, industrial bureaucracies, and computer systems not to dwindle, but to proliferate alarmingly, with the attendant costs being passed on to customers—cash and charge alike. In fact, the study reveals that people who use general-purpose credit cards write *more* checks per month than people who buy simply by cash and check.

The expense is staggering, and senior executives know exactly how staggering it is. They are aware of the cost of collection, of the value of their own time spent haggling with you about bills (by letter or phone), and of the cost of lost customer goodwill. They know that zealous collection of every penny due soon reaches a point of diminishing returns where the value of the labor and overhead spent collecting a debt exceeds the money that the collection will bring in. Unlike the local merchant, these executvies will often decide to avoid (or cut) their company's losses by resolving a collection dispute in the debtor's favor in the hope of making up the loss with profits from his next purchase.

Once you do credit business with large corporations, you should make sure that these corporations you do business with are established, reputable, even high-class outfits. Common sense suggests, and experience confirms, that the higher class a company, the higher its markup is likely to be. The higher the markup, the bigger the cash reserves, the less need for speedy collection, and the more leisurely and deferential the dunning procedures.

Brooks Brothers, for example, is reputed to write dunning letters whose tone implies to the debtor that the management is cognizant of the fact that the customer is merely waiting to clip the coupons on his gilt-edge debentures and that the store is writing merely to ensure a place at or near the top of the pile when that happy day arrives.

Georg Jensen's first dunning effort is a note clipped to the bill when ninety days overdue, asking if the merchandise is satisfactory and asking the customer to contact the store if there's any problem.

But perhaps the all-time record for deferential dunning goes to a society photographer who took photographs of a bride-to-be shortly before her marriage in April, 1970. After the picture had run in the New York *Times* and prints were delivered (albeit poorly retouched and printed), a bill for $90 came in the mail. Because of the poor reproduction quality, the bill has not been paid. He has yet to send a second notice.

Finally, complaints about merchandise quality, billing procedures, and the like are important for either self-defense or delay. Although reputable establishments are far less likely to provide grounds for complaint, they're far more sensitive to complaints when they do arise (the two facts are far from unrelated).

In summation, get open-account charge accounts, don't sign promissory notes, and do your credit purchasing with large national organizations. Locally, take out thirty-day charge accounts with establishments of such quality that you doubt they'd take the likes of you as a customer.

As you're about to see, that last little obstacle is far from insurmountable.

CHAPTER THREE

The Way to Get Credit Is to Prove You Don't Need It

THERE ARE TWO equally important factors in satisfying a debt: ability to pay and intent to pay. All the good intentions in the world are of no help to creditors when the debtor is stone broke. And all the money in the world is equally useless when the debtor hasn't the slightest intention of parting with it.

Creditors, as a rule, attach a great deal of importance to your ability to pay and since it's hard to measure, far too little importance to your intent. They assume that if the money is there, the intent to pay will also be present. So much weight is attached to ability to pay that creditors are far more lenient, deferential, and courteous in their dunning of rich debtors than they would be in dealings with us plain, simple, $30,000-a-year folk.

This overly deferential attitude toward debtors of proven (or at least assumed) means is rooted more in history than in logic. In medieval times, for example, those people who held a monopoly on wealth also held monopolies on land, military and police power, the courts, and anything else that wasn't nailed down. A tradesman trying to collect overdue debts from the typical medieval baron *had* to go easy, or else the costs of collection could include his head.

In the early seventeenth century, King James I of England had the power to promulgate a royal edict making it a criminal offense for people to dun him for debts incurred back before he made the big time and was just king of Scotland. The penalty for breaking this law was flogging and imprisonment.

As late as the nineteenth century, the mere word of a gentleman (i.e., a nobleman, member of the landed gentry, or on occasion, a capitalist parvenu who'd married well) was not to be questioned and constituted all the collateral the gentleman in question needed. Through Edwardian times, it was the custom of British gentlefolk to pay their bills (and servants' wages) on an annual basis, and never in advance.

Even today, many businessmen who should know better approach their richer customers like an Edwardian footman, bowing and scraping, hat in hand, to humbly beg that the money which had been rightfully theirs for as long as a year be paid to them. There are also many rich people who act as if all businessmen were expected to treat them that way, and actually get away with it.

One such case was reported to the *Wall Street Journal* by a Sunoco station owner in Rye, New York. It seems that one day in 1969, one of his customers pulled up in her Bentley and gave him a check for nearly $3,000 . . . in payment for all the gasoline she'd bought since 1968. "All of a sudden it hit me," said the gas station owner. "She lives in a monstrous million-dollar estate and pays her bills only once a year. I've got a wife and five children to feed and a $23,000 mortgage eating my gut, yet I have to wait a full year for money she owes me." Starting with 1970, the lady had to either pay cash or do without Sunoco.*

Fortunately for debtors, few businessmen show the good sense it takes to run a suburban Sunoco station. According to Robert R. Thiel, vice-president of the Na-

* Lee Berton, "It's Only Money," *Wall Street Journal*, September 22, 1969.

tional Retail Merchants' Association, most merchants handle "the wealthy with a velvet glove when it comes to overdue bills." Why? Apparently for no better reason than the fact that rich deadbeats are "used to being treated so." †

According to a New York attorney, "Many wealthy people are just oblivious to other people's financial problems. Collecting late bills from them is different from collecting from people of moderate income." At the time he was quoted in the *Wall Street Journal* piece, this attorney was representing a jeweler who had to sue Mrs. Susan Rosensteil (of the Seagram Whiskey Rosensteils) for some $347,885 worth of jewelry that she bought on credit and reportedly never paid for.‡

In 1970, when the Honorable Arthur J. Goldberg, former U.S. Secretary of Labor, former Supreme Court Justice, former Ambasador to the United Nations, ran for governor of New York State, his campaign staff booked the entire mezzanine floor of the Lancaster Hotel at the rental rate of $4,500 per month. Goldberg Campaign Headquarters checked in in April, 1970. When they checked out in July, the hotel management claimed, it was with $6,500 owing. According to the hotel managers, they had to turn off the lights and air conditioning to prod the Goldberg staff into making token payments. "Then someone would show up with $500 in back rent [less than four days' worth] and we would turn them on again."*

All things considered, Goldberg was far better off than the Honorable George McGovern, who racked up thousands of dollars in unpaid travel bills and had his airline and car rental credit cards revoked in mid-campaign.

The New York Telephone Company, which disconnects phones belonging to ordinary people when bills become 40 days overdue, somehow managed to let the New York State Democratic Committee enjoy continuous

† Berton, "It's Only Money."
‡ Berton, "It's Only Money."
* Grace Lichtenstein, "Hotel Says Goldberg's Staff Owes $6,500 Rent," New York *Times*, August 31, 1970.

47

phone service in spite of a bill of $90,000 owing over a period of 10 years.*

Also, New York City merchants are trying to collect an estimated $400,000 in unpaid bills run up by U.N. diplomats.†

And the city's Parks, Recreation and Cultural Affairs Administration is still owed $2,560 and $7,235.68 by, respectively, former mayors Robert Wagner and John Lindsay for food bills run up at Gracie Mansion. Wagner moved out of the mansion in 1965 and Lindsay in 1973. But it seems that collection attempts weren't started until 1975.‡

A Roslyn, New York, hardware dealer let a $203 bill run up by Winston Guest hang around for three years before going to court to collect. Why? "You could never catch up with him. He was either in Europe or South America or anywhere but home, and he didn't worry about who paid his bills." †

But for every businessman who wises up and hauls these rich stiffs into court, there are at least three or four who don't. Like the dealer in crystal, china, and silver who said, "We wouldn't dream of adding a carrying fee to our customer's charge accounts. It would disturb them . . . After four months we write them and delicately say it's overdue. We may telephone after six months." Or the owner of a dress shop who has to tie up a $20,000 cash reserve just to subsidize the bill-paying (or, more exactly, non-paying) habits of women rich enough to buy $200 and $300 dresses without batting an eyelash: "My customers aren't pressed to pay quickly. This is a small town, and so many of them are my friends—I see them at cocktail parties and at the country clubs—and I think

*Allan Wolper, "Democrats Ring Tel's 70G Bell," *New York Post*, June 29, 1972.

†"For the Record," *National Review*, August 1, 1975.

‡Mark Lieberman, "Wagner & Lindsay Failed to Fork Over for 10G Mansion Meals," *New York Daily News*, January 23, 1975.

† Berton, "It's Only Money."

they would be offended" if they were treated like dead-beats of lesser means.‡

To summarize, the advantages of the rich (aside from the obvious ones, of course) fall into three main categories:

1. *The rich are regarded as a breed apart*, and as such, they are very desirable for many otherwise sensible, hard headed businessmen to deal with. Many creditors find a certain magic in hobnobbing with, rubbing elbows with, and being able to drop the names of this charmed elite ("Let me tell you about the very rich. They are different from you and me"—F. Scott Fitzgerald), and this magic is so powerful that creditors actually subsidize the very rich—through slowed cash flow; loss of carrying charges, extra cash reserves, and capitalization; losses from nonpayment, and the like—for the dubious privilege of getting business from them.

2. *Their ability to pay is unquestioned.* As Joe E. Lewis once put it, "A bank is the thing that will always lend you money if you can prove that you don't need it." The rich don't have to prove it; it's an *a priori* assumption. In dealing with the very rich, therefore, businessmen keep their eye on the eventual payment, forgetting about the time and money they dissipate while waiting for that eventuality to arrive. Even when they don't forget, creditors really aren't geared to deal with their betters. Bill collection systems are set up, as a rule, to cope with people who can't pay, not with deadbeats who can pay but won't. Also, bill collecting itself doesn't pay very well and therefore doesn't attract practitioners from the upper crusts of society, so bill collectors are forced into combat against the rich with their own feelings of personal or social inferiority putting them one-down. As a result, it's easier to simply sit and sweat it out as the sums too "paltry" for a rich debtor to bother with mount up. And up. And up.

3. *The rich have the wherewithal to erect barriers to collection* which are usually unavailable to people of lesser means. By definition, the rich enjoy more leisure

‡ Berton, "It's Only Money."

time and more discretionary income than us common rabble. Putting these two things together, the rich can erect rather impressive *barriers of distance* through travel. It's hard, if not impossible, for a department store in, say, Chicago to work its collection tricks on a debtor taking an extended holiday in Samoa or Monte Carlo.

But the wealthy can be incommunicado even when they're comfortably at home, through their ability to erect *barriers of people*. In *Gulliver's Travels*, rich Lilliputians had in their personal retinues people called flappers, whose function was to swat the master on the eyes or ears with an inflated bladder when, and only when, the flapper deemed something worthy for the master to see or hear. Similarly, the wealthy can retain flappers by the dozen and so insulate themselves from whomever they wish to avoid confronting.

Servants can deny access ("Madame is not at home"). Their alleged foibles can provide excuses for nonpayment ("That blasted secretary! I told her to mail your check!"). And they can form a small bureaucracy whose very existence and complexity can bamboozle or delay creditors and give them a general runaround in the bargain. ("Mr. ————has instructed us to issue your check, but before we can, the accountant must approve it/the trustee must authorize it/the attorneys must clear it.")

And nothing is harder for creditors to cope with than inability to communicate with their targets. According to one Stanley Tulchin, "credit consultant" (a fancy term for bill collector), "If you can communicate, you can collect, but you can't collect a dime from someone you are not reaching."*

Finally, the rich can erect *legal barriers*, and often they inherit them. There's a saying to the effect that poor people save, while rich people invest. Much inherited wealth is the result of investments in corporations, and many estates are set up in such a manner that wastrel heirs can squander the dividends but not touch the basic

* *The Executive's Credit & Collection Guide* (Englewood Cliffs, N.J. Executive Reports Corporation, 1965).

capital. The legal mechanisms that project this capital from the heirs also work admirably against the heirs' creditors.

Both the self-made rich and the rich who have inherited their wealth have learned the advantage of protecting assets by putting them in the name of a legal entity—like a corporation or a trust—other than the entity in whose name debts are contracted. This enables the rich debtor to tap his assets practically at will, while keeping them inviolate from a creditor who, but for the legal niceties, would have a perfect right to get at them.

Of course, if you were as rich as some of the people discussed here, you'd probably be more than happy to pay your bills and enjoy a life of luxury on the money remaining. But you don't actually have to be rich to enjoy the rich man's ability to get credit.

You do, however, have to be at least well off. Many products and services are geared to mass sales and therefore to the "average" family as customers. Therefore, at the average income level there is access to virtually all gasoline credit cards and to charge accounts at lower- and middle-priced department stores. The top of the range enjoys, in addition, access to bank credit cards (with smaller debt limits) and can apply for car rental and travel-and-entertainment cards (although the applications will not be automatically accepted).

Upper-middle-income families should have no trouble with car rental and T&E cards. Affluent families can get charge accounts at most, if not all, department and clothing stores that offer them. Rich families can also get Air Travel Cards with relatively little difficulty.

Not surprisingly, the more the income, the larger the sum of money that the debtor can, with conviction and credibility, dismiss as too trivial to pay immediately. The below-average-income family can understandably get very upset when being dunned for six dollars when only five are in the cookie jar. But to, say, the upper-middle family, uptightness shouldn't set in for debts five times that figure. A former bill collector for Sears, Roebuck & Co. in Nebraska says that his hardest times came from upper-middle-class families with bills of $50 or less. These debtors were well able to pay the sums of money owing, but for some reason or other couldn't be bothered at the particular time Sears wanted to get the money. They failed to be intimidated by threats that would reduce debtors of less than average income to quivering jelly. In fact, upper-middle-class debtors would often become indignant that a bill collector had dared to invade their privacy. Eventually, they would pay the bills "in some sort of grand gesture" like mailing in the money in pennies or marching into the collection office and throwing a check on the floor. As you've read, this is the mental outlook that rich deadbeats have and get away with using on creditors; the only difference is the magnitude of the debt at issue.

Similarly, you don't have to be rich to enjoy a rich man's safeguards. All that's necessary is to understand the principles involved and apply them yourself.

The first principle to observe is: *Always separate your debts from your assets.* Before your creditor can get his hands on your money, he has to know where it is, and with a multiplicity of banks and other depositories for cash, this is almost impossible without your cooperation. On a credit application, you generally have to list your employer and one bank at which you maintain an account. Beyond that, a creditor has to conduct extensive, and therefore expensive, investigations that often make smaller debts more profitable to leave uncollected. With a court judgement, a creditor can garnishee your salary, but only within very stringent limits (see Chapter 12). Of course, if you've changed jobs since getting credit from him, that's going to make his job that much harder. And the bank account information you give him can apply only to your special checking account, which is unlikely to contain more money that you're likely to need for current expenses. But all other bank accounts will be hard, if not impossible, for a creditor to track down and attach.

One application of this principle suggests itself almost immediately. If you have a Master Charge, BankAmericard, or American Express Gold account at any given bank, don't keep your savings or regular checking account at the same bank. In the first place, a commercial-bank savings account is far from the best proposition to begin with; you can get more interest at a savings bank or savings and loan association, and even that won't be enough to keep up with the annual inflation rate. By the same token, a minimum deposit earning no interest at all in a regular checking account is stupid, especially since some commercial banks (like the Israel Discount Bank in New York City) offer checking accounts requiring neither monthly fees nor per-check fees nor minimum deposits.

But neither of these is the most important reason, and that is, in the event of a disputed bank credit card bill, your bank can automatically confiscate money from your checking or savings account for the payment on your Master Charge account. Without going to court. Without informing you in advance. And without even having to listen to your complaints.

Now, having decided not to keep your savings money where you do BankAmericard business, where *do* you keep it? Basically, that's an investment decision, and this is not an investment-advice book. However, there are certain methods which have been used not to guarantee high investment return on savings money but merely to keep that money inviolate from creditors, ex-wives, and other assorted predators.

One is called the W. C. Fields Method in memory of its most famous practitioner. Before he made it big on Broadway, Fields juggled and acted his way across America in many road companies. All too often, these touring companies failed to meet expenses on the road and would be canceled, in mid-tour, with the actors having to make their way back to New York unpaid and unaided. Fields never lost his fear of being left penniless in a strange town, so in his later years, even when he had no need to worry about money, he opened savings accounts wherever he went. Since Fields was a fancier of exotic names, he opened these accounts in fictitious names of his own devising. (Of course, back then, there was no requirement to give the bank your social security number. But even today, it is possible to apply for, and receive, a social security number which covers only the interest earned by the savings account.)

There was one major defect with the system. Fields kept all the names in his head and never made a list of his accounts. He died in 1948, and his heirs are still trying to figure out where the estate went. The defect in his system is one that can be remedied with a pencil and paper.

If the prospect of even as mild a subterfuge as the Fields Method depends on unnerves you, there's another, perfectly legitimate, method to guarantee your hard-earned savings will be inviolate. Several countries have laws protecting anonymity of bank depositors. Switzerland is the most famous of these, even though recent agreements with the United States have eroded its protections slightly. Under certain circumstances, Swiss banks may be required to divulge information to Uncle Fingers, but unless you're a suspected tax-dodger, Mafioso, or card-carrying Communist, you don't have to worry. Of course, if you don't have a Swiss bank account by now, there's no sense in trying to get one; Swiss banks no longer accept savings account applications from Americans not living in Switzerland. However, Lebanese banks, while not quite so prestigious as those in Switzerland, operate under equally stringent anonymity laws and, as of this writing, will probably welcome your business. Which brings us to still another method for separating your debts from your assets, and that is to set yourself up in business.

The most obvious form of business to set yourself up in is a corporation. The corporation is a legal entity based on the principle of limited liability. Under the law, your corporation and you are two separate and distinct persons, even if you own 100 percent of the stock, and even if the corporation in question exists only on pieces of paper on file in your desk drawer and with your state government. The corporation has the power to earn money, buy and sell merchandise, amass capital, contract for debts, and pay them. You have the power to do the same things. But your money and your debts are yours, while the corporation's money and debts are the corporation's.

54

As a stockholder of the corporation, you can receive dividends, the only upper limit on these dividends being the amount of money that the corporation has to pay out. As an officer of the corporation, which in a small, privately held corporation of your own formation you will surely be, you can receive a salary, an expense account, and a drawing account, all of which let you take money out of the corporation. But the flow of money between you and the corporation need not be two-way.

If the corporation gets into trouble with creditors, there are legal mechanisms by which those creditors can seize the corporation's money and property. There is no way, however, for creditors of the corporation to grab the stockholders' personal assets unless the stockholders want them to. Stockholders and officers can lend the corporation money when it's in trouble, but only if they want to. If the corporation is over its nonexistent head in debt and gets wiped out, the stockholders have lost their initial investment, which for private corporations can be as little as one dollar. And that's it.

It's a common technique among the rich—particularly those rich people who earn their wealth in the form of some kind of salary—to have their own corporations, which receive the money, buy "corporate" property which the principal stockholder enjoys sole use of, pay the principal stockholder's expenses, and so on. This kind of corporate setup reduces tax liability (the maximum federal income tax bite on corporations is roughly 20 percent lower than the maximum taxation rate for individuals), which is ostensibly, its main purpose. However, it can also be used to avoid personal debt liability and probably *is* used that way more often than you'd think.

In big cities throughout America, there are hotels notorious as centers of prostitution and drug traffic. These hotels are the property of corporations, which in turn are often the property of other corporations, and so on for a few generations back, until we find a corporation owned, at least in part, by wealthy, highly respectable people, who, of course, know nothing at all about what all those other corporations they indirectly own are up to. Which is quite understandable since the first corporation

—the one that "owns" the red-light hotel—and many of the intermediate corporations consist of nothing more than a few pieces of paper and a mail drop. These are known as "shell" corporations, because in the event of any legal or other liability which the stockholders want to avoid, the corporation is found to be nothing more than an empty shell.

Another shell corporation did a flourishing charter flight business. It took reservations, put charter groups together, leased aircraft, and generally raked in money. One day, at the height of the European travel season, several charter groups assembled by the corporation converged on the airports only to find no planes waiting for them. It eventually turned out that the operators of the corporation—and boy, were they operators—had paid the charter monies to themselves, and instead of booking airplane space for their charter customers, booked only tickets for themselves, to countries that accept American dollars but have few extradition agreements with the United States. When law officers closed in on the corporate offices, they found a room with a telephone and a beat-up desk. And that was it—the empty shell. Shell corporations are also used by large-scale slumlords to insulate themselves from legitimate tenant complaints.

According to the law, each different corporation is a different person, even if it has the same stockholders and address as another, similar corporation. A person is allowed to go bankrupt, i.e., wipe out his debts (see Chapter 13), only once every six years, and this is true regardless of whether the person in question is a flesh-and-blood person named John Doe or a paper person called ABC, Inc. However, while John Doe will always be John Doe, the stockholders of ABC, Inc., can also go into business as DEF, Inc., which is a totally different entity. So if ABC declares bankruptcy, the stockholders don't have to wait six years to have DEF go bankrupt, if bankruptcy is convenient before that interval has elapsed. They can take a bath on DEF, GHI, JKL, and all the way on through XYZ. Lots of biggies in the soft goods business do this as standard operating procedure, and the practice is far from unknown in the retail business, among others.

Corporations offer two additional advantages, even for people who haven't the slightest intention of incorporating for the purpose of getting away with hanky-panky.

Since it's rare for corporations to be set up just to create a legal entity (even rarer than the American who defaults on his bills), corporations are generally assumed to be going businesses, and going businesses routinely deal in sums of money exceeding those handled by individuals or families. In other words, creditors who would question your ability to pay the sums of money involved in typical consumer debts often assume that a corporation will automatically be able to pay debts of the same magnitude, with the result that people who have trouble getting consumer credit experience little, if any, difficulty getting the same credit from the same creditors when they incorporate. Vincent Marrapodi, an advertising executive, was refused a charge account by Bloomingdale's on the grounds that his wife, who'd opened a separate account, for herself only, in her own name, was behind in her payments, which came from her own earnings. Yet, a corporation in which both Marrapodis were principal stockholders had no trouble whatever getting a Bloomingdale's charge account *after* his application was denied and her account was suspended. In summary, then, the first of the two advantages we mentioned is that corporations can often get charge accounts even when their officers and principal stockholders can't.

The second advantage is that every corporation must have at least three officers—president, secretary, and treasurer—and being an officer of a corporation, even one you formed with your wife and mother-in-law, greatly enhances your apparent solvency as an individual. It may not be that way in fact, but somehow John Doe, vice-president and treasurer of the XYZ Corporation, seems to be a more solid citizen and a better credit risk than plain old John Doe. Robert Townsend, former president of Avis Rent A Car, noted the tendency to assume that corporate officers are somehow more responsible than average people, even though this assumption often con-

57

tradicts experience. "You might suppose that the higher you go in the ranks of business executives, the more word-keepers you find," he wrote. "My experience doesn't substantiate this. I've been welshed on by a big bank president, the number two man of a major finance company, and various investment banking house partners."*

Before you rush out to incorporate, however, you should be aware that a corporation of your own is not the universal panacea. Corporations have advantages, but they can also have potential drawbacks, the most important of which is cost. Corporations are chartered by state governments, and political rhetoric notwithstanding, nothing that a government does for the public is free of charge. Most states charge a charter fee of a few hundred dollars when you form the corporation, and you might have to pay for legal help in drawing up the charter. Also, since governments rarely impose one-time charges on anything they can keep hitting you for year after year, there's an annual fee varying from state to state and ranging from $25 to $100. Also, if a corporation has cash flow, which yours certainly will, it will be required to file income tax returns every year, and this can double either the time or the money you spend to prepare your income tax forms.

In some circumstances, it can be harder for a corporation to get credit than for the individuals who own stock in it, acting as individuals. A well-known male model (you've seen his face in dozens of advertisements) runs a small handicrafts business on the side. In 1972, he incorporated that business. In 1973, a year and a half later, he applied for a small business loan in the name of the corporation, and because it had been in existence for less than two years, the bank he applied to turned him down (although they offered a personal loan for the same amount, probably at a higher rate of interest). What's ironic about the whole incident is that he went to that particular bank because he had just finished posing for one of their ads which told people how easy it was to

* Robert Townsend. *Up the Organization* (New York: Alfred A. Knopf, 1970).

get loans there. Nobody knows for certain, but it's doubtful that the same problem would have arisen in applying for consumer-type charge accounts in the corporation's name, instead of business-type credit. Also, a simple expedient could have given this man a corporation that was already two or more years old before he even thought of forming it.

Many law firms that deal in corporate law often charter spare corporations in case a client will suddenly need one. They pay the fees to keep the corporations alive, even though the corporate operations are confined to the inside of a file drawer. Then, when a client needs a corporation, they sell it to him merely by selling its stock, for a fee that usually covers the fees and labor that went into forming the corporation, plus a reasonable mark-up.

Now, the advantages of incorporating generally outweigh the drawbacks, but if you want to forego the drawbacks, you can still hold onto some of the advantages. You see, a business doesn't have to be a corporation, and you can set yourself up in business without actually incorporating. If you do this, you'll forfeit the advantage of limiting your personal liability for the corporation's debts, but you'll retain many of the psychological and practical advantages of doing business with creditors as a business.

In most cities and states, turning yourself into a business involves little more than registering the company name with the appropriate government office and paying a very nominal registration fee. You will then be officially recorded as "John Doe doing business as The Deadbeat Co." but entitled to put all your business ventures under the label of "Deadbeat Co." And this kind of label can work wonders.

Just as creditors assume that corporations are going concerns with continuity, roots in the community, and assets, they make similar assumptions about unincorporated companies. Many creditor companies that do business with other companies have learned that it's often less expensive to automatically grant credit, within certain limits, and assume a certain proportion of the debts will be uncollectable than to lose money, time, and possibly customers by investigating each company that places credit orders. As was noted earlier, while the standard condition for consumers making purchases is payment on demand, the standard condition when businesses make purchases is 2 percent discount for payment within ten days, total balance (net) thirty days after billing. In other words, the mere placement of an order by a business, under normal conditions, automatically produces thirty days' credit. And thirty days' credit can easily be expanded into sixty days, ninety days, or longer, depending on how much the debtor is trying to get away with. Of course, in this kind of situation, it's highly unlikely that the creditor will allow the debtor company to place a second order, but there are so many other suppliers who gladly will that denial of a second order is equivalent to locking the barn door after the horse has been stolen—along with the other livestock and the manure spreader.

A man in Florida cashed in on this principle merely by ordering printed letterheads with a company name on them. Using this stationery, he placed first orders with more than 100 companies. The merchandise was shipped, he never paid, the suppliers found it cheaper to write off each small debt than to collect it. After a few years of this, the creditors began to get wise to him, so he made up a new company name, had new stationery printed, and started all over again.

At the other end of the scale, the Penn Central Railroad continued to receive merchandise on credit, even after the corporation achieved a certain amount of notoriety for being in severe financial troubles, which would limit if not totally do away with, their ability to pay for these purchases. One supplier even gave them credit for a purchase that should have been a dead giveaway—a large quantity of red ink.

There are other ways to make it easier to get credit, even if you apply for it as an individual rather than as a business.

For example, if you work in two different occupations, always list the more respectable-sounding one on your credit application. A few years ago, before teachers across the country got some well-deserved pay raises, the profession of teaching was not only poorly paid but seasonal as well (with a long unpaid period over the summer). One teacher applied for credit, listing his occupation as "school teacher." He was rejected. But during the long summer vacation he worked as a bulldozer operator, so he applied again, this time listing his occupation as "bulldozer operator." He made no effort to conceal that he was the same person as before, with the same annual income. His second application was accepted.

Acting is another problem occupation. In addition to seasonal and "between jobs" unemployment, it seems to have, at least to creditors, an air of disreputability, which is rather quaint so many years after the death of Queen Victoria. One actor who earns big chunks of money from doing two or three television commercials a year supplements his income by working between jobs and auditions as a used-car salesman. He spends more time selling used cars, but he makes more money acting. Yet he's learned that he can get credit by listing his occupation as "used-car salesman," but not as "actor."

Women are a credit disaster area, regardless of occupation. If they're single, credit is often more readily extended to men with lower incomes. If they're married, they must often sign pledges not to have children, or to abort any children they conceive, in order to be allowed to get themselves into certain kinds of debt. Moreover, many creditors automatically revoke a woman's charge account when they learn that she has married, and base a re-extension of credit privileges on the husband's financial and credit status.

Over the years, Carte Blanche has required that women who apply for their travel and entertainment card have their applications co-signed by a husband or other sponsoring male. For women belonging to the National Association for Female Executives (members must earn $10,-000 or more per year), however, there are special application forms that don't require co-signatures. According to *Business Week*, "P. K. Dunshire, marketing vice-president, says that Carte Blanche would like to hand the new application out to all women but felt that putting a second box of forms alongside the regular one at distributing points would be confusing."*

When a woman who practiced law in San Francisco got married, Macy's closed a charge account of long standing and demanded that she re-establish credit under her husband's name. But I. Magnin, a store that wouldn't give her the time of day on credit when she was single, sent her an unsolicited charge account application—also in her husband's name.

Thirteen states plus the District of Columbia now have laws which bar banks, finance companies, and stores from credit discrimination on the basis of sex and, in some jurisdictions, marital status. In California, a law enacted in January, 1974, requires that credit must be granted without regard to sex or marital status, that a married woman can have her own credit rating separate from her husband's and that violators can be compelled to grant credit and pay up to $500 plus provable cash damages. In January, 1975, another law took effect in California granting wives as well as husbands the right to incur family debts under the community property system.

There's also federal legislation (the Equal Credit Opportunity Act) which took effect on October 28, 1975, that helps matters somewhat, but is also a mixed blessing. The overall purpose of the law is to prevent women from being discriminated against on the basis of sex or marital status in the granting of credit. While removing a number of obstacles that women seeking credit faced, it also eliminated a number of loopholes that smart wives—or their husbands—once used to advantage.

When you apply for credit, the creditor is no longer allowed to ask you to specify your sex and marital status on the application. A creditor can no longer demand that you produce a male co-signer or "sponsor" simply because you're a woman. In evaluating your application, creditors must take your earning history into account, regardless of your gender. If they reject you, creditors must, on your request, give you a summary of the reasons for this decision within 60 days after it is made. Finally,

* "Credit-card Tokenism," *Business Week*, September 16, 1972.

you can sue creditors who discriminate against you on the basis of sex or marital status for your actual damages plus up to $10,000 in punitive damages. That's the good part; now for the rest.

Under this law, and in order to enforce it, the Federal Reserve Board was to draw up regulations for itself, the FTC, the Federal Deposit Insurance Corporation, the Comptroller of the Currency, and nine other federal agencies. As of 47 days before the law was to take effect, the Federal Reserve Board was first starting hearings on the subject.

Under this law, wives—especially non-working wives —may find it harder to hitchhike on their husbands' good salary or credit rating. The law specifies that accounts used by both spouses must be maintained in both names, and this subjects the wife's earning and payment history to as much scrutiny as the husband's. One widow, for example, found it easy to get credit in her late husband's name for the six years since he died. Now, with equal credit opportunity for all, she may find the going harder.

Though husbands and wives can maintain separate accounts, a wife with no income of her own will find it harder to get one. The couple will find it harder to practice separation of debts from assets—where one partner accumulates all the assets while the other runs up the debts. Ultimately, this could undermine the many state laws which keep the assets of one spouse from being confiscated to satisfy debts incurred by the other. (See pages 237–238.)

Upon getting married many women lose their charge accounts, or at the very least discover they have to reapply for them, and the Equal Credit Opportunity Act gives little opportunity for changing this situation. Creditors are still allowed by this law to reapply for credit after a change in marital status. (Thus, a woman who previously ran the risk of losing her credit when she got married, now may lose it under the Equal Opportunity Act if her husband dies or if she gets divorced.)

Believe it or not, many a bride loses her credit as the result of an inadvertent wedding present she makes to her creditors. Proud of her new name, she immediately requests a routine (she thinks) change of name on her charge-a-plate. This alerts creditors that a marriage has taken place, and the account is canceled. She is then required to reapply and creditors take her new status into account (whether she'll continue to work, how much her husband earns, and so on) as the basis of the decision to open or refuse to open a "new" account. Ironically, this is another example of the system working because of the voluntary cooperation of its victims, in this case women who call creditors' attention to the existence of their marriages.

According to the Equal Credit Opportunity Act, a woman may maintain a charge account under her maiden name, married name, professional name, or any name she's legally entitled to use. Moreover, in every state of the union except Hawaii, there is no requirement that a woman adopt her husband's last name on marriage. And even if she does, according to *Money* magazine, this need not stand in the way of getting credit, providing she applies for it as an individual, not as half a couple. "Couples who don't want to assume legal responsibility for each other's debts should apply for separate charge cards—the woman's in her own first name, her maiden name, or her professional name. When debts are contracted separately, the law generally protects husbands and wives from each other's financial mishaps. If one spouse runs up more debt than he or she can pay, the other ordinarily is not responsible for paying it."* Of course, creditors don't want debtors to take advantage of their legal rights against creditors, so they try and bulldoze married couples into taking out joint charge accounts or paying cash. That way, each spouse will be, for bill collection purposes, the other's keeper.

The second major principle of dealing with creditors like a person of means is: *Get as much credit as possible when you need it the least*. In other words, before you start any deficit spending on a large scale, open charge accounts with as many creditors as possible. This has several advantages.

* "Marriage as a Limited Partnership." *Money*, February 1974.

64

First, it's inevitable that any debtor who delays paying his bills or complains about merchandise with any regularity or persistence is going to be temporarily in bad with some of his creditors. There is a wide range of companies offering essentially similar merchandise and services on essentially the same credit terms. If you take advantage of this diversity, then when and if you're in trouble with one creditor, you can carry on with his competitors. It's a fact that creditors are much more concerned about your general credit standing *before* they grant you credit than *after*. Thus, if creditor A suspends your charge account and reports this fact to a credit bureau, you will have difficulty if you subsequently apply to creditor B. However, if you open accounts with creditors A and B simultaneously, creditor B will consult only his own credit records to see if your account is in good standing; he will not go to the trouble and expense of consulting external sources. Thus, your credit will be good with B after it has ceased to be good with A, until you start defaulting on bills owed to B also.

But there's another, equally important, advantage. Credit tends to breed more credit. Having a zero balance (this means either that you're all paid up or have never made a purchase, and creditors don't go to the trouble of finding out which) at one creditor—particularly one that's either prestigious or foreign or, better yet, both—makes a fine reference for getting charge accounts from other creditors, and some creditors—more than is really wise—will check no further than the references that potential debtors supply to them.

A librarian and her chronically unemployed husband arrived in San Francisco a few years ago with the sum total of ten dollars between them and little immediate prospect for earning more. He did, however, know how to look and dress like a respectable citizen, so he walked into Abercrombie & Fitch, made a purchase, and was offered a charge account. At the time, it was Abercrombie's policy to offer immediate charge accounts to customers who the salespeople thought were respectable-looking individuals. (They've since discontinued the practice, but other high-ticket retail stores still do it.)

Armed with an Abercrombie & Fitch charge account, he then went to Gump's, another San Francisco department store. Using his Abercrombie account as a reference —and it was a good reference, since it was too new to show arrears—he got a Gump's charge account. Then, with Gump's and Abercrombie as references, he proceeded to another store. And so on, until he and his wife were able to furnish an entire apartment, all on charge purchases.

A Canadian advertising writer who arrived in New York pulled the same stunt, only he went a step further. As soon as the merchandise he charged arrived at his apartment, he sold it, for cash, at a discount, and then lit out for London.

Other people have been able to build whole houses of credit cards simply because they went to the right colleges. In the past, it was the practice of many gasoline companies (although with the fuel shortage, and the resulting sellers' market, it's a practice they're not continuing) to obtain lists of graduating classes and offer each member his own credit card. Some department stores, like Barney's in New York, do likewise. Some credit organizations who realize the connection between availability of credit and likelihood of patronage obtain lists of holders of other credit cards and then send out mailings offering charge accounts of their own. When bank credit cards first came out, BankAmericards and Master Charge cards were sent unsolicited to virtually all checking account depositors and loan recipients who were keeping their payments current. And today, if you have a checking account, use a bank credit card, or have successfully repaid a loan, chances are you'll receive several mailings per year offering you more bank credit cards, a chance to apply for travel and entertainment cards, or invitations to open other kinds of charge accounts.

Just as money tends to attract more money, credit tends to attract more credit. In fact, creditors today regard the absence of debt in your financial background as somewhat shady. According to *Money* magazine, "absolute liquidity can be . . . a serious handicap, especially

66

for people over 40." The magazine went on to quote an executive vice-president of Diners Club who said, "If a man hasn't established credit by then [age 40], we wonder why."*

According to testimony given before the House Consumer Affairs Subcommittee by John B. Martin, consultant to the National Retired Teachers Association and the American Association of Retired Persons, "a clear pattern of discrimination against older persons by certain national credit card companies, department stores, banks, and other credit-granting institutions" exists. "Older persons often encounter credit discrimination when they try to establish credit for the first time after a life-time of paying cash." He cited the case of a 67-year-old physician earning $30,000 annually who applied for a mortgage loan "at a bank where he had been doing business for 37 years but was turned down unless he could obtain a 'young' co-signer."†

This where-there's-smoke-there-must-be-fire attitude "helps explain the plight of a prosperous New York lawyer who recently complained to the FTC of being refused a department store charge account because he had no credit file." ‡

A jeweler who emigrated from Europe to New York by way of Australia and California faced this problem when he arrived in the United States. He solved it by taking out a bank loan he didn't need and paying it back ahead of schedule. With a good reference from the bank, he got all the charge accounts he needed. He did have to pay interest on the loan, but he regards it as a good investment.

Of course, if he'd had credit references from overseas, he could have saved himself the money. Foreign credit references can often be better for a debtor than the domestic variety. In the first place, since Americans are still affluent compared to most average Europeans (devaluation notwithstanding), you're probably far more eligible

* Jean Carper, "The Reputation Merchants," *Money*, February 1974.

†Peggy Simpson, "See Bias On Credit For Aged," *New York Post*, April 24, 1975.

‡Carper, "The Reputation Merchants."

for a charge account at a European department store than an American one. In fact, European department stores periodically advertise to attract American charge customers, in the hope of obtaining additional business and additional dollars. Harrod's, for example, which is in London, has advertised in *The New Yorker*, and their ads included charge account applications. On a vacation that takes you to one of the principal cities of Europe, a famous department store is a good sight to see, and there's nothing lost in taking a few minutes extra to visit the credit department.

Since you're not likely to shop at these stores too often, unless you enjoy ordering things sight unseen by transatlantic mail, you will then have references showing zero balance, which, as stated before, often translates as "all paid up." The fact that you have accounts at stores in London, Paris, Rome, and Geneva also stamps you as a jet-setter who can afford to commute back and forth over the Atlantic, and this impression is often sufficient in itself to get you the domestic credit privileges you're after.

A Swiss or Lebanese bank account (or an account in another country with banking privacy laws) also gives you an excellent reference. When a potential creditor writes to a Swiss bank to inquire about your solvency, he receives a formally phrased, old-world letter informing him that Swiss banking laws forbid the divulgence of how much money you have on deposit with the bank, and this inevitably leads to the impression of a numbered account containing secret millions.

The trappings of the rich, or the affluent, or of a business are useful not only in persuading creditors to give you charge accounts but also in dealing with their collection attempts after the accounts have been opened.

For example, a little foresight and some small investments can provide you with a rich man's inaccessibility. The first piece of foresight is to never answer the phone yourself, particularly during the hours when bill collectors are most likely to call (for business debtors, from 10 AM to noon and from 2 to 5 PM; for individual debtors, during early evening hours). Legally, bill collectors are not supposed to talk to third parties—even third parties

68

who happen to be married to you—about your alleged debts, for if what they say turns out to be false, they're wide open to slander suits. Therefore, they'll just be able to leave a name and a message to call back, and they'll keep calling *you* back until they get you. However, your wife can also pose as your personal secretary and inform the bill collector that you're attending to business interests in Johannesburg and will be abroad for the next two months; this will tell the bill collector in question that (1) you have the ability to pay and that (2) calling back in less than two months will avail him nothing.

If you go the business route, you can order a phone with a "hold" button, and with this, your wife can claim you're tied up on "the other line" and convincingly put the bill collector on hold.

Secretaries, or apparent secretaries, are useful in reaching corporate biggies with a complaint, instead of getting shunted off to some junior assistant obfuscator. As a rule, women generally get cold receptions when they telephone large companies and ask for the president, unless they can say, "Mr. A———, please; Mr. B———calling." Single women posing as their own secretaries can make contacts they wouldn't have been able to by honestly admitting they were calling themselves. Eleanor Perry, the movie producer, ran into this problem when she was shooting a movie in New York. Every time she had to call the studio, secretaries there wouldn't put her calls through. The reasoning was that no woman could be a producer, and even if one could, no producer worthy of the title would place his or her own telephone calls to the Coast.

Single men who can't avoid answering phone calls can install a recorded-message answering service, and use it to screen incoming calls—forgetting those callers they don't want to talk to and immediately calling back those they do.

An unlisted phone number is also a help, but you can have the same advantage without paying seventy-five cents a month by having your phone billed to your name but listed in another one, preferably one that's hard to pronounce. This has the added bonus of making it possible to immediately spot callers who obtain your number from the phone book and then ring you up to sell you encyclopedias, cemetery plots, newspaper subscriptions, ranchettes in the middle of the New Mexico desert. If someone calls up asking for Mr. Dzugashvili, or whatever name you chose, he's immediately branded as a salesman and can be hung up on with no further time wasted.

If you do speak to creditors or bill collectors over the phone, you can put on a rich man's airs and use a rich man's excuses. Your payment check can be awaiting approval from the attorneys who handle your trust fund, or your business manager, or your accountant. Your secretary may be in the process of preparing the check, or she may be getting ready to put it on your desk for signature. Your business (if you're dealing with creditors as a company) can be expanding at such a rate that you're hard put to keep up with incoming orders, much less incoming bills. And, if you can sound convincing, you should have no trouble convincing them. And this is true even if your charge application listed an income barely hovering over the poverty level. The information you use to obtain the account is on file with the credit department. Rarely, if ever, is it consulted by collection, which is usually an entirely different department.

Creditors communicate not only by phone, but by mail, and it helps to have the right materials to write replies with. An electric typewriter is always classier than a manual, since everyone knows that electric typewriters are more expensive. However, *used* electric typewriters are comparable in price with new manuals and, especially if you're getting into debt in the name of a business, are essential in reinforcing (or even, perhaps, creating) the impression that you have the ability to pay, and only your present intent is at issue.

The stationery, of course, must live up to the typewriter. Tiffany, for example, not only does good letterhead engravings, but prints on its own paper with a distinctive, and legible, "Tiffany Co." watermark; nobody receiving a letter from you on this stationery could possibly believe you to be a deadbeat.

But in addition to helping you impress creditors, Tiffany stationery can also help you to obtain more of them. A year ago, a New Yorker walked into Tiffany's to order some stationery. After placing his order, he was asked, "Will that be cash or charge?"

"I'm afraid it'll have to be cash," he answered. "I don't have a charge account here."

"Well, sir," said the salesman, "may we open one for you?"

The salesman handed him a form which read, "You may open a charge account for me," and had blanks for his name, address, and signature. And from the minute he signed the form, he had a Tiffany charge account, no further questions asked.

Now, the gentleman in question only uses that charge account whenever he has to reorder stationery, so it usually shows a zero balance; and when someone is all paid up at Tiffany, where purchases can run in the thousands of dollars, that's a very good credit reference indeed.

In addition, there's a whole group of first-class retail stores in New York that will grant charge accounts to people who have accounts in current standing at other stores belonging to the group. In fact, their application forms are printed with boxes to check for charge accounts at these other stores, and that is often the only reference required. Thus, the Tiffany account led immediately to accounts at Georg Jensen (imported silver, china, housewares), Brooks Brothers (clothing), F.A.O. Schwarz (toys), and other stores. And all because he went to Tiffany to order some stationery.

Just as secretaries and other buffers are useful in dealing with creditors by phone, they can be equally useful in dealing with creditors by mail. If you write them in your own name, show that you can afford to have someone else do your typing by putting a secretary's initials in the lower left-hand corner. Or if you want to use an out-of-the-country or similar excuse, you can send out letters over the signature of your imaginary personal secretary.

Finally, another medium of communication from you to your creditors will be checks. (Yes, we're afraid you *will* have to write some.) If you're making a partial payment or a reduced payment on a bill for defective merchandise or services, nothing lends a check an air of substantiality, and of being computed on the basis of irrefutable business calculations, like a check-writing machine.

In Orlando, Florida, Michael Thomas Henson, age eighteen, was arrested after touring the world on a borrowed credit card and some 200,000 worth of phony checks. According to police, he had somehow gotten hold of a check-writing machine and some blank checks. The checks that resulted were so official-looking that banks around the world accepted them at face value, allowed him to open accounts and draw personal checks against them immediately. In Hong Kong, he drew up three phony checks for $25,000 each and converted them into American Express travelers' checks, apparently with no questions asked. "It's incredible," remarked an American Express official. "Who would accept a $25,000 check without checking it out first, much less three of them?" As the police sergeant handling the case said, "I have . . . trouble cashing . . . my checks [at home], and someone goes around doing it in strange countries."*

Now, nobody is suggesting that you use a check-writing machine to write phony checks. But if such a machine can make phony checks look credible and official, imagine what one can do for a real check, covered by cash in your account, but for a reduced payment that you have calculated is all a piece of shoddy goods is really worth.

Of course, in talking about all these rich man's defenses against creditors, we're getting a little ahead of ourselves. Because once you open accounts with creditors, the simplest thing to do about their bills, in the first few months at least, is to sit back and ignore them.

* "Around the World at Eighteen on Credit and Golden Pen," New York *Post*, October 26, 1973.

CHAPTER FOUR

The First Hundred Days

To A CREDITOR, a sum of money owed is a receivable.

And a receivable is a tangible asset.

He can reckon it into his profit and loss statement.

He can use it as collateral for a loan.

He can sell it, at a slight discount, to a factor.

Or he can merely wait until he receives it.

But one thing that all creditors always do with receivables is age them. That is, they compute the length of time that each receivable is outstanding and then use these computations as the basis for their collection and accounting procedures.

Exactly what a creditor does about a receivable of a specified age depends on the nature of his business. For example, the higher the markup, the more leisurely, as a rule, the collection. The same is true for businesses with large cash flows and relatively small amounts of capital tied up in product inventory. In short, all the things that improve a creditor's ability to survive without your money also tend to help receivables live to enjoy a ripe old age.

Businesses with low markups, small cash flows, slow turnovers of inventory, and a large proportion of assets tied up in product inventory have a harder time living without your money, so they start working to collect it sooner.

As a rule, therefore, large, fat corporations make outstanding prospective creditors. They show relatively little corporate anxiety over the absence of your money, and those that do concern themselves about it rarely exhibit their concern before approximately 100 days have gone by.

Once you understand the standard big-business 100-day billing cycle, you can cope with it with a negligible expenditure of either money or effort.

The first thing to do is learn the day of the month when the billing cycle begins. Or, to be more specific, *your* billing cycle begins. The larger the organization, the more charge accounts it has. And the more accounts it has, the less likely that it will compute statements for all of them on the same day. Some companies stagger their billing dates alphabetically. Others do it by account numbers; and still others, by methods known only to themselves. But with all of them, there's usually a line on your statement either listing the billing date or saying, "This statement includes purchases and payments made as of the —————of the month. Purchases and credits after that date will be reflected in next month's statement."

Despite the wording of this statement, payments are usually not reflected until *after* the interest has been computed. This means that, even when customers pay bills immediately on receipt, they're often socked with interest on the "unpaid balance." In New York City, a partially successful class-action lawsuit made creditors cut it out. The lawsuit was partially successful in that it also sought to have the court order the department stores in question (Macy's and others) to audit their records and refund interest charges previously collected in this manner.

When the U.S. Senate was debating the bank-card legislation described in Chapter 2, Senator William Proxmire and others attempted to have these retroactive interest charges prohibited on a national scale, but they weren't successful.

Once you've determined when your billing cycle begins, you can then time your purchases for one or two days immediately after. That way, it will be a full month before the purchases appear on your statement as a current balance—the first step in the aging process.

The aging cycle will start with the time of first billing, even though as many as thirty days may have elapsed since the purchase.* If your billing cycle starts on, say, the twelfth and you buy something on the thirteenth, the aging process won't start until the twelfth of the next month.

If the bill is not paid right away, the next step comes some thirty days later (sixty days after you bought whatever it was you were buying). At that time, the purchase goes from the current-balance blank on your statement to the blank for previous balance. Otherwise, relatively little notice of the debt is taken.

It's _only_ in the next step of the aging cycle (which occurs a month later, or after a lapse of ninety days) that the first concrete attempt at collection comes. This attempt almost invariably takes the form of a form letter, which generally reads something like this:

> DEAR CUSTOMER,
> If you've already paid last
> month's bill, please disregard
> this letter. But if it slipped your
> mind, please send your payment
> by return mail.

Other variations on this theme deal with how easy it is to forget things, or how this letter and your check may have crossed in the mail, or some other handy excuse that a normally conscientious bill payer might have had for not paying a bill.

But all such letters contain (1) an assumption that it is only an oversight that prevented the recipient (a con-

---

*It may be less. The payment agreement for a charge account at A&S department stores specifies that the customer agrees to pay charges on what the store calls its 30-Day Account within 27 days of the billing date.

scientious bill payer) from taking care of it (based, no doubt, on the principle of diplomacy: Always give your opponent a face-saving way to back down), (2) an apology for having sent the reminder, and (3) a request that payment be sent if it isn't on its way already. No attempt is usually made at this time either to shame or to bully the debtor into paying. That comes much, much later—after a long, long series of form letters.

Different corporations have different aging cycles, so if you're tempted to stall a bit but fear the consequences, hold off paying one creditor at a time, just to see what his cycle is. When you get a letter that frightens you, pay him, first noting the delay between the date of the letter and the original purchase date. You'll then know what amount of leeway you'll enjoy as a matter of course, with no personal risk whatever.

After the ninety-day letter, creditors will allow an additional ten days for it to reach you and for your check to reach them. So at this point the weak-hearted can go ahead and become conscientious bill payers, resting assured that without lifting a finger they have gotten 100 days' free credit (more than a quarter of a year's) that will have resulted in a savings of 3 or 4 percent on interest and about 2 percent on inflation.

Incidentally, it's strange that creditors' practices allow the first semiserious collection attempt to be so little and so late.

The longer a receivable remains unreceived, the more

How the value of a dollar of indebtedness shrinks with the lateness of payment*

current	3 months late	6 months late	1 year late	2 years late	3 years late	5 years late
$1.00	$.90	$.50	$.30	$.23	$.15	$.01

The more overdue the debt, the less it's worth collecting.

* CHART ADAPTED FROM *CREDIT AND COLLECTIONS,* THE NATIONAL CASH REGISTER COMPANY.

it costs to collect, the less likelihood there is of collecting it, and consequently, the less it's actually worth. In fact, there comes a point in the aging cycle where standard accounting practices no longer permit the receivable to be carried on the books as an asset of the company. Shortly thereafter, usually around a year overdue, a point is reached where the receivable actually costs more to collect than to write off.

But, as with new cars, the rate of depreciation is far from evenly distributed throughout the cycle. Statistics show that almost 50 percent of the value of the receivable is lost by the time the creditor sends his first or second feeble dunning letter, that is, when payment is three or four months overdue (four or five months after purchase). Why creditors wait so long is something of a mystery, but at least until they read this book, it's a mystery that you don't have to understand to take advantage of.

Some creditors, including gasoline companies, never even bother to send the first letter. Instead, they program their computers to add a finance charge and print across the bottom of the statements with ninety-day balances a message to the effect that this charge can be avoided by making payment now.

Others may never send you that ninety-day letter at all, but just keep on carrying the overdue amount as a previous balance.

And still others will have aging cycles that make a debtor's life easier in other ways. For example: Consolidated Edison, the company that supplies New York with electricity, used to send bills only bimonthly,* probably

---

* The company changed to monthly billing in the hope that the change would speed up their cash flow. The hope turned out to be misguided. What happened was that most customers merely ignored every other bill and went on paying bimonthly. However, they started complaining monthly, instead of every other month, and this increased Con Ed's customer relations expenses. The whole issue was complicated by the fact that while the electric company billed every month, they read the meters every other month, and estimated customer usage in the off-months. These estimates provoked even more complaints, both to the company and to the New York State Public Service Commission. In early 1974, Consolidated Edison admitted defeat and started, on what

77

because of the relatively low dollar amounts that monthly statements would amount to in comparison with the costs of tabulating and mailing them and processing the checks sent in payment.

As a result, each step of the aging process took twice as long. As if that weren't enough, many states have laws regarding payment of bills for utilities that prevent the gas or electricity from being cut off so long as the debtor is making some kind of payment on a regular basis. Thus, you could keep your unpaid bill going indefinitely by sending the electric company a dollar a month.

Still other types of creditors, notably insurance companies, offer you built-in grace periods, usually required by law, during which you can delay payment without having your policy canceled.

In states that require automobile liability insurance, for example, the insurance company usually waits thirty days before sending you a second notice and sends you a warning several weeks later that your policy will be canceled in thirty days if payment is not received by then. Such warning is required by state law, as is the additional thirty-day grace period.

With life insurance policies, there's even more leeway, since you can smash up cars many times in your lifetime, but you drop dead only once. And since there's no legal requirement for people to have life insurance (and therefore fewer policyholders than with auto insurance), life insurance agents anxious to keep on receiving commissions from your payments will do everything possible to keep the policy in force, even if your premium check is months overdue. Even after the grace period expires, they'll keep the policy alive by borrowing the payment— without interest—from the cash surrender value that the policy has built up. This means you can stall on your life insurance payments just as you can any other sort of bill, without worrying about what your family will live on

---

they called an experimental basis, to return to bimonthly billing, for customers using less than $18 worth of electricity per month, in selected neighborhoods.

should you get caught in an avalanche or step into an open elevator shaft.

However, no matter how hard you try to confine credit purchases to large corporations, you'll still probably have at least a few creditors a little nearer home, which is where the expenditure of effort required to avoid the expenditure of money increases. And this happens for several reasons. For one thing, neighborhood creditors are too small to process your account in a machinelike, totally impersonal manner. Therefore, it's much easier for them to draw the conclusion that you're a slow payer —and much more quickly.

They're also not huge bureaucracies with equally huge clienteles, so they're not bound to rigid collection schedules.

Finally, they lack the huge assets that cushion huge creditors from the efforts of delinquent debtors. At best, it's harder for them to get along without your money; at worst, it can be impossible. This means that by stalling on payments to small creditors you can at worst help to drive them out of business and at best subject yourself to more highly motivated—and thus more energetic, to say the least—collection efforts.

Consequently, the best thing you can do about a conscientious small tradesman who gives honest value for money and can't stand the loss of revenue from slow payments is to pay him.

Unfortunately, many merchants and tradesmen fail to fall into this category, so there are many other things to do about them.

Many tenants have weaned their landlords into accepting later and later rent payments by paying the rent a few days later each month. Eventually, a landlord will send you a statutory notice saying that he will initiate eviction proceedings if the outstanding balance is not paid within a specified number of days. If you reach this point, you can do one of two things.

You can pay the rent and then time future payments so that the rent check and the statutory notice cross in the mail. Or you can delay payment further until the landlord actually starts eviction proceedings, which he

79

must inform you about by summons. And then there are delays before your case comes up on the court calendar and additional delays that you can create yourself (see Chapter 11). Judges are usually not anxious to see tenants thrown out into the street, and the laws allow you to dispose of the matter any time up to (and even, in some jurisdictions, after) the actual eviction decree by paying the balance due (plus a nominal fee, usually under $10).

The same weaning technique works well with other local creditors, but since you don't depend on them for the roof over your head, there are other techniques to use instead.

One such technique is the *system* gambit, which was developed by an antique dealer and is particularly useful if you've registered as a business and are dealing with creditors sophisticated enough to know about data processing and its pitfalls. Basically, this technique relies on the inflexibility built into data processing systems (see Chapter 5). But the beauty of it is that you needn't actually have a data processing system to use this inflexibility as a scapegoat.

If you're a business, your purchases will most often be billed on a 2 percent 10-day, net 30-day basis. So, after thirty days, or perhaps a longer time, a creditor will call up to ask about his overdue payment. When this happens, you reply that "it's in the system."

From this, he will infer that you're alluding to a data processing system. He'll know from personal experience that if you were to do anything to dislodge his bill from its preordained niche in the system, it might be years, instead of months, before the system churned out a check with his name on it. This fear should suffice to hold him at bay for at least another few weeks before he asks for his check again.

From this point on, his repeated requests for payment can be met with the repeated explanation that the system has developed bugs, and his check will be forthcoming as soon as the debugging is complete. The only limits to this technique are your creditor's patience or gullibility and your knowledge of esoteric computer programmer jargon to use for explaining the bugs as they develop and are exterminated.

If you're not a business but have established yourself as a wealthy man, you can enjoy the tactics used by the *bona fide* rich described in Chapter 3.

You can blame the unpaid bill on "that confounded secretary" who was supposed to send the check out and rant on about how hard competent help is to come by these days, until the creditor gets bored, snowed, or sympathetic.

Or you can have your wife impersonate "that damned secretary" and explain, "I'm sorry, Mr. Smith is in Australia and I am unauthorized to sign checks in his absence."

If you're unlucky enough to pick up the phone yourself, you can exclaim, "I just got back from Kuala Lumpur, old man, and as soon as I get things sorted out, your check will be on the way to you." Alternatively, you can tell creditors that their bills have been turned over for payment to "my lawyer" or "my accountant" or "will be taken care of in due course," which is always a great catchall if delivered pompously enough. And if your creditor already "knows" you're well-to-do, you'll be able to make any one of these stick.

Or tell him you'd love to pay him if it weren't for the quarterly declaration of estimated income tax that was due, or the beginning or end of the fiscal year, or your legacy being held up in probate, or your Bosnia-Herzegovinan bonds being frozen, or all your cash being tied up in short-term convertible debentures. And as a confidant of one as rich and powerful as you appear, he'll be loving every minute of it.

CHAPTER FIVE

Fold, Spindle, and Mutilate

ON OCTOBER 5, 1960, a computer nearly brought civilization, as we know it, to an end.

At 3:15 Mountain Standard Time, it caused a red light to flash at North American Air Defense Command headquarters, indicating a 99.9 percent probability of ICBM attack on the United States. Specifically, the NORAD computer reported a large flight of missiles, presumably Russian, headed westward over Norway, at a range of 2,200 miles.

For being alive and well today, the people of the world owe a debt to Canadian Air Marshal C. Roy Slemon, senior duty officer at the time, who had the intelligence and sheer guts to question the computer's report before ordering a counterstrike launched in retaliation. Further investigation revealed that the large flight of missiles attacking the United States from 2,200 miles away was actually the moon, from a considerably further distance.

There's no record of whether Air Marshal Slemon was ever decorated for this, but he deserves the highest medal that could possibly be awarded him—not merely for saving the world but for having the bravery, courage, and intrepidity, above and beyond the call of duty, reflecting great credit on himself and his organization, to refuse to blindly accept the word of a computer.

In today's society, there are all too few like him. People in general tend to treat computer printouts with all the awe and credulity that their ancestors, in more spiritual ages, reserved for the words of prophets, oracles, and the deities they represented.

People trust computers to choose such things as their roommates, their jobs, their dates and spouses, their homes and their children's colleges.

No less implicit is the faith that the corporations you'll be dealing with (if you followed the advice of Chapter 2) place in their computers' purported infallibility. The results of this outlook are a bizarre combination of high tragedy and low farce. Because the object of all this faith and reverence is basically a very stupid machine— one designed to perform very involved numerical operations by the electronic equivalent of counting on its fingers, albeit very quickly. (If you question this statement, run, don't walk, to the nearest dictionary and look up the meaning of "digital," as in "digital computer.")

A few years ago, IBM programmed a computer to translate Russian into English and vice versa. To test its operation, they gave the computer some well-known English phrases and orders to translate those phrases into Russian and the Russian equivalents back into English again. Following this procedure, "blood, sweat, and tears" came out as "blood, body water, and eyewash" and "out of sight, out of mind" as "invisible, insane."

Of course, exactly what a computer does depends on the systems analyst and computer programmers who tell it what to do. And as you know from all those computer-school television commercials that always interrupt your favorite John Wayne movie, successful (note: success does not equal competence) computer programmers can be made from high school dropouts.

Between the innate limitations of its circuitry and those of its high school dropout programmers, the computer is not only fallible but capable of errors that even dimwitted human beings have the intelligence to avoid.

During the Lyndon Johnson administration, for example, Defense Department computers predicted that the United States would achieve military victory in Vietnam before 1966, and Secretary of Defense Robert Strange McNamara believed them. (After all, hadn't computer projections been invaluably helpful in helping him reach his decision of a few years before that to bring out the Edsel?)

"Had there been a computer in 1872," said Professor K. William Kapp, of Basel University, "it would probably have predicted that by now there would be so many horse-drawn vehicles it would be almost impossible to clear up all the manure."

According to the *Omaha World Herald*, in 1973, a Dallas, Texas, church called the Melrose Drive Church of Christ was receiving computer-typed letters from a correspondence school. These letters sold electronics courses and were personalized by a program that tells the computer to include the addressee's name in the salutation and body of the letter. Unfortunately, nobody told the computer how to distinguish between people and institutions, so the church got letters addressed to "Mr. Melrose Drive Church of Christ." One of the letters concluded by urging the church to "accept the challenge, Mr. Christ; don't waste your life in a dead-end, low-paying job."

The computer that handles New York's city income-tax collections blew five cents' worth of stationery and six cents' worth of postage (this was before first-class postage went up to ten cents) to send a letter to, of all people, a city councilman (Joseph Modungo) telling him that he owed the city the grand total of one cent from his previous tax return.

New York City's parking violation computer isn't so hot, either. On July 1, 1969, a Bronx man parked his car on West Fifty-sixth Street fourteen minutes too early and received a parking ticket from a passing policeman. On July 3, 1969, he pleaded guilty by mail and sent $10 in payment of the fine. Shortly thereafter, he started receiving a series of computer-printed letters branding him a scofflaw, raising his fine to $65, and by Septmbeer, 1970 (some fourteen months after he'd paid the fine), threatening to attach his property and wages. Letters and visits to the Parking Violations Bureau were of no avail, so he went to New York State Supreme Court for an injunction against these "continued acts of harassment and oppression" and a written apology from the bureau.*

The same computer had also had problems coping with parking tickets issued to out-of-state vehicles, completely ignoring protests from Connecticut and New Jersey drivers that its letters often get the make, color, and license number of cars wrong or ignore documentary proof that the cars in question were nowhere near New York City when they were allegedly ticketed there. It's gotten so bad that two neighboring states have withdrawn their customary reciprocity in this area.

Since 1965, New York City has had almost as bad luck with computers as it's had with mayors. But the blight of computers isn't confined to New York.

When a midwestern college turned its class scheduling over to a computer, they found it had put five classes into the same room at the same time and failed to put other classes into any room at all.

In Virginia, the state's computer suddenly refused to print paychecks for a state employee of eight years' standing, or even to acknowledge that she was, in fact, on the payroll. After seven unpaid paydays, the programmers fed her name in as a new employee, only to have the computer reject her as a duplicate. But when they asked the computer where in its records she was, it couldn't (or perhaps wouldn't) tell. Finally, they ordered it to go through its master list of employees, find her, and transfer her from wherever she was to the commonwealth attorney's office, where she worked. That worked, and she finally got paid.

The president of a company that services and programs the American Express credit card computers was billed for $644 he'd already paid. (To add insult to injury, the second billing was on somebody else's account number.) Which shows that nobody's safe.

Of course, it should be noted that computers are good

* Owen Moritz, "Driver Sues City: Call off Your Crazy Computer," New York *Daily News*, November 9, 1970.

85

for far more than making dumb mistakes; they're superb at compounding those errors by clinging to them with literally inhuman tenacity.

In May, 1969, a *Newsweek* writer charged a plane ticket to his Diners Club card, specifying that the charges be spread out over monthly installments. Apparently, this never got into the Diners Club computer, for he was billed for the entire fare. "I began writing letters to find out why," he said. "No answers came. But every time a dunning notice arrived, I wrote to the name signed at the bottom. Finally I got a form letter signed "M. Sandone' explaining that my inquiry was being investigated. All this time I was paying my regular Diners charges on schedule plus $25 a month on the plane ticket. I never heard from 'M. Sandone' again."*

Another Diners Club cardholder, a computer salesman living in Venice, Florida, had to fight for two and a half years to get his account credited for a $244.39 airline ticket he had canceled. First, instead of crediting him for the $244.39, Diners Club billed him for it a second time. Then, after months of interest charges and dunning letters, Diners suddenly wrote him that he had a $270.65 credit. He wrote for a check, only to be informed he now had a zero balance. However, before the matter was finally resolved, he was dunned several times by Diners Club for the 270.65 "credit."†

A Colorado deputy district attorney sent a creditor a check for $76.39. His account was credited for only $16.39, but his bank's computer debited his checking account for the full face value. For nine months, the creditor's computer kept sending "seriously overdue" notices for the $60 difference, even though the deputy D.A. had called, written, and sent photocopies of the canceled check.†

In 1969, Alfred Bloomingdale, then chairman of Diners Club, said, "I can remember the time when, if some-

* James D. Synder and Robert F. Hickox, "The Revolt Against Computerized Billing, *Parade*, May 31, 1970.

† Marguerite Tarrant, "Coping with Credit-Card Computers," *Money*, June, 1973.

† Tarrant, "Coping with Credit-card Computers."

thing went wrong with a member's account, I called in two little old ladies who rushed to the back of the shop and straightened out the problem in a matter of minutes. Obviously, with today's volume of business the little old ladies are gone, and a monster machine is fed with various data, and if the input happens to be wrong, God help the human being involved! It triggers off a series of dunning notices, legal letters, telegrams, it warns the collectors to start calling on the phone, and sends a letter of misinformation to everyone concerned. To repair the damage and reprogram the computer with correct information takes months. Just how to humanize the computer and the people who work with it is going to be a very big job because . . . the machines are programmed to protect us from . . . abuses, taking no cognizance of the poor, honest man who gets caught in this mess through no fault of his own." ‡

Mr. Bloomingdale is no longer at Diners Club, and the plight of the "poor, honest man" is something his successors seem not to care about.

And this is unfortunate because it takes very little for a poor, honest man or woman to get into "this mess" that Mr. Bloomingdale was talking about.

Quite often, all it takes is a common last name. Mrs. Kate Goldman of Woodruff Avenue, Brooklyn, was for years billed by B. Altman (a department store) for purchases made by Mrs. Katherine Goldman of Woodycrest Avenue in the Bronx. This billing continued after Mrs. Katherine Goldman moved from Woodycrest Avenue in the Bronx to a street of some other name in Far Rockaway, Queens. It continued after letters of apology from the office of the store's president and even after (the president's promises of correction going unkept) Mrs. Kate Goldman closed her Altman's account in disgust.

The American Express computer assigned the same account number to two gentlemen named Greene. One lived in Connecticut, one lived in Maryland, and both had

‡ E. B. Weiss, "Credit Computer Systems Aren't Programmed for Public Relations," *Advertising Age*, October 27, 1969.

different first names. That took six months to straighten out.*

Sometimes, *Parade* magazine reported, "even James Davenport is too common a name for an aerospace executive in McLean, Va. He's dunned repeatedly by a department store for $100 owed by some phantom namesake." † He should get down on his knees and give thanks that his name isn't John Smith.

When people don't get into trouble with credit computers because of their names, sometimes they get folded, spindled, or mutilated because of their addresses.

In May, 1969, an army lieutenant colonel wrote American Express that he was being transferred to the Panama Canal Zone. In fact, he wrote them twice. "On August 15," he stated "I received a bill which had been apparently sent to my old address in the States and forwarded by steamship to Panama. I paid the bill the same day, then began to receive a strange series of communications. The first was a receipt for my payment. Then came a computer letter canceling my account for 'delinquency.' Next came a bill for my new credit card [i.e., an annual fee for the renewal of the travel and entertainment card that had just been 'canceled']—all still bearing my old address!"

Even when the debtor's name or address isn't at fault, a computer can take it into its transistors to zap him for some capricious reason known only to itself.

A woman in Seattle ordered $7.99 worth of merchandise from a local department store. The merchandise never arrived, but the bill did. Her complaints produced another bill, this time for double the amount ($15.98), but still no merchandise. *Newsweek* magazine, which reported the story, had no idea, at the time of publication, what the final outcome would be, but there was a good indication. "In a previous transaction with the same store, she bought $900 worth of furniture, was billed for $1,400 before even signing a contract, and the bill itself was

* Marguerite Tarrant, "Coping with Credit-card Computers."
† Snyder and Hickox, "The Revolt Against Computerized Billing."

stamped 'past due.' That matter was cleared up, but it took six months of correspondence."*

When Congressman Jonathan Bingham of New York received an unsolicited BankAmericard with his name misspelled, he sent it back with a letter of explanation. In reply, the bank sent him a statement of indebtedness: to wit, a bill for a "$10.79 purchase my wife had made by mail from S. S. Pierce Co.—and which she had already paid by check." He sent off another, angrier note, *Life* reported, and "the computer was completely unimpresed." All he got for his trouble was another statement, this one with 16 cents interest added and a 'sharp reminder' of his financial delinquency." †

Of course, with simple computer errors of this type, the best procedure is to send a letter of complaint—not in the hope of any corrective action but just for the record (keep a carbon copy for your files)—and then sit tight awhile. Admittedly, to someone conditioned to believe in the positive moral value of prompt bill payment, a string of dunning letters—even impersonal dunning letters addressed to "Dear Customer" by a computer and "written" by a punch card—can be a frightening and guilt-provoking experience, regardless of whether the debt is disputed or legitimately owed. But it needn't be. If you have to, you can get the error rectified through use of complaint techniques that circumvent the whole computer bureaucracy. These are described in detail in Chapter 6.

However, up to the point where computer dunning ceases to be a nuisance and starts to be a threat (i.e., when they say they're taking your credit card away,) it is to the debtor's advantage that computer errors be prolonged and, when possible, compounded.

Once you bring the computer error to the attention of someone responsible, and he ultimately does something about it, all the moral advantage is going to be on your side. This gives you the leverage to make demands and have your demands acceded to. The longer their delay, the greater your leverage. Specifically, your demands

* "Credit: The Great Snafu," *Newsweek*, September 15, 1969.
† Paul O'Neil, "A Little Gift from Your Friendly Banker," *Life*, March 27, 1970.

should include removal of all interest charges accrued during the life of the computer problem (which means you've gotten a long-term, interest-free loan), a written apology, and reimbursement of out-of-pocket expenses in overcoming the incompetence and insensitivity of your creditor's computer bureaucracy.

These expenses include, but are not necesarily limited to, long-distance phone calls to their corporate headquarters and filing fees for any small-claims court summonses. But in order to make your position justifiable, you must first take certain steps to put your complaint on record in such a way that makes it certain to be ignored.

If you had a computer-type complaint that you wanted to solve immediately, the worst thing you could do would be to write a letter to the person whose signature appeared at the bottom of the computer letter and then mail it in the self-addresed envelope provided by the creditor for payment. This is because the person whom that signature represents may not be a person but a pseudonym created by the computer. The Humble Oil and Refining Company used to send letters signed "T. B. Abrams," which was funny to people sufficiently familiar with the gas station business to know that "T.B.A." was an industry expression standing for "tires, batteries, and accessories." When the person does, in fact, exist, addresing a letter to him doesn't in the least guarantee that he (or she) will get it. There are several reasons why.

One is that mail is delivered to offices twice a day, but it's delivered to post office lock boxes hourly. Therefore, a large credit corporation will have checks sent to a post office lock box instead of their offices, so that they can receive and deposit incoming checks sooner. The incoming mail is usually taken from the post office to an office full of clerks and key-punch operators, who then process the checks and computer-bill stubs and generally ignore everything else.

In other operations, the everything else, which includes complaint letters, is taken to one or more of the people whose name appears at the bottom of form letters. But the actual addressee may not be on hand to receive your letter, and it will take time for it to be forwarded through interoffice mail.

An example of how this works: A customer received a computer letter from BP Oil Company, threatening to revoke his credit card because a balance of approximately $25 had gone unpaid for approximately six months. The letter was signed by one M. Webster. On September 28, 1972, the customer wrote a letter to Miss, Mr., or Mrs. Webster (it turned out to be Miss) stating that there was a mail-theft problem in his building and asking that photocopies of the last three months' transactions be sent. On October 9, in the absence of any reply, other than another dunning letter, he placed a telephone call to the real Miss Webster at company headquarters in Ohio. Her end of the conversation revealed that his letter had arrived the day after he had sent it had been read by another member of her department (whose job it was to screen incoming correspondence that day), had been forwarded to her, and had just that morning crossed her desk.

In response to his righteous indignation over BP's delay, she promised immediate reinstatement of the account, a credit for the cost of the long-distance call, and the requested photocopies. (They arrived marked "Air Mail," "Special Delivery," and "Rush.")

Had it not been a case of suspending credit privileges, he could have merely kept a carbon copy of his letter and ignored the fact that they hadn't answered it until he was ready to make a complaint to someone on a higher level.

Communications between creditors and customers should be two way, but thanks to the anonymity of the computer's system, it's one way for anything but checks and punched payment cards. Legislation was introduced in Congress to require that computerized bills and statements bear an address or phone number (preferably both) that customers could use for complaints, but the bill was never passed. (Some companies, like Shell Oil, list a toll-free complaint number in their computer-written dunning letters. Others in the same industry, like Sunoco, do not.)

Of course, when the computer and its human attendants haven't made an error, it's easy to get them to create one. The request for a billing summary, described above, is just enough out of the ordinary to create delay in getting an answer.

Another way is to fold, spindle, staple, or otherwise mutilate the punch card. This will not stop the system, but it will slow things down because a human being must then redo your card to make it fit for the computer. As with anything touched by human hands, this affords the certainty of delay and the possibility of human error, which you can complain about later.

Mutilating the punch card can divert human attention to your problem. When a Washington, D. C., computer salesman can't get action on his billing complaints, "I mutilate the computer billing card and send it back. When the computer kicks it out as a reject, some human has to write to me and ask why I committed such a dastardly deed. Then I pounce on him with my problem."*

A way to ensure that the computer system will grind to a halt is to deny it its lifeblood: numbers and punch cards. Apparently, there's no way that a creditor can cope with a check that arrives unaccompanied (and legally satisfies the demand for payment). A telephone user once sent a check to the New York Telephone Company, which kept sending it back because there was neither a punch card with the check nor his phone number on it. The check was, however, imprinted with his name and address, and using these, they could have gotten his number simply by phoning information.

In another instance, a customer sent the Citgo Oil Company an unaccompanied check for $7.39 and for the next year received letters from them inquiring what the $73.90 (sic) was in payment of. It was only months later that the check was actually debited to his checking account.

Aside from the delays gained by withholding account numbers and the like, there are some moralistic points to be gained as well. After all, your creditors pay their people to keep records, and you pay (eventually) your

* Snyder and Hickox, "The Revolt Against Computerized Billing."

creditors, so why should you be called upon to do their record keeping for them?

Sometimes, you can create more error and delay by enclosing your punch card than by omitting it. Provided you indulge in a game called *Computer-card Roulette* by its inventor, an anonymous gentleman residing in London.*

The equipment required for this game consists of a razor blade and some punch cards. The rules are as follows: You take the razor blade, cut a few extra holes in the punch card, send it in for processing, and complain about the result. (An X-acto knife will work even better.)

He did this with a magazine subscription card and received twenty-three copies of the magazine each week, along with a thank-you note for using it in his current-events class. (Naturally, he doesn't have a current-events class.)

A group of Harvard mathematicians recommend the same technique, but for a different reason. "The computer," they say, "will check your altered card with its own memory tape, will notice the discrepancy, and will get very nervous. If your friends are all doing the same thing to their punch card[s], so much the better." And from month to month, move the extra holes around. This creates an impression of many random, nonpersistent errors in the computer. "They'll get paranoid. Many random mistakes are the industry's Achilles' heel. This system works to destroy them." †

A method for the more timid is to enlarge the holes with the tip of a ball-point pen. This will make the punch cards illegible to the computer and will cause it to reject the card for no apparent reason. You can picture the delay that this will cause as people keep feeding the card in and the computer keeps throwing it out.

Some computers are programmed to bug you only if you send no payment at all. So if you have a no-interest

* Guerilla War Against Computers," *Time*, September 12, 1969.

† "How to Stop Worrying and Love the Computer," *Newsweek*, July 27, 1970.

charge account, you may be able to keep it current by sending in token payments every month.

Other computers are so unsophisticated that they can handle a balance due but not an overpayment. If you send in a one- or two-cent overpayment, the computer may go "tilt" and kick out your check. You will have tendered payment without your checking account actually being charged for it.

The computer may be a very massive machine, but it's also a very delicate one. Its vulnerability to outside elements is such that even the air in a computer room must be cleansed of dust and all other impurities lest the machine have a nervous breakdown. Using this knowledge, the inventor of Punch-card Roulette has also invented the following method for rendering a computer unable to cash your check (along with anybody else's): Mail your check with its punch card in an envelope heavily soaked in cheap perfume. Even after a day or two in the mails, enough perfume molecules should still remain to knock the computer out of kilter.

Finally, however, some computers seem to have minds of their own, albeit retarded ones. For six months, a Pittsburgh truck driver received past-due notices and increasingly obnoxious letters from an appliance store's computer. The balance due was $0.00 (i.e., zero dollars and zero cents). Phone calls and letters didn't help, so he finally sat down and wrote out a check for the full balance—$0.00. The computer sent him a thank-you letter for his payment, but the computer at his bank's clearinghouse reportedly underwent a nervous breakdown.

CHAPTER SIX

The Joys of Shoddy Service

THERE IS A theory prevailing in the land that what consumers need is some sort of surrogate, preferably governmental, to do their complaining for them. In 1969, Ralph Nader went on record as advocating a sort of sub-cabinet-level Federal Bureau of Kvetching. The same attitude has been reflected in magazines like the radical-chic *New York*, which published an article entitled "How to Complain." The article turned out to be nothing more than a list of governmental agencies to complain to, and as anybody who's had any dealings with any governmental agency knows, having a government address to complain to is the beginning, not the end, of the problem. In any event, Nader's and New York's working assumptions seem to be that the individual is powerless to register a complaint and that a government agency—any government agency—is his salvation.

Neither assumption is true, and before getting into what the individual *can* do, it is important to realize what government agencies *can't* do. One of the best illustrations of the latter is a story published in the very same

New York magazine that worships at the feet of paternalistic government. What was involved was a man with water leaking through, and plaster falling from, the ceiling of his rented apartment. Instead of pursuing other remedies, like the city Landlord and Tenant Court, for example, he took his problem to the appropriate governmental agency: the city's Rent Control Commission. He submitted his complaint in duplicate. His complaint was sent to the landlord. The landlord answered it, in duplicate. He was sent a copy of the landlord's answer. He rebutted it, in duplicate. A building inspector came. He inspected. He filed his report, in triplicate.

Then a final order for the repairs was drawn up, in duplicate, and sent to both the landlord and tenant, with copies of the inspector's report. Then the inspector came to inspect again, to see if the repairs had been made. They hadn't, and he filed another report. Again, in triplicate.

Each of these steps is supposed to take place within ten days of each other, but backlogs and bureaucracies being what they are, there's usually at least sixty days between steps one and two and at least thirty days before each of the succeeding steps. So finally, after more than a year had gone by, the forces of government drew themselves up to wreak administrative justice on behalf of our deserving hero. The redress: His rent was reduced by the princely sum of one dollar per month.

Of course, this case is not typical of all government bureaucracies. In the case of industries totally regulated by government, like utilities, a government agency can be useful and even highly effective. But government effectiveness, as a rule, is almost as much a contradiction in terms as military intelligence or democratic socialism; and the debtor with a problem would be better advised to take it elsewhere (he could lose his credit, be sued, and file for bankruptcy while the rebuttal forms were still going back and forth in duplicate). Government agencies are more effective as potential threats than as actual remedies. And should you have a complaint that needs solving in a hurry, your creditor's complaint department is even less helpful. It, too, is a bureaucracy, but one working for the organization you're complaining about, which implies a certain lack of disinterested objectivity.

Dealing with most complaint departments is enough to give most people the inescapable impression that these bureaucracies have been designed expressly to capitalize on the fact that far too many people don't know what their rights are and how to fight for them. One measure of people's inability to fight for, or fear of fighting for, their rights is a calculation made by the New York State Public Service Commission that in more than half the complaints made to Consolidated Edison Company, consumers fail to get satisfaction.

However, the very qualities that make the creditor's complaint department totally useless as a source of relief make it highly useful as a source of time; namely, bureaucratic inefficiency and a vested interest in getting rid of you rather than helping you.

Like most bureaucracies, the creditor's complaint department is composed of people who spend most of their time dealing with bits and pieces of paper; including the letter of complaint you write, the pieces of paper pertaining to your transaction, other pieces of paper describing the merchandise, still other pieces of paper confirming or denying the existence of similar complaints, the piece of paper that tells you your complaint has been received, and finally the piece of paper that's supposed to dispose of your complaint. Not "solve," . . . "dispose of." To make it go away, with any satisfaction you get being purely coincidental.

In addition to the paper situation, there's also the employees' vested interest, which is to handle your problem with a minimum of actual work, in such a manner as will please, not you, but their immediate and ultimate superiors. And insofar as complaint bureaucrats know, their superiors are most pleased by (1) not being personally bothered by your complaint and (2) not losing any money over it.

When you complain through channels, what you end up with is (1) an unsatisfactory answer, (2) an inordinate delay in arriving at it, and (3) for debtors who can afford to press the issue, still further basis for complaint to someone higher up.

A 1972 case in Federal District Court (Southern New York district) illustrated this principle. A seventy-seven-year-old Brooklyn woman, on welfare, received electricity bills several times as large as her usual monthly charges. While paying Consolidated Edison the usual monthly sum, she asked them to investigate the cause of her high bills. They discovered that in a private energy-conservation program her landlord had been tapping into her power line for his own electrical needs. In spite of this discovery, however, the electric company continued to bill her for the landlord's stolen electricity. In May, 1971, Con Edison cut off her electricity, and after three weeks, the woman got an emergency check for the amount demanded from the city's Social Services Department, hand-delivered it to Con Ed, and got a receipt for it. Her service was restored, but less than two months later, Con Ed bill collectors showed up at her apartment to demand another $175 and threaten another one-woman blackout if she didn't pay it. The woman went to Legal Aid and sued Con Edison.

In its reply to the lawsuit, the electric company denied that they sent representatives to her apartment or that they had any record indicating that the landlord tapped her power lines. But "in a flat contradiction" of this contention, Federal Judge Harold R. Tyler wrote in his opinion, the company furnished a letter it had sent her, informing her that two representatives (bill-collectors) had been sent to allegedly verify the bills. "However curious this may appear," Judge Tyler continued, "it is mild stuff when considered against the story of what happened to the check with which [she] attempted to finally end her ordeal." The check was received and credited to her account and then sent for deposit to Manufacturers Hanover Trust. "But with remarkable self-satisfaction under the circumstances," the judge wrote, "Con Ed then asserts: One, the check was lost at the bank; two, the bank notified the company that they had not received the check; and three, the company, by unknown employee, then reentered the deficit on [her] account."*

To the customer who's made his purchase by cash and wants his money back, experiences like these are very frustrating. But to the customer who's charged his purchase and kept his money in his own pocket, they're a source of delay. Which means a source of profit.

The way most large companies work, any complaint automatically puts the dunning and interest-charging procedures on hold; and even where it doesn't, you can easily demand, and automatically receive, a credit for interest covering the period during which your complaint was being handled, regardless of the outcome.

When you write letters of complaint to the Hertz Rent-A-Car customer relations department, for example, their first response is a form post card, arriving about two weeks after, acknowledging receipt of the complaint, stating that an investigation is being initiated and will take six to eight weeks and that the results of the investigation will be sent shortly after its conclusion.

This investigation consists of verifying the rental agreement with the issuing office and looking up your file to see how often you rented and whether you'd complained much before. Then, after a waiting period of eight weeks minimum to twelve weeks maximum, an answer is forthcoming. But throughout the entire eight-to-twelve-week period—in other words, for almost a quarter of a year—payment is neither asked nor expected.

Diners Club has a similar procedure, up to the post card. After that, they completely forget about your complaint and keep on billing you, with interest.

The important thing here, and this cannot be repeated too often, is not the final disposition of your complaint, because unless it's satisfactory to you, it's not final anyhow. What is important is (1) the fully acceptable delay in payment and (2) the fact that for future reference and for future defense against any bill-collecting procedures, you've put your complaint on record.

Of course, the people you're dealing with don't realize

* Marvin Smilon and James Norman, "Judge Pulls Con Ed Fuse," New York *Post*, October 31, 1972.

that this is what you're after, so they'll proceed to delay and "frustrate" you, in the hope of losing you, like most complainers, by attrition. If you handle your complaint in such a manner as to "cooperate" with their system, they'll play right into your hands.

To do this, you should first complain by letter rather than telephone. There are several reasons for doing this. First, to the normal delays, you'll be adding the delays of the U.S. Postal Service, which are far from inconsiderable. Second, a telephoned complaint can be handled quickly by return phone call, but a written complaint necessitates a written reply, which, in turn, necessitates sorting by the mail room, internal routing, initiation of a file, dictation and typing of a reply, and further mail room handling, all of which take time. Third, there's no way to make a carbon copy, for the record, of a telephone call.

When you write your letter, make at least one carbon copy. If you don't have access to a Xerox machine, make several carbons. You'll probably need them later on.

When you state the nature of your complaint, it often helps to keep it a bit sketchy. This creates the need for them to write you for more details.

If you send a copy of your bill with your letter, make sure it's not your only copy. Make a copy, or, better yet, have them search the files for *their* copy. This takes even more time.

Address your letter to the company, but not to any specific individual. If you must address it to someone, address it to the complaint department. This will add more time while they figure out which department to send it to and which person in that department.

According to Professor C. Northcote Parkinson, each organization has what he calls a "standard delay," this being defined as the length of time it takes your letter to get from the bottom to the top of the "In" basket and then out to you in the form of a reply. Note the length of the standard delay, and take slightly longer in sending your reply to their reply. (Turnabout is fair play.) Or if you really want to confuse things, send them another letter a few days before the standard delay is up. This will drop your letter from the top of the "In" basket to the bottom again.

Resist all blandishments to provide your creditors with information that you have reason to believe already exists in their records. Tell them that you already pay them to do this through their profit margin and that you have no intention of doing their work for them. In addition to being right as a matter of principle, this will add more time as they delve into the records.

Whenever possible, answer their questions with questions. Question their definitions, circumlocutions and jargon. But bear in mind that if you're dealing with the right kind of company, they'll provide all the obfuscation you could possibly need.

A perfect example of the way this works in practice is how an American Express cardholder's complaint about a billing error was, pardon the expression, handled.

In 1965, he had gone into the London Terrace Florist in Manhattan to have a bouquet of flowers delivered by Florists' Telegraph Delivery (as it was called then) and asked that the purchase be charged to his American Express card. Rather than pay American Express a 7½ percent commission, the florist offered to take his personal check, using the American Express account as a reference (a procedure that constitutes a breach of contract with American Express, by the way).

Having paid for the flowers by check, the cardholder was astounded next month to see, with his American Express statement, a charge for the flowers and a form stating: "Your account has been charged for purchase from an FTD florist. If further information is required please write us."

Not wanting to pay twice for the same bouquet of flowers, he wrote. He explained that he had paid by check and would not pay again unless American Express could send him a copy of a sales ticket with his signature on it (which they couldn't, because none existed). He paid his outstanding balance, less ten dollars for the flowers.

A month went by.

He then received a reply from one D. G. Smith, stating

that the files were being searched for the charge ticket and that a photo-copy would be on the way shortly.

Another month went by.

American Express started dunning him for the ten dollars.

He received another letter from D. G. Smith, proudly enclosing the photocopy. The photocopy was of the card that said "Your account has been charged for a purchase from an FTD florist. If further information is required, please write us."

He wrote again, challenging D. G. Smith to find his signature on this document, demanding one that did have his signature, and refusing to pay his entire account balance (a total of $104) until either the documentation or a credit was provided.

Two more months passed.

A total of about four months having elapsed from the start of correspondence, D. G. Smith replied that the customer should write to FTD in Detroit for a copy of the charge slip. The customer wrote back asking whether it had taken all of four months to come up with that.

Another month went by.

Smith wrote, apologizing, stating that he was writing Detroit for a photocopy of the right slip.

Two months went by.

Smith wrote, stating that FTD only kept charge slips on file for six months and that the slip was "missing or destroyed." (The possibility that it was nonexistent had still failed to register on his mind). Therefore, he was giving the customer the benefit of the doubt, crediting his account for the ten dollars, and removing all interest charges for the last six months. "Your patience in this trying matter," he concluded, "is greatly appreciated."

As a result of this long affair, attenuated by American Express' blundering and stupidity (typical of any large credit organization), the customer, through an error, had gotten more than six months' interest-free credit on $104 worth of purchases. Had he thought to omit his account number and other information useful to the creditor, there's no telling how much longer it might have dragged on.

Of course, the one thing that any debtor needs to engage in a stall like this is a good complaint, and these days, at least, a good complaint is not hard to find.

A New York television station demonstrated on the air that about half the net weight of canned fruit products is taken up not by fruit but by a solution of sugar in water.

According to Senator Frank Moss, during the seven-year period ending January, 1974, some 40 million cars, trucks, buses, and other vehicles have been recalled for safety-related defects. In the sixteen months ending January, 1974, the Consumer Products Safety Commission found more than 5 million butane lighters, gas ovens, space heaters, color-television sets, lawn mowers, ski boots, and other products to have "substantial product hazards." And each year, an estimated 30,000 Americans are killed and 110,000 permanently injured in accidents involving consumer products from hair dryers to roller skates.*

Many brands of ice cream are made with such tasty ingredients as ethyl acetate (also used as cleaning fluid), amyl acetate (also used as a solvent for oil paints), piperonal (also used as a louse killer), and propylene glycol (also used in germicides and paint removers), and artificial flavoring and coloring.

The pages of *Women's Wear Daily* have been full of articles about customer complaints about dresses that lose buttons and split seams on the first wearing.

When long-lasting stainless-steel razor blades first came out, according to financial writer "Adam Smith," one manufacturer kept profits up by putting the boys in the lab to work on reducing the number of shaves per blade from 16.4 to 12.7.

Dollar-bill changers at the new Dallas-Fort Worth Regional Airport give ninety-five cents change; boarding ramps take as long as thirty minutes to hook up to planes; local phone calls cost twenty-five cents; mechanical baggage-handling machines rip luggage to shreds, and automated passenger-transport vehicles head for the

* Living Dangerously," *Newsweek*, January 28, 1974.

wrong destinations. "Considering the size and scope of the facility," said the mayor of Dallas after the airport's first few weeks of operation, "I'm really elated there weren't more foul-ups." †

Consumers Union analyzed federally-inspected pork sausages and found that one-eighth of the samples contained "insect fragments, insect larvae, rodent hairs, and other kinds of filth."†

In November, 1969, the U.S. Department of Transportation announced that one out of every four tires it tested failed to live up to the manufacturers' own quality standards.

From August, 1965, to January, 1973, the ten-cent Hershey bar shrunk from two to 1.26 ounces (the price remained constant).

Two-by-four boards now officially measure 1½" by 3½", and McDonald's hamburger stands have gotten into legal trouble because their "quarter-pounder" burgers started life as less than a quarter pound of raw meat.

In December, 1974, Nabisco, Inc., shipped gift fruitcakes to its stockholders, only to find out that a rancid ingredient had made them turn sour.‡

New York City health inspectors discovered hundreds of pounds of spoiled food, moldy cheese, rotting baby food in jars, slime-covered poultry and black meat being sold on the shelves at 96 supermarkets—ranging from A&P to Zeitzer Food Corporation.†

Other inspectors discovered that Weight Watchers frozen diet foods were helping dieters lose weight in a totally unexpected way—by packing less food, by weight, than was specified on the packages.

To show that nothing is sacred, Consumers Union ran radio commercials to sell subscriptions to *Consumer*

---

*"Airports: Debugging the Future," *Newsweek*, February 4, 1974.

†"The U.S.'s Toughest Customer," *Time*, December 12, 1969.

*"Nabisco's Fruitcakes Fizzle," *Advertising Age*, January 27, 1975.

‡William Sherman, "City Shops the Food Markets, Finds Some of the Goods Stink," *New York Daily News*, November 8, 1974.

Reports. These commercials featured the low price of "a full year's subscription of 11 monthly copies."

Services provide almost as many grounds for complaint as goods. Our egalitarian society assigns low status to people who earn their living by giving service. Service has come to be reviled as merely servility, which is to be avoided at all costs. One outcome of this point of view is the surly, cavalier attitude of many sales and service people toward the customers who supply their livelihoods. Another outcome is a relatively short supply of people in service trades and positions, who are allowed by the law of supply and demand to do pretty much as they please, as opposed to what the customer pleases.

The shoddiness of services actually manages to outstrip the shoddiness of goods.

In 1968, when the Boeing 747s were making their debuts, the *Wall Street Journal* reported that a man arrived at San Francisco as the only passenger aboard one of these flying great white whales, only to discover that the airline (Pan Am) had managed to lose his luggage. And this example is neither as extreme nor as isolated as it may appear to the uninitiated.

When the New York City Department of Consumer Affairs tested television repair shops by asking them to fix sets with no problem more serious than a single bad tube, only one shop in eight did an honest job in the customer's home and charged a reasonable service fee. The others took the sets away, made unnecessary repairs, or charged for work that wasn't done.

In 1973, the Conference Board commissioned an opinion survey to find out whether consumers rated each of 44 products and services as good, average, or poor values for money spent. Only 5.8 percent of the respondents rated auto repairs "good," while 59 percent rated them "poor"; 5.3 percent rated appliance reparis "good," while 57.3 percent rated them "poor"; similarly, a mere 4.4 percent rated home repairs "good," while 57.4 percent rated them "poor." (These were the three worst ratings in the survey. By contrast, the best was for eggs, which 41.5 percent rated "good" and 12.4 percent rated "poor.") *

But perhaps the booby prize goes to the U.S. Postal Service, which, according to *Time* magazine, "regularly exceeds its own heroic standards for inefficiency. [In 1970] one letter took sixteen days to move from Massachusetts to New Jersey." †

Americans spend more than $2.5 billion per year on drycleaning, and according to a 1972 survey made by the National Institute of Dry Cleaning, 25 percent of the customers had their garments damaged, 13 percent had items lost, and 7 percent received clothing belonging to someone else. Add them all together, and you get 45 percent, which means that nearly half the people who are dry-cleaning customers get taken to the cleaners in one way or another.

We have become the society that John Gardner warned about, where shoddiness in philosophy is honored because philosophy is a high and noble calling, and excellence in plumbing is scorned because plumbing is a humble and menial occupation. As a result, neither the theories nor the pipes hold water.

If goods and services fail to offer any grounds of complaint, there's always the vague, subjective complaint, like "I don't like it," or "It's not right for me (my room, my house, my dog, my car, and so on)," which is as hard and time consuming to pin down and prove or disprove as an army malingerer's complaint about a back injury.

Even if you don't have a very major complaint, it doesn't hurt to raise it, and for advantages beyond the time gained before you have to finally pay. For one thing, you'll be pulling the same tactic your creditors pull on their creditors—to stall for months with complaints and then use the complaints as the basis for haggling down the price. Second, you will, by merely stating your complaint, be working to improve goods and

* The survey was conducted in May, 1973, by National Family Opinion, Inc. Questionnaires were mailed to a representative sample panel of 10,000 households. The response rate was about 83 percent.

† "America the Inefficient," *Time*, March 23, 1970.

services for the millions of people who have stronger grounds for complaint but are too weak-hearted to do anything but silently nurse their dissatisfaction.

At the very worst, you'll have gotten your creditor to review, if only cursorily, his products and customer services. At best, you'll have gotten delay and redress.

Don't worry if you lack sufficient facts to fully describe the nature of your complaint. According to Infact Systems, Inc., 75 percent of complaints received by businesses and government bodies can't be acted on because pertinent facts are missing.

Now most of the techniques discussed so far assume that you have all the time in the world to get your complaint settled and that every added delay is on your side. But if you're in a situation where your merchandise doesn't work right, the seller won't take it back, and the credit department is ready to take away your plastic if you don't pay up regardless of whether or not you're getting what you pay for, an entirely different set of techniques is called for. Just as the foregoing techniques were designed to maximize delay, the following ones are designed to all but eliminate it.

The key to eliminating delay is the principle discussed earlier, but in a different context: if you want to win, pick on a bully. The "bully" in this case is the second highest placed relevant official in the company you're complaining to. Some definition and explanation are called for here. "Relevant" means relevant to customer problems, sales, and profits (and possibly lawsuits) from customers' transactions. In other words, if some furniture you ordered is two months overdue, the head of the Shipping Department (who cares about shipping) is far less relevant to you than the Sales Manager or General Manager (who has to be concerned about revenues and, by implication, the customers who provide them). The "second highest" means you don't go screaming to the chairman of the board on your first call. This is not because there's anything particularly sacrosanct about board chairmen, but simply because, if the official you talk to can't or won't help, you want to allow yourself at least one level of appeal within the company hierarchy.

The one person you don't want to talk to is someone in the Complaint or Customer Relations department, for several reasons.

The first is that, being closer to the level where your complaint originated, the complaint person is in a far better position than the company officer to investigate its validity.

An experiment with Macy's department store proved this point. In mid-February, 1970, a customer wrote a letter to the linen buyer (in department stores, the buyer is the de facto head of the department). The letter set out the following complaint: On January 29, he had placed a phone order in response to a white sale ad in the New York *Times* (the page number of the ad was quoted). He also ordered merchandise from another department. On January 31, the merchandise from the other department arrived, but not the marked-down, slightly irregular linens. On calling the store to find out about the missing linens, his letter of complaint continued, he was told by a saleswoman that the linens were all sold out, and besides, the January white sale was over. The letter concluded that according to any calendar, 30 days hath September, April, June, and November, but January had 31; and since it was a January, not February, white sale, what right had this salesperson to say that the month ended on the 28th?

Immediately upon receiving this letter, the Macy's linen buyer called the customer at home to offer the same quantity of the same size and color sheets—but first quality, not irregular—at the marked-down sale price. The buyer, keeping good customer relations in mind, obviously made this offer without even bothering to investigate the complaint, because the most routine investigation would have turned up no record whatever of any January 29 transaction between him and the linen department, for the simple reason that none existed. The buyer merely assumed the inefficiency, rudeness and inconsideration of the people in his department and acted on this assumption.

This is not to imply that company officers are a bunch of dummies. They're not. They just happen to have a different order of priorities than flunkies lower down in the hierarchy and the executive order of priorities works more to the advantage of the complaining debtor.

Unlike the complaint department bureaucrat, an officer doesn't want to get rid of you. He wants you to come back again. He has the authority to bend the rules in doing this, while the complaint bureaucrat lacks both the authority and, often, the inclination.

One customer's dealing with the Bloomingdale's phonograph department provides a case in point. About six months after purchasing a KLH stereo there, one of his speakers went mute, and he called the department to have the speaker picked up and repaired. The salesman he spoke to said the store would do this if he repacked the speaker in its original carton, which he hadn't bothered to keep. Voices rose, and the discussion got nowhere.

He then had his call transferred to the store manager and asked whether Bloomingdale's policy was that all customers had to relegate one room of their apartments to storing empty cartons just in case the merchandise had to be returned to Bloomingdale's for repairs. Unlike the salesman, the manager was able to set aside the rulebook and use his head. He merely had an empty carton delivered to the customer's home and then had it picked up, with the speaker inside, a few days later.

The executive also has a different perspective on money from that of the complaint clerk. The $300 you may be refusing to pay for a defective television is a large sum of money to a clerk who may be lucky to take home half that sum every paycheck. But for the executive who routtinely deals in hundreds of thousands, if not millions, of dollars of the company's money, your $300 is relatively trivial.

The executive is aware of other economic values that the clerk is unaware of. For example he's aware of the value of the company's time spent in investigating and processing your complaint. He's aware of the value of his own time to the company. He's aware of the amount of money that the company has spent (through advertising and promotion) to solicit and retain your business.

And finally, since senior executives tend to be senior in age as well as position, they are aware of the fact that companies do not exist in a vacuum, of and for themselves, without customers. Taken together, this means that the senior executive is likely to save time and money invested in himself as an employee and you as a customer by deciding disputes in your favor rather than the company's, and with a profuse apology to boot. Provided that your complaint is made in such a way as to convince him that if he doesn't, you're going to cost the company a lot of time and money.

The first step in complaining to a senior executive, of course, is finding out the name and address to complain to. Sometimes, when the company you're complaining to is in your city, this is as easy as making a phone call and asking for the president.

If you live in New York and have a complaint about phone service (which is probably often), you can pick up the phone, dial 394-4141 (the number of the New York Telephone Company's executive offices, listed in the Manhattan directory), and ask for either "the president" or "Mr. Ellinghaus." You won't get President Ellinghaus, but you will get one of a circle of high-placed flunkies assigned to deal with customer problems in the name of the president's office.

These people buck the complaint down the line to the people who would've gotten it had you called the business office to complain in the first place. But there's an amazing difference in time and attitude, because the complaint people handle complaints entirely differently when they come down from the top.

When a vice-president sends a note down saying, "Take care of——," he may mean "Get rid of him" or he may mean "Be very nice to this friend of mine." Any clerk who wants to hold his job for a while is going to asume the latter, since there's no penalty for being nice to a customer, in contrast to what happens when you get rid of a customer who's the vice-president's friend. As a result, the repairman comes in a few hours instead of a few weeks, the bill is adjusted promptly instead of never, and so on.

Incidentally, the phone company formalizes what is merely a matter of custom and psychology in most non-monopoly, non-government-regulated companies. With other companies, complaints made to officers tend to receive much more deferential treatment than those made to complaint clerks, but this is merely the result of the vested interest of the clerk in question. With the phone company, however, this disparity of treatment is the result of company policy. According to a former New York Telephone Company business representative, company regulations require that complaints be classified into three distinct orders of priority. First priority goes to customer complaints filed with the state Public Service Commission. There is a teletype link between the offices of the PSC and those of the phone company, and whenever a phone user complains to the PSC, a summary of the complaint is sent to New York Telephone over the teletype. Phone company employees are under instructions to start settling the complaint as soon as the last period is typed, if not sooner. Second priority goes to "executive appeals," which are calls to the president and his circle of high-placed flunkies. These take priority over anything but complaints to the PSC and almost invariably get same-day service. (When one New Yorker had repeated troubles in reaching his own home phone from his office, he made an "executive appeal." Within two hours, an installer and a supervisor arrived at his apartment to check out the problem, much to the surprise of his wife, who had accidentally knocked the receiver off the hook.) Third priority goes to complaints directed to business representatives, repair service, operators, supervisors and so on. These complaints take precedence over nothing and therefore often takes days, if not weeks, to satisfy. And while other phone companies may handle routine complaints faster, they all seem to have the same kind of procedure for giving precedence to non-routine complaints.

One thing to be said in New York Telephone's favor, though, and it's probably the only thing, is that they do put most men straight through to the president's office. Apparently, women are too diffident on the line to get through, as the experience of far too many women have shown. The best thing for a woman to do in this circumstance is to pretend to be her husband's secretary and announce herself over the phone as such.

Many other companies, notably Macy's and Abraham & Straus in New York, train their switchboard operators to keep calls away from the president at all costs. The procedure works like this:

"Macy's."

"The president, please."

"*Whom* do you want?"

"The president."

"Of what?"

"The president of Macy's."

"Oh. What is your call in reference to, please?"

And from this point on, unless your call is in reference to his committing adultery with your wife, you'll be switched to some complaint clerk.

Fortunately, there are two books that can get you around this kind of promise. One is *McKittrick's Directory of Advertisers*, and the other is *Standard & Poor's Business Directory*. Both are big, red books, containing the names, addresses and phone numbers of all major American companies and the names and titles of their key executives, and either can be found in the business or reference section of any large library.

If you know the name of a key executive and ask for him by name, you can usually get by the switchboard. Or, even if the switchboard gauntlet is still too heavy to run, you have a name and address to write to.

How you make your complaint is almost as important as whom you make it to. The first thing you want to convince your target of is the fact that you are a customer of value and a person of substance (these always being assumed to be customers of value). If you want to save time by making your complaint over the phone, then place your call person-to-person. He's not going to know you're a person with enough means (or enough money) to place long-distance calls unless he knows you're calling long distance. And in these days of direct dialing, he won't know you're calling long distance unless there's a person-to-person operator to say, "Mr. Smith, please, long distance calling." (If the company is local, you can achieve almost the same effect by having your secretary—or some woman around your office who puts help to the needy ahead of Women's Lib—place the call for you.)

Don't worry about the cost of the call. In complaint cases, these are readily repaid to customers who demand it. If you write instead of call, this is where your engraved stationery, IBM Executive typewriter, and "secretary's" initials in the lower left-hand corner will carry the same weight as an announced long-distance phone call.

The value of communicating your personal importance cannot be overstressed. Richard Tarlow ordered a hand-made table from an establishment called the Yellow Barn (in Westchester County, New York) in June of 1972, and September delivery was promised. In October, with no table having arrived, he called the store to complain.

He was told that the carpenter who made the tables took his vacation from June to September and that the table would therefore be ready in December, and that the store had no explanation for why they hadn't made this little fact known in advance. "Then what do I tell President Nixon and Secretary General Waldheim when they come to dinner next week?" he asked, "To eat on the floor?"

The next day the Yellow Barn's executive vice-president called up to apologize and to offer to deliver in person a rosewood table that Tarlow could use until the one he'd ordered was ready. "Will seating for eight be sufficient?"

Sometimes either the complainer's position or the circumstances surrounding his complaint establish him as a valuable customer automatically. In 1968, the vice-president and copy director of a New York advertising agency wrote a letter to United Airlines complaining about inedible food, served cold and late, when he flew first class from Chicago to New York. His position as a principal of an advertising agency and the fact that he flew first class impressed the airlines sufficiently to make them refund the difference in price between first-class and economy fare for that flight.

113

Donald Spector, a vice-president and copy group head at Needham, Harper & Steers, Inc., found that his title and the fact that he had patronized one of Restaurant Associates' more expensive restaurants (the one at New York's La Guardia Airport) accomplished the same for him. He wrote to complain about the surliness and grudging service of the maitre d'hôtel. The vice-president who answered his letter was impressed enough to offer Spector and his family a free meal at the restaurant, with the maitre d' ordered to serve as his waiter and to treat the family with tender, loving care.

Instead of being vague about facts, to add delay, you should be as specific as possible in order to reduce it, and in order to give your case an air of credibility. In the Macy's white-sale letter, one reason that the linen buyer didn't double-check the facts was that there was such a profusion of them: the color, size and quantity of the linens "ordered," the prices, the merchandise numbers, the time of day the phone order was "placed," even the page number of the *Times* on which the white sale ad appeared.

Also, when you marshal your facts, be sure to notice any that make the creditor's actions look particularly fishy, because then you're in the strongest of bargaining positions. The mother of a soldier at Fort Dix, New Jersey, sent him a telegram, paying seventy-five cents extra for messenger delivery. Prompt delivery was necessary, since the soldier was due home on pass the next day, and the family's phone number had been changed.

Now, Western Union is no longer known for giving the best of service. The New York *Times* once, as an experiment, gave Western Union offices throughout New York City the same message to send to the same address, with messenger delivery. Delivery times varied from a few hours to a few days, and less than 25 percent of the telegrams were free of garbles and spelling errors. Western Union protects itself from the consequences of bad service, however, with a masterfully written contract. The contract is on the back of a telegraph blank, and you signify acceptance of its terms by filling out the front. This contract obliges Western Union only to *attempt to* deliver the message and not necessarily by telegraph, either. They can send it by telephone, carrier pigeon, camel caravan, hot-air balloon, or U.S. mail, which, in the case of the soldier's telegram, was exactly what the Wrightstown, New Jersey, Western Union office did. The telegram arrived by mail in the middle of the following week.

Technically, Western Union could have quite legally told the soldier's mother to jump in the lake with her complaint, but the very absurdity of the situation, coupled with her persuasive argument that if she'd wanted to send a letter, she wouldn't have paid Western Union's rates for a telegram, got her a full refund.

Another example: In mid-1972, a driver left his two-year, 40,000-mile-old Plymouth Duster at a Bridgeport, Connecticut, Plymouth dealer to have the front disc-brake calipers—which had become inoperative—replaced. Since disc brakes were optional equipment, the parts were not in stock, and the dealership placed an order for them. Three days were allowed for delivery of the parts and the necessary installation. After four days, a phone call was made to the dealership, during the course of which the service manager explained that the calipers originally supplied with the car were no longer listed under the original parts number, and, since Plymouth had failed to update the parts list, it took a day and a half—until the order came bouncing back—for them to discover this. In 1971, the calipers had been modified and given a new number. Unfortunately, the nearest warehouse was out of the new parts and said they would be for about a week, and the dealer knew of no way to speed up the process.

The car owner went to a copy of *Standard & Poor's*, got the name and phone number of Plymouth Division's general manager, and placed a call to Detroit. In this conversation, he recounted the history of the disc brake calipers in question, noting that the part probably wouldn't have been modified if there hadn't been some kind of problem in the original design; that while the warranty on that part expired after one year or 12,000 miles (both of which had long since come and gone), it covered only defects in workmanship and materials, leaving the question of design defects wide open; and that if the parts were not delivered to the dealership immediately, he would be all too happy to explore this open question in a court of law.

The general manager promised that someone who could deal with the problem more directly would call back within the hour. Within the half-hour, an apparently shaken-up executive from their regional office in White Plains, New York, was on the line. His main concern was to mollify the car owner into not taking legal action for breach of warranty. The owner said that if the parts were delivered in time for the car to be picked up the following evening, his only action regarding them would be to issue a check in full payment for parts and labor, but if the parts weren't delivered, he would not be that forbearing. The executive said he'd make some other calls and then call back. He did, after about two hours, said he'd located the parts, and that they were on their way to the dealership.

This whole story brings up another aspect of the technique of complaint, and that is to demonstrate that if your complaint is brushed off you're not going to let it ride. One way is to threaten legal action in a manner that indicates you've taken the trouble to at least bone up on the law (as the Plymouth owner did with the law of warranty).

Another way (and a common lawyer's trick) is to actually initiate legal action, even though you may not intend to go through with it.

A New York lawyer once ordered some books on art treasures from the Time-Life Book Club. A month later, he failed to exercise his negative option (i.e., "Check off here if you don't want us to send it") on their next selection, which dealt with Italian cooking and was sent back as soon as it was delivered. When the bill came, however, it covered not only the art book he'd ordered, but the cookbook he'd sent back. To make matters worse, he hurriedly wrote a check in payment of the total asked, without checking the itemization.

When he realized what he'd done, he wrote the Time-

116

Life Book Club asking for a refund. There was no response. So one day shortly thereafter, when he was in the Manhattan Civil Court building on business for one of his clients, he took a few minutes to stop by the small claims section and file suit against Time Inc. to get his money back. Once the papers were served, he got a grudging phone call from someone in the Time-Life Book Club legal department offering a refund of his money. Our friend gave Time-Life the same attentive response they'd given him and reminded them that he was legally entitled to be reimbursed for the three dollars and change he'd spent to institute the lawsuit and would not settle until he got it. Apparently, this became enough of a problem for Time Inc. (see Chaper 9 to find out why) for the company's chief counsel to step in. He called the lawyer with a complete and sincere apology and a promise that a check for the overpayment plus the filing fee would arrive shortly. It did, that afternoon, by messenger.

In dealing with customer complaints, many companies feel they can "solve" the complaint by answering it with some superficially reasoned argument based on alleged company policy or assertions whose pompous language lends them an air of authority. On close examination, these arguments and assertions turn out to be quite specious, but unfortunately too many people fail to either examine them or challenge them.

One "argument" popular with car rental companies in replies to frequent complainers is that the company can't grant an adjustment because they've granted adjustments to the customer before. Logically, this argument holds about as much weight as the assertion that, since a coin comes up heads 50 percent of the time, a flip where it's come up tails must be followed by one where it comes up heads. As any statistician will tell you, each flip is a separate incident, and only over a very large number of flips will the heads and tails average out to fifty-fifty. Similarly, each car rental is a separate incident, and that's the first answer to this kind of argument. A second and more effective way is to answer a challenge with a challenge. In this case, to call or write the boss of the person who made this reply and ask, "Do you mean to say that your continuous record of failures in the past relieves you of liability for additional errors? And that the more mistakes your company made in the past, the more it's entitled to make in the future? Your rental contract says nothing about this. Moreover, it promises that the cars you supply will be in good mechancial condition."

The *reductio ad absurdum* plus the indication that you know your legal rights (which, in turn, implies that you're ready to fight for them) is usually enough to make creditors give in just to get rid of you.

Another example of the creditor's argument reduced to its natural absurdity: On September 21, 1972, Mrs. Lynn Ortenzi, of Lodi, New Jersey, wrote Norman Wechsler, president of Saks Fifth Avenue, to complain about the store's refusal to grant her full credit on a $65 dress she charged and later returned. After two paragraphs showing she was a good customer of Saks, she wrote:

> With the dress and sales slip in hand, I was told by one of your seventh floor people that the dress was now on sale for $20 less than the original price. She insisted that if I returned the dress, I would have to suffer the $20 penalty. There was no question in the saleslady's mind that the dress had not been worn, since it was still in its original wrappings.
>
> It hardly seems proper that I should have to suffer a loss because you marked down the dress. However, in spite of my protestations, the saleslady was adamant. I was sent to a floor manager and thence to customer services,

118

>   where I received the same deci-
>   sion, as well as shabby treatment.

By September 27, her complaint filtered down from
the president to one W. Boelker (Miss), assistant manager, customer services, who wrote, in part:

>   According to our records, there
>   was a dress charged to your ac-
>   count in the amount of $65.00
>   purchased on July 21st from the
>   Seventh Floor. . . . Our time limit
>   on returns is ten days or two
>   weeks but under extenuating cir-
>   cumstances, we would extend it to
>   a longer period.
>
>   Although our policy governing ad-
>   justments is a most liberal one,
>   we do not feel we are being unfair
>   in offering you the last selling
>   price of $44.90. . . .
>
>   In view of the above explanation,
>   if you still desire to return the
>   dress, please do so to the at-
>   tention of the writer and I will
>   see that the above credit is
>   issued. (Note the attempt to add
>   an air of authority through the
>   use of bureaucratese.)

In her reply to this smoke screen, on October 6, Mrs.
Ortenzi answered, reducing the store's initial argument
to absurdity and making a threat of litigation.

>   Your letter of September 27 . . .

119

stated that the time limit on returns would be extended under extenuating circumstances. As I told personnel in your store (even if this weren't true, there'd be no means of verifying or refuting it), my husband was in the hospital with pneumonia in August and early September (ditto).

Between working and running to the hospital, I was in no position to shop, let alone return.

. . . I fail to see why I should be penalized because you put the dress on sale. If you used the theory of the last selling price, would you give me more of a re-fund if the selling price of the dress rose between the time I bought it and the time I returned it? I don't think that would be the case, so why give me less than I paid?

If you remain adamant in your point of view, you can institute a court action (to collect the original $65). I would be happy to appear in court and explain my position to a judge.

I am truly angry at this situation and demand an immediate reply to this letter.

The reply from W. Boelker (Miss), sent on October 12, was not immediate, but it was, although grudging, satisfactory:

> . . . Since we are now desirous of closing our records on this transaction, we suggest that you have the dress returned to the attention of this writer. Immediately on receipt, a full credit will be issued.

In discussing regulatory agencies earlier, we concluded that they were of limited usefulness for fast remedies of complaints. However, threatening to go to a regulatory agency is a way to show an executive whom you're complaining to that your complaint is in earnest. But when you do it, you must word your threat to imply very strongly that you've either had dealings with the regulatory agency and thus know the score, or that you've studied the agency's procedures enough to make your complaint with a minimum of delay and floundering.

In 1965, a planeload of people was kept waiting five hours in Baltimore because of ineptitude and prevarication on the part of Eastern Airlines. As the airplane was taxiing to take off for a flight to New York, the pilot discovered that a one-dollar hydraulic fitting had burst. The passengers were kept locked in the plane out on the runway for twenty-five minutes. During this time, Eastern was searching for a replacement part and a mechanic to install it and discovering that they had neither in Baltimore. They then called the nearest mechanic, who was in Washington, D.C., to get up there as fast as he could. By car, that is.

Now, Washington is one of the few cities in the world designed from the ground up, and the purpose that L'Enfant designed it for was to impede a cavalry charge on the Capitol. The design features that were to impede a cavalry charge in the nineteenth century work excellently

121

to impede the flow of traffic in the twentieth. National Airport, where the mechanic worked, is just across the Potomac in Virginia. This mean he had to drive all the way across Washington before he could reach the highway to Baltimore. And since all this took place at about 4:30 P.M. he had to do it fighting rush-hour traffic both ways.

Meanwhile, back at the airport, Eastern people were telling the passengers that a "special" plane was being readied and would be available momentarily. This "special" plane was really the next scheduled flight to New York. All in all, what should have been a flight of less than an hour took more than five hours including waiting time, and if Eastern had told the truth in the first place, the passengers could have gotten to New York quicker by bus.

The next day, one of the passengers looked up Eastern's regional sales manager in *Standard & Poor's*, threatening to complain to the Service Complaint Section of the Civil Aeronautics Board if Eastern failed to come up with a damned good explanation and some restitution. Note: His letter said the Service Complaint Section (which, he'd found out by a phone call to the CAB, was the relevant body). Not "the government." Not the FAA. Not the CAB. But the Service Complaint Section of the CAB. Eastern sent the New York sales manager and another executive to the passenger's office to apologize and explain in person.

When you don't know specifically whom to threaten a creditor with, common sense can often help you fake it. A married couple in New York restored a brownstone that used to be a gas-heated boarding house and, in the process, had it switched over to electric heat. But for months after the switch, Consolidated Edison, instead of sending someone around to read the meters every month, charged them for "estimated" use based on the previous monthly gas consumption of a gas-heated boarding house. With not one gas appliance in the house, they were being charged for enough gas to run a small bakery. Telephone conversations and letters got them nowhere until they happened to recall the role that the Irish have played in New York politics and patronage. In the last of his phone calls to Con Ed, the husband threatened to go to "Mr. McIlhenny at the Public Service Commission, and you know what he's like." A meter reader was dispatched posthaste to the house, the bill was corrected, and Mr. McIlhenny turned out to be very influential for a man who doesn't exist.

Many lawyers in New York are Jewish, and Jews seem to hold many posts in the State Attorney General's office. Furthermore, mere mention of a Jewish lawyer is enough to strike fear into the hearts of nonlawyer executives at WASP creditor organizations. One complainant used these facts to advantage when complaining about a year of lackadaisical service from one of the travel and entertainment credit card companies. He felt that since he had received little or no service over the previous year, his $15 annual "service" charge should be refunded. And when he threatened to go to Sheldon Greenberg of the Bureau of Consumer Frauds in the Attorney General's office, the credit card company decided that $15 was a small price to pay for not having to do battle with Mr. Greenberg. While the law of averages leads us to suspect that there must be a Sheldon Greenberg in the Attorney General's office, the Sheldon Greenberg used as a threat was purely mythical.

Senior executives of creditor companies are acutely aware of what they spend for advertising to favorably impress the consuming public, and particularly in "heavy user" service industries, where a small segment of the population uses a large proportion of the available services (air travel and car rental are two of the best examples; more than 60 percent of the flying and 80 percent of the car renting are done by business executives, who comprise less than 20 percent of the population), you can work wonders by throwing a company's advertising (or its main competitor's advertising) back at them.

When Avis was starting its "We try harder" campaign and talking about how they promised to try harder by cleaning out their ashtrays, it was possible to get a refund by checking the ashtrays of Avis cars and mailing in the cigarette butts along with a covering letter admonishing them for not really trying very hard. At the time, Hertz was smarting from the Avis advertising, so complaint letters to Hertz could produce fast action by including the suggestion that they, too, try harder.

Over the years, the advertising slogans have changed, but the technique works as well as ever. In 1971, Peter Hegedus rented a Hertz truck for moving furniture. The truck didn't run right, and someone also made a whopping error in recording the mileage. Hertz was then countering Avis with the slogan, "You don't just rent a car; you rent a company." Hegedus wrote to the president of Hertz. In his letter, he explained his difficulties and concluded, "I didn't want to rent your company. I just wanted to rent a truck, and Hertz wasn't up to it." Hertz refunded the entire rental price.

Finally, you give yourself more bargaining power by knowing in advance what kind of adjustment you're entitled to and asking for it. Reimbursement of long-distance phone charges is always in order, since the creditor's defective merchandise was what necessitated the phone calls. And when return or replacement of your merchandise is impractical (because you've had it too long, for example), a partial refund is in order, too.

In 1968, a man bought two suits for a total of around $400 from Paul Stuart, a New York clothing store. There were some minor errors in the tailoring, but not enough to make the suits unwearable. He telephoned the store's billing department to complain about the discrepancies and to refuse payment until they were corrected. For about a year thereafter, the only letters he received from Stuart were advertising circulars and bills with the $400 marked in the "past due" column and nothing marked in the "interest" column. At the end of the year, he received his first dunning letter and phoned the company president. He explained that the tailoring had made the suits unwearable, even after it had been done over at the store, and that he finally had to take the suits to his own tailor to have them made right. He demanded a credit for the $45 allegedly spent for the tailoring, and Stuart's president had the adjustment made. So, a year after the suits were purchased, they were paid for. At slightly better than 10 percent off.

Infact Systems, which we mentioned earlier, sells a complaint kit, including a complaint form called Telagripe. An officer of the company sent a Telagripe to the president of a styrofoam-cup-manufacturing company, complaining that some cups he'd bought were ripped. Within the month, he received a case of 480 styrofoam cups and a letter from the president thanking him for helping them find a flaw in the production machinery.

Professor David Klein of Michigan State University believes that the way to obtain redress for shoddy goods and services is to "behave outrageously by current standards," and according to his track record, his belief has considerable merit. On arriving at the Queen Elizabeth Hotel in Montreal and being told that his confirmed room reservations wouldn't be honored, he told the clerk, "I will give you three minutes to find me a room. After three minutes, I am going to undress in the lobby, put on my pajamas and go to sleep on one of the sofas."* He got his room.

Whenever he has to devote his own time to untangle a problem that a creditor corporation should never have gotten him into, he charges for his time and expenses— at the rate of $10 per letter and $2 per phone call. Out-of-pocket expenses like photocopying are billed at cost. "I simply deduct the amount from my monthly charge account bill. I add the total amount of time spent on letters and telephone calls when I'm billed incorrectly, or if orders come incomplete, or if merchandise is unsatisfactory."† And a surprising number of creditors credit him for these "charges."

In the absence of any cash or in-kind restitution, your creditor may offer to make repairs, in which event you are really in luck. The couple who redid the brownstone bought a large air-conditioning unit for it. The unit was installed with the wrong mounting plate. The husband called the air-conditioning company, who sent an installer to fix it. He then made a partial payment (see Chapter 7 for the rule of thumb on partial payments). In the process

*Enid Nemy, "If Businesses Wrong Him, This Consumer Makes Them Pay," *New York Times,* December 8, 1974.
† Ibid.

of changing mounting plates, the installer managed to do something to the condenser, which caused water to condense on the carpeting. More mechanics were sent to fix this. The couple demanded money for repairing the carpeting.

Every few months, they discover another "problem" with the air conditioner and call the company to gripe about it. The company has stopped sending mechanics, but it's also started maintaining a low profile by not trying to collect the rest of the money owing. The air conditioner works fine now, but the husband still calls periodically. And the company executives are so busy trying to avoid him that they fail to notice how he's avoided them.

CHAPTER SEVEN

Using the Mails to Delay

TO MOST PEOPLE, a dunning letter is, short of an envelope with a Black September return address, the most fearful item their postman could possibly deliver. But it shouldn't be.

Of all the media of communication, a letter is probably the easiest to ignore. You can mark it "Return to Sender." You can open it, read it, and then throw it out unanswered. Or you can throw it out unopened. Collection letters are easy to spot from the outside, simply because of the lengths that credit departments and bill collectors go to conceal the fact that a piece of correspondence is, in fact, a dunning letter. Of all the letters sent to you with typewritten addresses and metered postage (instead of stamps), they're the only ones to arrive with either no return address, a return address with a room or box number instead of a name, or the name of one of your creditors.

Why, then, do bill collectors rely so heavily on such an ineffective means of communication? Because it's such a cheap one. Including printing, postage, and processing costs, collection form letters can cost as little as 16 cents apiece to send. At that price, if they're sent to every overdue debtor, and if the collection rate is as high as 20%, the mailing will be a howling success. To you, this may seem a minimal return (it is), but it's achieved at less than minimal effort.

However, even collection departments have come to realize the relative ineffectiveness of ordinary letters, and some use other types of "mail" in the hope that the medium will convey more of the intended message of fear.

Since certain types of summonses are served by registered mail (this provides proof that the document was actually received, which can be important with some documents in some court cases), creditors sometimes send dunning letters by registered or certified mail to imply the threat of legal action. If a postman comes to your door with a certified letter, however, all you have to do is remember that the letter can do you no damage if you haven't received it, and you are under no obligation whatever to accept and sign for it.

Other creditors use night-letter telegrams to give you a feeling of fear and urgency, because we are all conditioned to regard telegrams as important, often ill-boding, documents. Surprisingly, night-letter telegrams offer the creditor another advantage. In most instances, they cost less to send than a non-form collection letter.

According to the U.S. Postal Service, companies spend a minimum of $2.96 to have letters dictated, typed, addressed, processed, and mailed. This is a minimum figure, assuming letters dictated by recording machine, to a steno pool, by a lower-echelon office worker. When a vice-president dictates a letter to his executive secretary, who sits in his office taking it down, the costs can be as high as $10 per letter. An office managers' trade magazine estimated the cost of a business letter as ranging from $2.30 to $5.05 depending on how they were dictated and by whom (see chart). A night-letter telegram costs no more (and often less) than a business letter and is harder to ignore. At least for people who don't know any better, as you now do.

Another variation on this theme is a thing the Postal Service and Western Union have teamed up on called a Mailgram. It looks like a telegram, but is delivered by special postmen, and it costs the sender less than $2.

But what's even more distressing than the form of these letters is the content—or at least the purported content. Collection letters often use key words and phrases to make you think you'll really be in legal trouble if you don't fork over the money. "Don't hurt your credit standing" is a phrase that often crops up, implying an unfavorable report to your local credit rating bureau. "Our attorney," "our collection agency," and "our legal collection representatives" often crop up, along with "avoid yourself expense, inconvenience and embarrassment" and "spare yourself lawyers' fees and court costs." But all these threats are more apparent than real.

Crediors do not, as a rule, voluntarily turn in reports on debtors who stiff them. First of all, they run the risk of a libel suit should the debtor have a valid reason for not paying or should their accounting department have committed a billing error. (See Chapter 12 for more details). Also, doing this kind of gratuitous credit rating job simply costs them too much to be worth the bother. (American Express, for example, repeatedly asserts that the only information given out about debtors is whether or not they have an account.)

In the rare instances where information *is* volunteered, it's given out grudgingly (because giving out information costs money that the company can't charge for, and then only when specifically asked for by another creditor who had been given the first creditor's name as a credit reference).

What about the threat of collection agencies? This, too, is not much to worry about. In the first place, the dunning process will go on for months before your account is actually turned over to outside bill collectors. When it finally does go to them, it will be only with the creditor's great reluctance because outside bill collectors don't work for nothing. They charge a percentage of the money they collect, and this reduces the cash return to

129

Sending a Business Letter Costs Much More Than $.13 In Postage

The following figures are based on 250-word business letters, dictated at the rate of twenty per day or transcribed at the rate of thirty per day, during a seven-hour day. Ten percent of labor cost was allowed for unproductive time, and 40 percent for overhead.

| | LETTER WRITTEN BY | | | | | |
| | CLERK ($175 per week) | | JR. EXECUTIVE ($250 per week) | | EXECUTIVE ($400 per week) | |
	Dictated to secretary ($100 per week)	Dictated to machine	Dictated to secretary ($110 per week)	Dictated to machine	Dictated to secretary ($125 per week)	Dictated to machine
Dictator's time (8 minutes to secretary, 7 minutes to machine)	$ .66	$ .58	$ .95	$ .84	$1.52	$1.33
Secretary's time (letters per day)	1.00 (20)	.66 (30)	1.10 (20)	.74 (30)	1.55 (16)	1.04 (24)
Unproductive time	.17	.12	.20	.16	.30	.24
Overhead	.66	.50	.82	.63	1.22	.94
Mailroom time ($85 per week, 100 items per day)	.18	.18	.18	.18	.18	.18
Postage, handling, sealing, etc.	.17	.17	.17	.17	.17	.17
Stationery	.09	.09	.09	.09	.11	.11
TOTAL LETTER COST	$2.93	$2.30	$3.51	$2.81	$5.05	$3.01

the creditor. And finally, bill collectors themselves are far from impossible to cope with. (See Chapter 8.)

What goes for outside bill collectors goes even more for outside attorneys. Attorneys cost even more than bill collectors, so your debt will probably have to be over $250 before a creditor will engage an attorney to do anything more than send you a letter.

If an attorney should take you to court and win a judgement for the full amount (which is unlikely, as you'll see from Chapters 10 and 11), the day in court will cause more embarrassment and pain for your creditor than for you. Since you can appear on your own behalf, it won't cost you anything for an attorney. And, if you lose, you won't necessarily have to pay your creditor's legal fees and court costs. Judges may assess these charges, but they don't automatically do so. Even when these charges are added to the judgement, they cover far less than your creditor's actual out-of-pocket costs. In New York State, for example, court costs are $5 for the first $50 awarded in judgement, $5 for the next $50, and $5 for each additional $100 up to a maximum cost of $150, which covers any judgement from $2,900 to $10,000. Furthermore, despite what creditors' collection letters might threaten, the law does not require you to pay the winning side's attorney fees. You're only bound to pay this kind of fee when you agree to it in advance, when it's one of the conditions in a retail installment contract you sign, so to avoid this kind of cost you have only to read contracts before you sign them.

Collection letters may state that any court case will become a matter of public record, and this is true, but not in the way the creditors imply. A transcript will be made of the trial, and this transcript will become a part of the court archives, available to any member of the public who wants to research it. In this sense, a record does exist, but it's a far cry from the criminal or police record that creditors would have you think it is.

There is one disadvantageous aspect of the public record. Credit rating agencies check lists of pending lawsuits and unsatisfied judgements to obtain raw data for their credit ratings. However, there are ways that you

131

can protect yourself from this kind of stigma, under the Fair Credit Reporting Act, and these are fully described in Chapter 13.

Of course, when a creditor threatens litigation, he leaves himself wide open to the threat of counter-litigation. The wife of a New York attorney once booked reservations at a hotel in Atlantic City. On arrival, the only room available to her was one that was not made up (and, she was told, couldn't be cleaned up or get fresh towels and linens until the following morning) and next to a loud piece of machinery. She checked out of the hotel right after checking in, without paying. Two weeks later, the hotel's collection agency sent her husband a letter threatening court action and "the full penalty of law" (which was nonexistent, aside from a court judgement that she owed the money). Her husband replied, on stationery that showed he was an attorney at law, explaining her legal defenses against having to pay and outlining his intent to have the bill collectors prosecuted for violation of the federal laws against extortion, which he quoted both in language and by title and paragraph number. He and his wife never heard from them again.

Finally, another good answer to the threat of litigation is to indicate that you'll be all to happy to take your creditor up on it. In 1970, an executive ordered a book called *The Executive's Credit and Collection Guide* for shipment to a friend. He gave no instructions as to how the purchase price of some $45 should be billed. The book arrived and, shortly afterward, a string of collection letters. Since the recipient had not ordered the book, which was, to his knowledge at the time, unsolicited merchandise, he ignored the letters until one came threatening legal action. To this, he replied as follows:

> Gentlemen:
> I am in receipt of your letter
> threatening legal action for non-
> payment of $45 for The Executive's
> Credit and Collection Guide,

which I allegedly ordered from you.

First of all, I did not order this publication from you. My company is an advertising agency, not a collection agency, and my business is writing commercials, not dunning letters.

Second, before you sue me for not paying for this book, you'd better be prepared to prove I received it. I don't think you can.

Third, if I did receive it, it was unordered by me and, as such, is unsolicited merchandise, which I am entitled by law to keep without payment.

Fourth, I am not the least bit frightened of the prospect of a lawsuit, since it can only be decided in my favor, leaving you with all the embarrassment and expense.

If you have an order form with my signature on it, please send me a copy, and I'll be happy to pay you. If not, I'll see you in court.

He never received another letter on the subject. He did, however, receive form letters offering him additional merchandise. On credit.

Another of the implicit threats to be disposed of is that of the "legal collection agency," which implies a lawyer but actually means a collection agency that manages to operate within the letter of the law.

Along with the implicit threats, there are two techniques to be aware of. You should be aware of the first technique in order to know why you shouldn't take it seriously; you should be aware of the second so you'll know how to turn it to your advantage.

The first technique, originally developed by corrupt cops for shaking down local merchants, is known as the "good-guy-bad-guy technique." The way it works is that the cop playing the "bad guy" threatens to fine or jail the merchant for some violation and frightens him within an inch of his life. The other cop then steps in as the "good guy," taking the merchant aside and offering to intercede with the bad guy, provided the merchant will put up a payoff to mollify him.

Collection letters often use the same technique, with a clerk (the "good guy") offering to intercede with the credit manager (the "bad guy") on your behalf if you'll only pay a little something. Other letters may be ostensibly written by the person who approved your account and will now allegedly be fired if you don't pay up. Apparently, creditors must think debtors are very gullible, because they send out these touching personal stories on what are obviously mass-produced form letters. They make mildly interesting fiction, but are insufficient grounds for payment.

The second collection-letter technique is to try to open lines of communication with you, since experience has shown creditors that the debtor who writes or talks to them is usually the one who eventually pays them.

This is why dunning letters are invariably studded with phrases like, "We've written you three times, but you haven't answered us," "Is there a complaint you haven't told us about?" and "Why haven't we heard from you?"

At the end of this chapter is a collection of dunning letters that illustrate this point, but none proves it better than one from a New England furniture company, whose collection manager regards it as 89 percent effective. Its

response pattern, as tabulated by the company, works
like this:

39%	full payment
22%	partial payment
26%	promise to pay
2%	complaint about goods or services
89%	SUBTOTAL
11%	no response
100%	TOTAL

But collection letters are really effective only to the
extent that they help the company recover full payment.
Partial payments may remain partial, promises to pay may
remain unkept, and if you've read the previous chapter,
we don't have to say anything about complaints. Therefore, the letter's true measure of effectiveness should be
reduced by the percentage of debtors who string the
creditors along with complaints, partial payments, and
promises. And when this is done, a totally different picture emerges:

11%	no response
26%	promise to pay
2%	complaints
39%	SUBTOTAL

To this subtotal must be added some percentage for the
partial payments, since they are ineffective to the extent
that payment is not in full. In a few pages, you'll be
reading about the rule of thumb for partial payments,
and taking the maximum payment under that rule—25
percent—we can assume that the 22 percent partial payment responses represent three-quarters ineffectiveness.
Thus, continuing our calculations:

22%	"partial payment" responses
×75%	partial balances still outstanding
16.5%	percentage of "partial payment" category that is ineffective

135

+ 39%	Subtotal of other ineffective responses
55.5%	TOTAL INEFFECTIVENESS

100.0%	
− 55.5%	
44.5%	ACTUAL EFFECTIVENESS OF DUNNING LETTER

In other words, instead of having an 89% effectiveness rate, as the creditor who sends out the dunning letter calculates, the actual effectiveness, in terms of payments received, is exactly half that or 44.5%

As a result, the debtor has two alternative responses to dunning letters. He can either ignore them and let the string run itself out and escalate to the next stage of collection; or he can answer them and bog down his creditors in a long, meaningless string of correspondence.

Professor C. Northcote Parkinson sets down two methods for tangling your creditors up in their own collection machinery, the "Western" and "Asian" methods, named for the parts of the world where they're practiced. Both can be practiced by debtors here, with good result.

The Western method takes advantage of the Standard Delay, which, you may recall, is the length of time it takes your letter to get from the bottom to the top of the "In" tray. Timing your first exchange of letters and subtracting in-transit time should give you your creditor's Standard Delay. This interval having been determined, you then send your creditor a letter timed to arrive the day before the Standard Delay ends and he starts to answer your first letter. With luck, this will cause your file to be pulled out of the top of the "In" tray (so your new letter can be added) and sent down to the bottom again.

The Asian method was developed for use in the Far East, where bureaucracies function far too erratically to be the more-or-less well-oiled machines they are here. The Standard Delay doesn't fit any standard interval, so another method had to be substituted, and this was to baffle your correspondent with obviously well-calculated but just as obviously confusing and contradictory balances of money.

In reply to a demand for payment of, say, $100, the debtor sends a letter enclosing a check for an "adjusted balance" of, say $45.72. Two things are significant here. First, no explanation is given as to how the adjusted balance was arrived at. Second, the balance is always an odd sum, to imply that it was calculated down to the penny. While the creditor tries to figure out the arithmetic, but before he can reply with a demand for the rest of his $100, the debtor sends another letter, apologizing for an "error" and asking refund of a $2.68 "overpayment." With the creditor getting more bewildered every step of the way, yet, like most creditors, not wanting to risk harsh action that would cost him the debtor's repeat business, the debtor keeps sending continuous recalculations of the balance until the creditor gives up and takes whatever he's finally given.

There are other, less devious ways to prolong the correspondence, and the simplest is to write raising a question about your bill. Sections 703 and 705 of the General Business Law of New York State illustrate the amount of delay that can be achieved by doing this. This law is of no use to debtors who live outside New York State, and of next to no use to debtors who live inside. Banks and other major creditor organizations had an important say in drafting these sections, so they're written pretty much the way creditors want. However, they do shed a great deal of light on the pace at which creditors like to handle customer questions.

Under this law, creditors are required to include in every statement of account an address that the customer can send inquiries to. If a debtor has a question about his bill, he must then send to his creditor, at the specified address, a letter containing "sufficient information to enable the creditor to identify the consumer and the account, the amount and the transaction shown in the statement . . . and the facts providing the basis for the consumer's belief that the statement is in error." This letter must be written on some piece of paper other than the statement itself and sent by registered or certified mail, return re-

137

ceipt requested, within thirty days of the mailing date (this is the date the envelope went through the creditor's postage meter; it is not the date that the bill was received and often not the date it was actually mailed, both of which are usually a few days later).

The creditor then has thirty days (as many as sixty days after the mailing date) to acknowledge receipt of the debtor's complaint and an additional sixty days (which brings us up to as many as 120 days after the mailing date of the statement) to either rectify or refute the customer's complaint. Until the creditor actually does this, he is forbidden by law from contacting either collection agencies or credit reporting agencies regarding nonpayment of the disputed amount, although creditors, as a rule, do not call in outside agencies this early in the game.

One stall commonly used by your creditors on *their* creditors is to ask for duplicate statements. An amateur racing driver buys three to four hundred dollars' worth of gasoline for his racing car and tow car during a racing season. Most of this is charged to his Sunoco card during July, August, and September, and the charge tickets start to trickle in from Watkins Glen, New York, Loudon, New Hampshire, and Warren, Ohio, just in time to meet the annual Christmas bills in his mailbox. To complicate matters, Manhattan's West Side, where he lives, is notorious for mail thefts, and many of the thieves lack the intelligence to differentiate between checks and bills, so one year between the Christmas mail rush and the mail thefts, statements for about $250 worth of gas bills never arrived. Along about February, however, dunning letters for that sum did. So he sent a letter to Sunoco's credit card center in Tulsa, Oklahoma, secure in the knowledge that it would be either ignored or mishandled.

It was. The only reply to his letter was another form letter, in March, stating that his credit card was canceled. He then placed a telephone call to the company's vice-president in charge of customer relations, explaining the problem, relating that the letter had been sent and not answered, noting that the sum demanded was more than the average family spends on gasoline in a year (a subtle way of showing he was a better-than average customer)

138

and refusing to pay that kind of money without better substantiation than a form letter.

The vice-president asked for a Xerox of the initial letter, reinstated the account, credited the customer for the 1½ percent-per-month interest charges, and promised that duplicate charge tickets would be sent. Requesting and reading that copy was all the investigation of the complaint that the company undertook. This presents a very interesting implication. Apparently, an executive's belief in a Xerox or carbon copy is as great as, if not greater than, his belief in television news and the printed word. Even if the customer had merely pre-dated a letter, run it through a Xerox machine, and sent the resulting copy (or phonied up a carbon copy the same way), it would have carried just as much weight as a copy of a letter that was actually sent.

One debtor uses Xerox copies to "substantiate" sob stories to creditors, in which he explains how natural disasters impaired his ability to pay and asks for leniency until he recovers from those disasters. His favorite excuse is that he's just recovering from injuries sustained in an auto accident. In replying to dunning letters, he explains the circumstances and encloses a Xerox copy of the "accident report" to prove it really took place. Now, blank accident report forms are available at any police station, anyone can fill them out, and anyone with access to a Xerox machine can make a copy of the filled-out form and send that copy to a credulous creditor— even though the original is on file not with the police but in the bottom of some waste basket.

There's another way to guarantee relief from dunning letters and actually put yourself back into your creditor's good graces, but it costs some money. This is to send a partial payment with the promise of more to come at some unspecified future date. (With some creditors, you can even get off the hook for a while by writing a *promise* of partial payment a few weeks before you pay it). Experience has shown that as little as 10 to 25 percent will make a creditor happy enough to leave you alone for as long as three or four months.

Of course, all the foregoing is based on the assumption

that your creditors will be crass, dumb, and tasteless in their dunning-letter efforts. In the rare instances where they show a little consideration or intelligence, they deserve to be rewarded by payment, to the extent that your finances will allow. This doesn't happen too often, but when it does, it's worth the money to encourage them to keep it up.

The following letter from Evergreen Press, and one customer's reply to it, are self-explanatory. But after you read them, compare the Evergreen letter to those that come immediately after.

A GOOD DUNNING LETTER (no, it isn't a contradiction in terms):

EVERGREEN
CLUB 315 HUDSON STREET / NEW YORK, N.Y. 10013

Dearest Venerable Sir:

In my country, India, it is customary for a creditor to hang himself on the doorstep of one who is . . . how do you say . . . a "bad debt."

Naturally, before even considering such action, I wanted to allow you ample time to pay this paltry sum you owe.

Please send by next week.

Imagine, if you will, the embarrassment of having a dead Indian
dangling at your front door. What
would you say to the neighbors:
("Oh, that dead Indian! Funny you
should ask! It all started when I
was a little late on paying Evergreen.")

> I bid you all the
> blessings of Vidy-
> adevis, the thou-
> sand-eyed goddess
> of Tranquility, and
> may Vishnu keep you
> safe from harm now
> and for ever.

S. Ramekrish narangga

Swami Ramakrishnarangga

SR:dd
P.S. I'm only kidding. Just send
the money.

Creditors who take the thought and effort to send letters like this deserve to be rewarded. So give them some encouragement to keep up the good work. The following letter is a good example of encouragement. The check that went with it was even better.

Evergreen Club
315 Hudson Street
New York 13, N.Y.

Gentlemen:

When I received your form letter reminding me that I owed you money, my first reaction was not to pay you.

After all, hanging Indians aren't exactly the most commonplace doorpost decorations, and I wanted to be the first on my block to get one.

My second reaction was that if I didn't pay you, you'd stop sending your debtors nice, funny letters and start sending them rude, nasty ones. So I'd pay you.

Then I realized that if I did pay you, you wouldn't send me any more funny letters.

So now that I'm sending you a
check, would you be good enough to
pretend that I didn't, and send
me the rest of the dunning letters?

                    Sincerely,

You would have no way of knowing. . . .

But as Credit Manager, I was the one who okayed your account in the first place, for I felt you would be a very desirable customer, and I had the utmost confidence in your integrity and business ability.

No payment has been credited to your account since it was first opened, and the balance is becoming seriously in arrears.

It appears that both of our reputations are at stake. Yours because you have not replied to our courteous correspondence about your overdue account, and mine since it looks as if I may have misjudged you.

We are withholding legal action on your account, until you can advise just what has happened, for we do not want to resort to that unpleasantness.

Let us hear from you within the next week or ten days, please.

A dodge used by con men, cops taking bribes, collection agencies and other shakedown artists is the "good guy—bad guy" routine.

This routine owes its effectiveness to the victim's belief that one of the two partners in the shakedown is about to nail him (the victim) to the wall, a fate that can be avoided by cash from the victim and intercession by the other partner in the shakedown.

In the case of credit collections, the bad guy is always the collector's immediate superior, who, when the situation demands, will get on the telephone to insist very harshly on immediate, full payment. This will allow the collector to be a good guy by arranging a compromise payment from you, which the bad guy will then go through his act again to jack up a bit.

In the case of collection by letter, the bad guy's existence is only hinted at (see the first sentence of paragraph 4), but the structure of the con is still the same. To counter it, don't ever believe that any creditor's representative is on your side. He knows who pays his salary.

←FROM THE *DARTNELL FILE OF CREDIT AND COLLECTION LETTERS* (CHICAGO: DARTNELL CORPORATION).

NAME
ADDRESS
CITY & STATE

Gentlemen:

We were wondering if you would
send us the name of the attorney
who handles your legal affairs.

You see, we are preparing the
papers our attorney service requires to collect the $ due on
your account.

If you will just jot it down at the
bottom of this letter we will have
our attorney service contact him
for payment.

Cordially,

Credit Manager

This letter is designed to convince you that they actually mean business and are ready to sue.

Of course, if they did, they wouldn't want the name of your attorney. They'd just have theirs send you a summons.

In your reply, you should state:

- You have no attorney, but have the time and desire to spend years in court yourself, if necessary, to obtain justice.
- You have all kinds of interesting depositions, photographs, and so on, which they will no doubt enjoy seeing in court.
- You would welcome service of summons.

←FROM THE *DARTNELL FILE OF CREDIT AND COLLECTION LETTERS* (CHICAGO: DARTNELL CORPORATION).

Gentlemen:

It seldom becomes necessary for us to turn an account over to an attorney for collection. And on those few occasions when circumstances leave us no other alternative, we consider it only fair to tell the customer exactly what we intend to do.

Certainly, you must realize that we have made every effort to be fair and patient in requesting that you settle your December account of $107.20. We have written to you several times, asking that you let us know how we could cooperate with you in getting this indebtedness straightened out.

Your continued silence leaves us no other alternative than to refer your account to our attorney for collection—a step that we sincerely regret. So won't you respond to this final appeal for your cooperation, and thereby avoid a procedure that can only

mean embarrassment, inconvenience, and additional expense to
you?

Unless we hear from you by February 22, we shall be compelled to
transfer your account to the
office of our attorney. Please use
the enclosed reply envelope to let
us hear from you.

Cordially,

Credit Manager

"A procedure that can only mean embarrassment, inconvenience, and additional expense to you" actually means a great
deal of inconvenience and additional expense to them. For you,
there's the prospect of legally getting out of an estimated
$50.00 of $107.20 should the case actually come to court and
you come up with a valid complaint. See Chapter 11.
Note, also, the value placed on two-way communication in
paragraphs 2 and 3.

←FROM THE *DARTNELL FILE OF CREDIT AND COLLEC-
TION LETTERS* (CHICAGO: DARTNELL CORPORA-
TION).

Dear Sir:

An important decison was reached in my office this morning—a decision that vitally affects your interests.

Your subscription payment is now seriously overdue. Though we have sent you several invoices and two letters, your check has not been received. Neither have we had any explanation for your non-payment.

And this morning we decided, reluctantly, that there was nothing more we could do—that your account must now be given over to a legal collection agency.

Frankly, we dislike taking this drastic step. With a businessman like yourself, it is not a question whether you will pay, it is only a matter of when. However, we have already gone to considerable expense, at your request, to send you The Import Bulletin every week. Do you think it fair that we continue to do so without some payment or word from you?

Of course, we would much prefer to keep you on as a regular paid subscriber. Your subscription is important to us, just as the information that The Import Bulletin brings you about your business is of value to you.

Wouldn't it be easier and better for you to settle the account now, and not force us to other methods to effect payment? Surely as a businessman, you can see the logic of this arrangement.

Write a check now, attach it to the enclosed invoice and mail it to us AT ONCE in the enclosed self-addressed envelope—so that the matter may be cleaned up without further trouble to anyone!

Very truly yours,

A "legal collection agency" (paragraph 3) is supposed to make you think they're about to get a lawyer to sue you, but actually all it means is a collection agency that operates within the outer limits of the law. See Chapter 8.
The last sentence of the second paragraph shows how readily some creditors will accept excuses in lieu of checks.

←FROM THE *DARTNELL FILE OF CREDIT AND COLLECTION LETTERS* (CHICAGO: DARTNELL CORPORATION).

Dear Mr.   :

Although this is my final letter
to you, yet it is not the type of
letter you may have expected—
sarcastic and threatening.

Frankly, Mr. Brown, you have me
nonplused. Your silence is that of
a Sphinx—why, I can't understand.
If you would only talk, my job
wouldn't seem half so difficult.

That $92.00 isn't such a large
amount and the prospect of collecting it offers no real obstacle,
either. I am concerned, however,
in saving you court costs and
attorney fees; also, I want to
spare you the humiliation that
any court action would entail.

Won't you call on me or phone me
for a friendly chat? Let's talk
things over. If you are in adverse
circumstances, for goodness' sake
tell me, so that I can arrange
matters to help you out of your
dilemma and, at the same time,

protect your credit standing. You know the old truism—"Two heads are better than one."

The future holds something for the man who keeps faith in it, and I have faith in you, Mr.   —don't let me down.

                         Yours very truly,

This letter just goes to show how willing otherwise intelligent creditors are to take practically any excuse you're willing to hand them. The only thing they can't stand is silence.
By the way, to show how hypocritical creditors are, you'll note that after supposedly being nice guys, they threaten you with "court costs," "attorney's fees," and "humiliation" of court action. (The good guy—bad guy routine strikes again!) Court costs come, usually, to under $15. Your creditors will have to pay attorney's fees, but you won't unless you're a corporation. And humiliation is in the mind of the beholder.

←FROM THE *DARTNELL FILE OF CREDIT AND COLLECTION LETTERS* (CHICAGO: DARTNELL CORPORATION).

Dear Sir:

I feel that it is part of my duty
to keep in personal touch as much
as possible with our customers,
and to investigate all cases
where the normal course of a pleasant business relationship has
for some reason been interrupted.

Our Credit Department has called
my attention to the fact that for
some reason unknown to us, our
repeated communications concerning the unpaid balance on your
account, in the amount of $....,
have met with no satisfactory response. Although we would not
pretend to be disinterested in
the money itself, please accept
my assurance that we are far more
concerned about our good relations
for the future.

If some circumstance has arisen
to alter the conditions under
which you sought and obtained the
extension of credit from us, will

you please take a moment to tell me about it? Perhaps you will find it convenient to write on the back of this letter, using the enclosed stamped envelope which is marked for my personal attention.

Yours very truly,

Treasurer

This is the famous collection letter with an 89 percent effectiveness rate that on closer examination turns out to be only 44.5 percent effective.

All the letter is, is still another exercise in the good guy—bad guy technique, with the treasurer, in whose name the letter is sent, being the good guy and the credit department, which actually sends it, being the bad guy.

There's one very bad flaw of logic in this letter. A treasurer usually outranks a credit department, so any treasurer who lets himself be cowed by a credit department (see paragraph 2) is worthy of sympathy. This notwithstanding, he shouldn't get it.

"Love thine enemy" is something which works better in church than in debt avoidance. If you're anything other than merciless with creditors like this one, they'll be nothing short of merciless with you later.

The way to be merciless with them, incidentally, is not to flatly refuse payment, but to use the stalling techniques which the company's own statistics show they revel in receiving: complaints, promises, or partial payments (the 10 percent to 25 percent rule of thumb).

←FROM THE *COMPLETE CREDIT AND COLLECTION LETTER BOOK*, JOHN D. LITTLE (ENGLEWOOD CLIFFS: PRENTICE-HALL, INC. 1964).

Regarding Your Unsettled Account
of $

Dear Friend:

You asked us to trust you and we
did—

As a matter of fact, when you
asked for credit, we had no reason
to doubt that your word was <u>good.</u>
It never occurred to us that you
might fail to pay an honest debt.

Frankly, I don't know what to say.
All my letters and pleas have
brought no response from you . . .
not even the promise of payment.
You've received several statements and letters from us, po-
litely requesting you to settle
the account. We even offered you
an easy way to clear it up through
small, regular payments. Still
no reply.

Since I don't believe you would
deliberately let your credit
standing sink into serious jeop-

ardy, I feel there must be something wrong. Perhaps we've done something to offend you, or we've been unfair in some respect. Whatever it is, I would personally like to hear about it. If there's something wrong with our end of the transaction, every effort will be made to straighten it out.

To tell the truth, we've made a special concession in your case in carrying the account far beyond our usual limit. But we've gone as far as we can. The Credit Association is now pressing us for the regular report on your account. They require that we tell them how you've taken care of your credit with us, and this report will become a permanent part of your credit record.

This report must go in without fail in the next five days.

Your response to this letter will determine what kind of rating you will receive in the future.

The report we send the Credit Association will not be written by us . . . it will be written by you. We want it to be a favorable one, but the final decision rests entirely with you. You have five days to do something about it.

Which will it be?

Yours very truly,

"Love thine enemy" combined with "Shame, shame," combined with extortion. Be as insensitive to abuse and plays for sympathy as bill collectors revel in being, but don't let on.

In paragraphs 3 and 4, they're just begging for standard stalling techniques to be used on them.

Also, since they're threatening you, you might return the threat implied in paragraphs 4, 5, 6, and 7 by the threat of a suit for defamation if their threat materializes.

Incidentally, credit-rating bureaus rarely, if ever, solicit reports on individuals on a periodic basis, much less "pressing" for them. And, under the Fair Credit Reporting Act, adverse reports can be used not permanently, but for up to seven years.

←FROM THE *DARTNELL FILE OF CREDIT AND COLLECTION LETTERS* (CHICAGO: DARTNELL CORPORATION).

Name
Address
City

Statements and letters, Gentlemen—

—have been sent to you regarding
the long-overdue account for
$00.00.

In reviewing the file, it appears
that every opportunity has been
given you in which to <u>arrange</u> for
settlement.

However, before placing your
account with our Collection
Representatives, we request once
again, "Your check before Month
15, please."

Thank you.

This letter threatens to turn your account over to Collection
Representatives. In all likelihood, however, this may represent
nothing more than a routine transfer of your account from the
billing to the collection department. You still have lots of time
before they invest their money in an outside collection agency,
even though they'd have you believe otherwise.

←FROM THE *DARTNELL FILE OF CREDIT AND COL-
LECTION LETTERS* (CHICAGO: DARTNELL CORPORA-
TION).

Good morning!

One of the toughest things in the world is "harsh talk" to a friend or customer.

It is YOU who has put us on the spot to resort to "harsh talk."

Your time is valuable—so is ours! Do you realize you received four letters from us—and not even a phone call, or a single word from you about paying your account for $174?

A brilliant lawyer once said, "Silence is evidence of guilt." Why not tell us why you haven't paid?

If we don't have your check by November 1, our next step may be much more costly to you—and think of the unpleasantness!!!

DON'T HURT YOUR CREDIT STANDING!

One of the most important principles of stalling creditors is that the more time they spend talking and writing, the less time they'll spend actually collecting. The thing they get most uptight about is a debtor's failure to answer and give them some complaint, or excuse, or promise that will give them a rationale for continuing to carry your debt as a receivable asset (see paragraph 3).

Paragraph 4 is a device designed to lead the unwary who read it and the following paragraph into believing that legal action, which is actually very inexpensive to everyone but the creditors, is imminent.

By the way, any lawyer making the probably apocryphal statement quoted in paragraph 4 would be likely to have his cases thrown out of court on two grounds. First, non-payment of bills is a civil, not criminal, matter, and in civil matters there is no such thing as guilt or innocence (the court merely finds for either plaintiff or defendant). Second, the Fifth Amendment, which protects us all from self-incrimination, is in direct contradiction to such "brilliant" legal philosophies.

FINAL DEMAND FOR PAYMENT
before SUIT

_____

_____

     Debtor
     To

_____

_____

     Creditor   Claim No._____

TO THE ABOVE NAMED DEBTOR—*You will take notice:*

1. That you are indebted to the above named creditor in the sum of $_____

2. That account is overdue and unpaid.

3. That payment has been duly demanded.

4. That, therefore, unless you remit to the office of_____

_____, or otherwise make provisions for settlement, on

or before the_____day of_____, 19____, suit will be instituted

forthwith for full amount, together with interest, all costs, and disbursements in their behalf

expended.

     Dated at_____, State of:_____

this_____day of_____, 19____.

_____

                    Creditor.

Above, a collection notice designed to look like a legal document—specifically, a summons—and so scare a debtor into paying. While purporting to be a legal document, it represents a highly illegal practice, which Chapter 13 tells you how to handle. By way of comparison, a real summons follows. Note the difference and similarities.

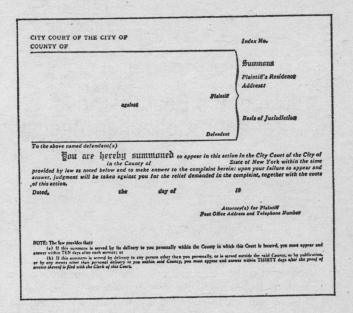

CITY COURT OF THE CITY OF
COUNTY OF

Index No.

𝔖𝔲𝔪𝔪𝔬𝔫𝔰

Plaintiff's Residence
Address:

against

Plaintiff

Basis of Jurisdiction

Defendant

To the above named defendant(s)

𝔜𝔬𝔲 𝔞𝔯𝔢 𝔥𝔢𝔯𝔢𝔟𝔶 𝔰𝔲𝔪𝔪𝔬𝔫𝔢𝔡 *to appear in this action in the City Court of the City of in the County of State of New York within the time provided by law as noted below and to make answer to the complaint herein: upon your failure to appear and answer, judgment will be taken against you for the relief demanded in the complaint, together with the costs of this action.*

Dated, *the* *day of* *19*

Attorney(s) for Plaintiff
Post Office Address and Telephone Number

NOTE: The law provides that:
(a) If this summons is served by its delivery to you personally within the County in which this Court is located, you must appear and answer within TEN days after such service; or
(b) If this summons is served by delivery to any person other than you personally, or is served outside the said County, or by publication, or by any means other than personal delivery to you within said County, you must appear and answer within THIRTY days after the proof of service thereof is filed with the Clerk of this Court.

Finally, an old Jewish anecdote offers a classic way of handling dunning letters. When a merchant from Lodz placed an order with a dry-goods firm in Brisk, he received a letter stating, "We regret we cannot fill this order until you make full payment on the last one." The merchant wrote in reply: "Please cancel the new order. I cannot wait that long."

CHAPTER EIGHT

A Debtor's Best Friend Is His Creditor's Collection Agency

A DEBTOR'S FIRST exposure to a collection agency takes place long before the collection agency's exposure to him. Somewhere in the creditor's internal dunning cycle (i.e., that of its own collection department), the collection agency will be introduced as a shadowy threat—a kind of bogeyman to whom the debtor's account will be turned over if payment is not forthcoming, and who will hound said debtor to the very death to collect the money due.

Thus, a bill collector's first utility to a creditor is as a deterrent weapon. Unfortunately for creditors, and fortunately for debtors, the collection agency's first utility is also its major utility, for, like all deterrent weapons, ranging from New York City's uniformed but unarmed Auxiliary Police to the United States nuclear umbrella, it is designed to deter merely by its existence. The one thing it's *not* designed for is to be used.

With relatively small debts, creditors, for all their threats, don't turn to collection agencies either eagerly or rapidly because collection agencies do create several problems.

First, they cost the creditor money. Collection agencies are not charities, as anyone who's ever dealt with one must realize. Collection agencies are profit-making businesses, and their profit is paid by the creditors who hire them, in the form of a piece of the sum or sums owing.

They make their money in two ways, either of which reduces the amount of money the creditor ultimately recovers. One way is by factoring, which means that the creditor sells his receivable debts at a discount. The other way is by paying the agency a commission—a percentage (as much as 50 percent) of the money it actually collects.

Until now, your creditor has been doing all his bill collecting internally. That is, he has used his own computers, his own people, his own postage, and so on, and because of this, collection expenses have come out of his general overhead. In other words, his efforts to collect your money up to the point of hiring an outside bill collector have been figured into his markup. His customers have paid for his collection efforts merely by buying his merchandise, and that includes not only customers who don't pay on time, but also those who do.

But with the retention of an *outside* bill collection service, the economics of the situation change. The creditor cannot collect your money without incurring an extra expense. Therefore, a process of attrition starts to set in. Rather than pay a disproportionately high collection expense, a creditor will make one last effort to collect his smaller, older debts, and then write them off as uncollectable.

When this happens, all is not lost for the corporation, since bad debts are tax deductible. For a corporation affluent enough to be paying the maximum federal income tax rate, this means that about half the face value of the debt will be picked up by the government. If you add the write-off value on state and city corporate income taxes, where applicable, and compare them to the decreasing value of receivables with age, a creditor can

165

sometimes recover more by writing off a debt than by going to a lot of expense to recover part of it.

With each successive outside service (e.g., lawyer, court, and so on), there will be a successively increased expense. So with each further step, many creditors will lop off more debts from the bottom of the pile. By the time a debt gets to the civil court stage, anything under about $250 becomes more profitable to forget than to fight for.

In the past, many of the larger creditor organizations had a best-of-both-possible-worlds solution to forgo the expense of an outside collection agency while still enjoying its psychological clout. This was through the establishment of an internal "collection agency" that had a separate name and letterhead, but was actually a department of the creditor organization, and, as such, merely a part of the overhead. Coventry Collection, a subsidiary of American Express, was one of many examples.

The Federal Trade Commission, however, has found this to be a misleading practice and has prohibited it. The prohibition also extends to in-house attorneys, even though they may be fully accredited counselors at law, empowered to take you to court on behalf of their employer. (This is not to imply that creditors can't have collection departments or lawyers on payroll; it's just that if they do, they must label them as such and not try to intimidate you by passing them off as independent, outside services.)

When your first collection agency or attorney's letter arrives, it will therefore pay to check the return address and see if it's the same street and number as your creditor's. If so, call the regional office of the FTC. Since your creditor is illegally making trouble for you, you might as well legally make some trouble for him.

If your debt is relatively very small, a creditor who has threatened to sic the bill collectors on you may forget the whole thing rather than incur the expense of making good on his threat. And if he goes ahead, certain features implicit in the economics of bill collection help the system to work against him.

166

With the factoring system, the creditor sells his receivables to a factor at anywhere from 60 to 85 cents on the dollar, and the factor then earns his profit by attempting to collect at the rate of 100 cents on the dollar. In the war of creditors on debtors, these are the economics of defeat. By setting his break-even point at 60 to 85 percent of face value, the factor has conceded that 15 to 40 percent of the receivables he has bought are uncollectable. Once the break-even point has been reached, or barely passed, many factors refuse to waste their employees' time (and therefore their own money) on increasingly time-consuming and decreasingly productive hard-core cases.

The commission system, on the other hand, is even more self-defeating. It tends to give bill collectors a "found money" attitude about the commissions earned through collection. If they can recover the full sum, that's great. If they settle for any sort of partial payment —no matter how small—they still make money. And if they fail to collect, they still haven't lost anything.

As with the factor system, there is a strong temptation to take the agency's cut on the easy cases (those that can be gotten with two or three letters or phone calls) and pass the tough ones along to a lawyer. Which brings us to the second major failing of bill collection agencies.

Unlike the Royal Canadian Mounted Police, bill collectors often fail to get their man. Part of the reason for this is economic, as we just discussed. But another cause is a situation of diminishing returns. You may recall from Chapter 1 that 95 percent of the U.S. population pay bills on time, 4 percent pay late, and only 1 percent are total stiffs. By the time a debt gets into the bill-collector stage, the collection process deals less and less with the easy 95 percent and more and more with the recalcitrant 4 percent and the 1 percent incorrigibles. As a result, more and more time and effort must be spent to produce results from a more and more difficult group of debtors.

Their reputation of inexorability notwithstanding, bill collectors lose their man more often than they get him.

The reputation is not so much the result of successful collection as of successful self-promotion.

In 1971, the head of Standard Collection Agency, located in New York City, was indicted on forty-six counts of extortion, coercion, harassment, grand larceny, and criminal impersonation for putting the arm on debtors in the way that most bill collectors would like you to believe is standard procedure. According to the indictment, he told CBS-TV newscaster Pia Lindstrom that he would wreck her career if she didn't pay a $200 restaurant bill that a friend of hers had run up. And that was one of the mildest forms of wrecking he threatened. He reportedly threatened one complainant with broken arms and legs unless he paid a $350 bill and told another he would chop off his arms and legs and shove him out a twenty-sixth-story window unless he forked over $396.55 allegedly owing to the Doral Park Hotel. He approached some fifteen other complainants with similar threats in establishments ranging from Sardi's, the Colony, and the Russian Tea Room in New York to, of all places, the Watergate Hotel in Washington, and passed himself off as all kinds of fearsome personages, from an FBI agent to Thomas (Tommy Ryan) Eboli, a gangster.

But despite his display of zeal, in eighteen cases, at least, the bill collector got in trouble with the law instead of getting his clients' money.*

A collection agency characterized as one of the most successful by the *Wall Street Journal*† was quoted as boasting of its 33 percent collection rate, which, they further boasted, was achieved mostly through immediate responses to the first letter in their dunning cycle. Now, think about these statements for a moment. You'll discover they contain very little to boast about.

A collection rate of 33 percent means a failure rate

* Lee, Vincent, "46 Counts of Extortion Charged to Bill Collector," *New York Daily News*, January 20, 1971.

† Danforth W. Austin, "Putting the Arm On: Bill Collectors Busy as Nervous Consumers Can't or Won't Pay," *Wall Street Journal*, July 2, 1970.

of 67 percent, or more than two failures for every success.

The high proportion of those 33 percent successful collections that results from the first collection effort could indicate one helluva scary first collection letter, but it could also indicate something more damning; namely, that the proportion is high by default, and that for debtors who refuse to roll over and play dead upon receiving the first letter, follow-up attempts are either half-hearted or ineffectual. In view of the over-all 67 percent failure rate, the latter would seem more likely.†

Failing number three: Like the creditors themselves, outside collection agencies have their own dunning and aging cycles. These cycles are not as drawn-out as the creditor's initial cycle, but they can run thirty days or more. While the bill collector's cycle is running, this adds a buffer of time. As a debtor, you know that as long as you can keep the bill collector's attention engaged, the agency will not move your account along to the next step, which is usually a lawyer.

Handicap number four: Theoretically, at least, bill collectors are honor-bound to investigate any complaints about the product or service and ascertain from the creditor whether the complaint is valid. They don't always do this, but if you had a complaint that wasn't satisfied, you can bring it up again, and the resulting investigation, if the bill collector actually undertakes one, will add a few more days' time.

The current state of the economy is handicap number five. Instead of chronic deadbeats, who can be relatively easy to cow, bill collectors find themselves dealing with more and more middle and upper-middle class debtors who are not the least bit inclined to sit back and accept harrassment from people they regard as their social inferiors.

Creditors everywhere report that delinquencies are up drastically. BankAmericard reports that cardholders ·

† According to the same article, while this collection agency was boasting of a 33 percent success rate, the average collection rate for all agencies in the nation was 28 percent, which means a 72 percent failure rate.

with outstanding balances jumped by 20 percent in 1974, Master Charge's cardholders by 27 percent.

But while receivables are increasing, so is the difficulty in collecting them. One Los Angeles bill collector is startled to find that debtors are starting to harrass him back. He receives obscene letters, returned with his dunning letters and signed by the debtor, and he's even gotten an anonymous telephoned bomb threat. Even the more passive debtors are causing him no end of trouble. As his company's volume of business increases, so do its operating losses. In September, 1974, he stated, "it cost me $12,000 to work . . . We cannot make money off people who haven't got it. Nor can we live off $5 or $10 payments . . . There was a day, not too many years ago, when if a client assigned business to us and we could not recover 35 percent of it, we got rid of the client. Today, if you can find a client of which you can collect 35 percent, you get down on your knees and praise Allah." ‡

The final handicap that bill collectors must labor under is that their most effective gambits are now either civilly actionable or criminal (see Chapter 13). Legal restrictions have forced them to behave almost like legitimate businessmen, and many of them find this limiting.

Because of the economic and legal restrictions, the most that "clean" bill collectors can do is write or phone you a few times with threats limited to legal action (in due time, of course), psychological intimidation, and general nuisance value.

Basically, there are three ways of dealing with collection agencies. Two have the end result of gaining delay while your debt proceeds to the next stage. The third puts an end to your collection cycle, but at some cost to you. The first is simply ignoring bill collectors until they move on to the next stage. The second is using their own communications as a device for delaying and temporizing with them, until they give up and move on to the next stage (often a month or two later than would be the case with the first technique). The third is putting

‡"A New Class of Debtors Costly to Bill Collectors," *New York Times*, October 20, 1974.

an end to collection efforts by arranging a lenient settlement.

Before you adopt any technique for dealing with letters and phone calls from bill collectors, you must first be able to recognize them. Thanks to the postal regulations, defamation laws, and human psychology, recognizing bill collectors is usually easy.

Federal laws and postal regulations prohibit the mailing of post cards or envelopes on which is printed matter reflecting on the character of the recipient, and this matter could even be construed to include the collection agency's name in the return address.

According to the libel and slander laws, even a phone message that "Mr. Jones of the XYZ Collection Agency called" can be defamatory.

And human psychology dictates that a letter or phone message containing the name of a collection agency will be the last to be opened or answered.

Because of this, collection agency letters come in envelopes that have room numbers or post office boxes instead of company names in their return addresses. (So do solicitation letters from some charities, for the same psychological reason.) When a bill collector telephones you, he leaves his name and his number, but not his company name. (So do insurance salesmen, and for the same psychological reason.)

Once you've spotted a letter from a collection agency, you can deal with it in any of the ways you'd handle a dunning letter from a creditor's collection department. (See Chapter 6.)

Phone calls are a new weapon, and the best way to handle them is, first, to screen them. In an office, if you're lucky, you already have a secretary who screens your calls. At home, your wife can be prevailed upon to perform the same function. This will leave you with messages consisting of names and phone numbers. The next step is to determine whether the numbers belong to collection agencies. To do this, simply call back the number and ask the switchboard operator, "What company is this?" Often, your question will be answered with the question, "Whom do you wish to speak to?"

171

An effective tool of the collection agency trade is a peremptory attitude that often works successfully to demand information that you have the right to withhold. So when they ask you a question, remember that you asked them one first. "I don't want to speak to anyone, I just want to know what company this is." If they don't tell you, you can be 99 percent sure it's a collection agency. And if they do tell you, you'll be 100 percent sure.

By the same token, if a collection agency calls your home, gets your wife, and demands to know your business address, make sure she knows in advance that it's none of their business and has no compunctions about telling them so.

During his year-long battle with American Express over a $10 overcharge, the customer described in Chapter 6 was at one point phoned by Coventry Collection Agency. In the course of the conversation, they asked, "By the way, do you still live at 255 Spring Street?"

"No," he replied, "I've moved."

"Then could you tell us your present address?"

"I could. But I won't. Goodbye."

They never bothered him again, although the correspondence with American Express continued to drag on.

If you should have the misfortune to pick up the phone yourself when a bill collector is calling, you can still handle the situation, provided you keep your perspective and remember a few things.

First, bill collectors, as a rule, are not the smartest or most energetic people in the world, and therefore don't use the sharpest telephone technique. For example, a company clerk in the National Guard had to telephone Guardsmen absent from drills to find out the reason for their absence. Giving the matter a little thought, he realized it would be smarter not to officiously announce, "This is Specialist Bauman from the National Guard," but instead to ask, "Hi. Is Charlie there?" While the first way would never get Charlie to the phone, the second one would, unless he was seriously ill, out of town, or otherwise truly inaccessible. Bill collectors, as a rule, rarely use this kind of thought.

Whenever someone calls and asks for you by initial (the way your name is listed on your bills) or last name, chances are overwhelming it's a bill collector. Once you realize this from the first words out of his mouth, you can instantly prepare yourself to deal with him, and this is where the sense of perspective comes in. Although a telephone is by its nature a peremptory device, this bill collector has used it to make himself an uninvited guest in your home. Therefore, you are perfectly within your rights to eject him from your home (by ending the conversation) if he doesn't mind his manners—or, for that matter, even if he does.

If you have a hold button on your phone, you can keep putting a bill collector on hold, while you "answer a long-distance call on the other line." Everybody's patience has limits, and if you keep it up long enough, so will a bill collector's.

One accountant got rid of a bill collector by pretending to have a message-recording device. When the bill collector called, he made the mistake of identifying himself before the accountant could even get a "hello" in. The accountant, talking in as mechanical and stilted a tone as possible, said, "I am not in now. This is a recording. When you hear the click, please record your name and phone number. Thank you." The click in question was the sound of the accountant's phone being hung up.

Once they've gotten you to talk to them, those collectors who are good at their jobs will attempt to scare you, bully you, anger you, manipulate you, or keep you off balance, all the while keeping perfectly cool themselves. It's your job to turn the tables on them, or that failing, end the conversation as quickly as possible.

For example, collection agents may threaten to ruin your credit ratings or call your employer. Should they take these actions, your remedies are discussed in Chapter 13. Be sure you're familiar with them and don't be afraid to answer a collector's threat with an appropriate counter-threat.

If they threaten to sue you, answer, "If that's what you want, it's fine with me. I'll be glad to take service anytime."

If it's a disputed bill, the collector may be willing to listen to your complaint. If not, you can merely state, "This is a disputed bill. Your client refused to even consider my complaints, so if he wants any money from me, he'll have to go to court to get it."

Sometimes a collector will attempt to use psychology and ask, "Why don't you clear this up? Why keep it hanging over your head?" to which you can answer that you're perfectly happy with it hanging over your head.

Another psychological tactic is the good-guy-bad-guy technique employed by implication in dunning letters. Here there will be a supposedly lenient collector who will agree to an easy settlement and a bad guy, allegedly his boss, who supposedly has to approve the settlement. After making an arrangement with you, the good guy will ask you to hold while he checks it out with his "boss." After a pause for effect, the "boss" will then come on the line breathing fire and brimstone, hurling abuse, and rejecting the settlement terms. After he's done, your friend the good guy will come on the line again, either with a sob story about losing his job if you don't pay in full or with an offer to intercede with the "boss" if you can make a better settlement.

This technique, as we said, was developed by crooked cops for shaking down merchants at Christmas time. It has a long history and is a set piece. Don't be taken in by it. When the bad guy starts yelling at you, threaten to terminate the conversation if he doesn't mind his manners. And if he keeps on, hang up on him. The worst that will happen is, he'll make four or five tries to get you back and then either drop the matter, try another day, or pass it on to an attorney.

In a less elaborate version of this ruse, a bill collector may throw himself on your mercy by "candidly" telling you that if he doesn't collect your bill, he'll be fired. Tell him that his relationship with his employer is no concern of yours.

Using the peremptory power of the telephone, bill collectors may threaten to hang up on you if they feel you're not sufficiently responsive. Many debtors who don't know any better will respond to this approach by actually trying to coax the bill collector to stay on the line. The right way to handle this situation is as follows:

COLLECTOR: If you're going to continue to be unreasonable, I'm going to have to terminate this conversation.

DEBTOR: Fine. I didn't ask you to start it in the first place. You're the one who called me, remember?

Bill collectors will search for the slightest opening to make you lose your equilibrium, and you should do the same to them. One gambit is to ask bill collectors, "How are you?" This is totally unexpected, throws them off their pace for a few seconds, and puts them psychologically one down. Should one brush aside this politeness with a rude remark, you can treat him to a long and pompous dissertation on good business manners.

By the same token, it always puts bill collectors one down when you interrupt them to correct their grammar, their pronunciation, or their manners.

Again, they often try to get you into an emotional state, so it never hurts to turn the tables. At the first rising inflection, say, "Don't raise your voice to me." The inevitable reply will be, "I am *not* raisng my voice to you," some thirty decibels higher. You'll actually hear the adrenalin flowing, and when the adrenalin flows, thought congeals.

Many bill collectors are used to insults, name-calling, and other forms of abuse, and therefore don't respond to them. This makes them suckers for a kind word or compliment, which (like a "How are you?") throws them completely off stride and often makes it psychologically very hard for them to be ruthless.

Of course, if you can't face up to a discussion with a bill collector, or if the sound of a ringing phone drives you up the wall, or if you'd like to gain a few more days' delay before you actually talk to a collector, there are some intermediate tactics you can use.

175

First, you can have your secretary (or wife) use the good-guy-bad-guy routine on the bill collector, with you cast in the role of bad guy: "I was supposed to send you a check last month, but I forgot, and Mr.————/my husband will be furious and fire/divorce me if he finds out I didn't. So please, let me send you a check, and please don't call again, or I'll lose my job/marriage."

If you're good at voices, you can handle the intermediate delaying tactics yourself. For example:

Phone rings.

SMITH: *(in French accent):* 'Allo XYZ Company.

COLLECTOR: Is John Smith there?

SMITH: Non. Zees ees Monsieur Deschamps from ze Parees offees. You see, we've an exshanje program, and eenstead of working at my office in Parees, I am 'ere een New York.

COLLECTOR: Don't bother me with that. I want to speak to Smith.

SMITH: I am sorree, 'e ees not 'ere. You see, weez ze exshanje program . . .

COLLECTOR: The hell with your exchange program! Where can I reach Smith?

SMITH: Ah! Zat ees very easy. You can téléphone heem at Orly 47 25.

COLLECTOR: I never heard of that kind of number. What kind of phone number is that?

SMITH: Monsieur, I told you zat I was 'ere on exshanje program and not at my offees in Parees. Well, zat is ze number of my offees in Parees, and while I am 'erein New York, Monsieur Smeeth is at my offees in Parees.

The possibilities are endless. A Rochester-type valet, a Chinese houseboy, and a Yiddish-speaking father or grandfather are just three of them.

For people who are good at sonorous, unctuous voices, the Reverend Oberwegger routine is also a natural:

COLLECTOR: This is Mr. ——— of the ——— collection agency. Lemme speak to Smith.

SMITH: Mr. Smith cannot come to the telephone, my son, but he'll be so happy to know that you called to pay your respects.

COLLECTOR: Who is this? Whaddya mean, pay my respects?

SMITH: This is the Reverend Oberwegger, and I am here to help the Smith family in their hour of trial.

COLLECTOR: Hour of trial?

SMITH: Yes, my son. In a few short hours, brother Smith will meet his Maker, and on his behalf and his family's, I want to thank you for calling to give your good wishes at the end.

When less drastic measures are called for, you can speak to bill collectors as yourself, giving excuses for nonpayment ranging from automobile accidents to operations on nonexistent children, to what, judging by its effect on people, is probably the world's most dread disease, cancer. Cancer is usually reserved only for emergencies (i.e., troublesome collection agents with big balances owing), and the most effective way it's used is in returning calls to collectors who have left messages:

DEBTOR (*in a disgustingly gravelly, raspy whisper*): Hello, Mr. ———?

COLLECTOR: ——— speaking. Who is this?

DEBTOR: This is John Doe.

COLLECTOR: Who is this? Speak up, I can't hear you.

DEBTOR (*softer*): I'm speaking as loudly as I can. I wanted to return your call earlier, but. . . .

COLLECTOR: What? I can't hear you.

DEBTOR (*still softer. The collector, though repelled by the voice, is straining to hear it.*): I wanted to call you earlier, but I was in the hospital (*wheeze*), being operated on for throat cancer. (*wheeze.*) I know I have some bills to pay the hospital and the throat surgeon, but as soon as I can see my way clear, I'll pay you. (*Wheeze*)

At this point, if the collector isn't completely turned off by the combination of cancer and the sound of Doe's voice, Doe will launch into a discussion of the gory details of his operation and the chances of his needing further operations. Sooner or later (generally sooner), this will elicit the reply, "Don't you worry, Mr. Doe. You just get well and send us a check when you're on your feet again," followed by a quick click of the phone, followed by a sigh of relief from both ends of the conversation.

Aside from the telephone and the mails, collection agencies can use personal solicitation. They don't do it very often, for the costs of time and labor make it impractical for any but relatively large debts. But in dealing with business debts, and in cities whose business districts are concentrated into one or two small areas, it's sometimes done, so you ought to know how it works.

The idea is to send one of four types of professional collector around to your office or place of business to hang around and embarrass you into paying. There are, as we said, four variations on the basic theme, but what all four have in common are their persistence, their triumphant personal obnoxiousness, and their lack of shame.

The first type is the retired policeman. Since policemen can retire in their middle forties, a retired cop isn't necessarily an old one. Therefore, until age starts to creep up on him, the retired cop will have the very obvious look of an active plainclothesman about him. He will come to your office and ask your receptionist to see you as if he were still on the force and carrying a warrant for your arrest in his back pocket. His manner alone is usually sufficient to gain him admittance, and about the only way to deter him is to make sure the receptionist asks for his credentials or identification before treating him as a peace officer.

The second type looks and smells like a Bowery bum, and if he's not admitted to see you, he'll gladly wait—in your reception room, which he will stink up with his clothes and body. He'll also change his seat often, moving closer to other business callers, who are trying to avoid him, and doing anything else that comes to mind as a way of embarrassing your receptionist into admitting him to your office just to get him out of the reception room. You might tell your receptionist to spray some roach killer. Not only around him, but on him.

Mr. Garlic is a variation on the Bowery Bum. While much more reputable in appearance, his very pores reek the odor of garlic. And when he opens his mouth to speak (which he'll probably do often), forget it. You might try having him sprayed with room deodorant. Particularly when he opens his mouth.

Finally, there's the Loudmouth, who usually combines this approach with either the Bowery Bum or the Mr. Garlic technique. In addition to looking generally disreputable, he'll sit around the reception room all day loudly inquiring of all within earshot (which sometimes means everyone within a half-mile radius) when you're going to pay him the money you allegedly owe.

The basic problem in coping with these four types is that they have the legal right to hang around your office and embarrass you. Legally, since most offices do business with the public and are set up to receive business callers, an office is a semi-public place. So you can't call a cop and have them ejected. And if you use force to do it yourself, you run the risk of a suit for bodily injury. (There's even a case where a second-story man, while committing a burglary, tripped over a rug, hurt his leg, sued his victim for damages, and collected.)

When confronted with one of these personal collection tactics, there's only one sure-fire way to deal with the collector, and that's to give him a check. But first, see Chapter 9.

CHAPTER NINE

How to Make a Good Check Bounce

INTO EVERY DEBTOR'S life, a little payment, like a little rain, must fall. Every now and then, it may be necessary to grit your teeth and send a check to one or another of your creditors. But, painful as the experience may be, it has its justifications.

For example, a payment—even a partial one—can get particularly troublesome creditors off your back for at least a while. At worst, you'll have a breather in which to husband your energies and brace yourself for the next onslaught; and at best, because of the way debts lose their value to creditors with age, you may get permanent relief from the creditor in question.

Another example: If your creditor is one of those rare companies that believe in satisfying customer complaints instead of losing them through attrition, and if they make an adjustment in your favor, there's a strong moral commitment to pay them.

In either case, there's a practical problem. If you're a committed, resourceful debtor, living life to the fullest on creditors' money, you may be overextended to the point of having too little cash on deposit in your checking account to cover those checks you have to write. (And this is not a bad state of affairs; if you don't watch it, writing checks to pay bills can get to be a $50-a-day, or worse, habit.)

Therefore, when you have to pay creditors, you ought to first take steps to ensure that your check will either (1) take practically forever to clear, or (2) be tendered in good faith, but, through an apparently innocent error, not be worth the paper it's written on. Which is far less risky than you'd imagine, because in both a legal and a practical sense, there is a double standard of rubber.

From the time most people learn what checks are, they're taught that a bouncing check is, in effect, a hand-written invitation to the nearest penitentiary. This just isn't so, for if it were, the jails would be so filled with New Math victims who couldn't balance checkbooks that no room would be left for real criminals.

True, there's a law against passing bad checks, but this law distinguishes between people who write bad checks by mistake and people who do it as a course of conduct, for a living. Thus, enforcement of this law is generally lenient, except in the case of certain circumstances which would lead a prosecutor, judge, or jury to infer criminal intent—if you've written bad checks repeatedly, if you've written one for an exceptionally large purchase, or if you've hung bad paper all over town. If these criteria don't apply to you, then if an occasional check bounces back marked "Insufficient Funds," you don't have to worry about being jailed for it. You do have another worry, however, and that is that creditors don't, as a rule, trust people who bounce checks on them, and trust is an important condition to continued credit. Also, banks generally charge fees ranging from one to three dollars for bounced checks, and unless you're bouncing a very large check (which is a legal no-no, for reasons already discussed), this fee is unconsicously large "interest" to pay for what is generally not more than a week's delay.

Fortunately, there are other checks that are apparently not "bad" (in the sense of not being covered by sufficient funds), but will be returned to the creditor before they can be debited to your account. These are checks which, through "errors" on the part of the writer, lack one of the five essential elements that make checks negotiable.

Legally, a check is (1) an unconditional order to a bank to pay on demand (2) a specified sum of money (3) to either a specified person or corporation or the bearer (e.g., a check made out to "Cash") (4) as of a specified date (5) authorized by the signature of the payer. In simpler terms, this means that your check, to be valid, must have five things written on it:

1. the name of the bank
2. the name of the person or company it should be paid to
3. the amount to be paid
4. the date
5. your signature

With these five elements, a check can be written on birchbark, toilet tissue, or the side of a cow (there is precedent for all three) and still be valid. (If you're in New York, visit the Chase Manhattan Bank's money museum; you'll see some valid checks that are real weirdos.) Without any of these elements, your check can be printed on bank safety paper, pre-numbered, perforated for easy tearing from the checkbook, and encoded with magnetic numbers for easy computing, but it still will come bouncing back from the clearing house—before it can even be determined whether you have sufficient funds on deposit to cover it.

Unlike a check marked Insufficient Funds, there is no stigma attached to such an occurrence, since you have obviously tendered your payment in good faith, but in your rush to pay, became the victim of common, all-too-human error.

Moreover, modern clerical standards being what they are, a ridiculously long interval may pass between the time your check is returned to your creditors and the time they take cognizance of the error, process the check, and return it to you for correction.

One customer deliberately "paid" Bloomingdale's some

six weeks late with an unsigned check. Another six weeks went by before the store sent him the check and a form letter asking him to correct his oversight. (During this time, he was billed for a one-month, 1½ percent "service" charge. He got this charge rescinded by telephoning the manager with the argument that while he was to blame for the initial "error," Bloomingdale's was to blame for the inordinate delay in detecting it.)

Of course, if you're going to "forget" one of the five vital elements, you ought to make sure it's not one that can easily be filled in by someone else, like the payee's name. Many companies have rubber stamps expressly for this purpose, and, should your check be large enough, a dishonest employee could "forget" to use the stamp and write his own name in instead.

Similarly, should you leave out the amount to be paid, but include your signature, the results could be disastrous, particularly if the bill is a disputed one.

Leaving out the date can't get you into trouble, but it doesn't help, either, since it can be easily filled in.

But if your signature is missing, the check is legally invalid, and therefore cannot legally be paid by your bank. And if you're lucky, your creditor won't notice the lack of a signature until after the bank returns the check to him, and this, as we've seen, can add considerable delay. In all fairness, it should be noted that if you're unlucky, the bank may cash your check even though it is legally invalid. This is because checks are generally processed by computer, and computers are designed to read coded numbers, not human signatures. Should your bank cash an unsigned check, you owe it to yourself to get the branch manager on the phone and read the riot act to him; after all, if a pickpocket were to swipe a whole book of unsigned checks, fill them out (except for your signature), deposit them to his own account unsigned, and have them clear, you could be wiped out by the bank's acting not only negligently but illegally! Of course, the best of both possible worlds is to have your creditor's computer "read" the check and credit your account while your bank's computer bounces it back, uncashed, for lack of signature.

If the check is made out for two conflicting amounts, the bank's computer won't "know" which amount to debit your account for. The check will go back to your creditor, who'll have to do without your money until he contacts you to correct the mistake.

Legally speaking, there's nothing wrong with an old check. A check held for a year after it was written is just as valid as one presented for payment before the ink on the date is dry, but as a practical matter, banks generally refuse to honor checks dated more than ninety days before they're deposited. If there is an error on the month or the year, it is just as certain that the check will be returned unpaid as if it had two conflicting sums for payment. This is particularly useful to remember every January, when it's perfectly natural to write checks that are one year out of date through sheer force of habit.

Also, there's nothing legally invalid about checks written in pencil (admittedly, these can be erased, but the safety paper your check is printed on will show up erasures) or with items crossed out and written over. But the clearing house will generally return such checks, too, for correction or replacement.

As much room for common error exists in the way checks are mailed as in the way they're written. A very common mistake people make is to write perfectly good, legally valid checks, and send them to the wrong creditors, who then cannot deposit them. This error is the natural outcome of the way credit accounts are billed and the way checks are printed.

Although some creditors stagger their billing so that the same number of statements go out on any given working day of the month, many still send all their bills out at once—on the first, fifteenth, or thirtieth of the month. Thus, most debtors generally have a lot of bills to pay simultaneously. Now, most checks come bound together in checkbooks, so, when a debtor has a lot of checks to write at once, it's easier to write them all first and match them up with the statements and return envelopes later. As you can see, it's very easy for a conscientious debtor, with speedy payment of bills paramount in his mind, to mix up some of the checks and envelopes, with the result that at least two creditors get prompt, valid checks made out to some other company.

In this kind of situation, it's little help to the creditor that the check arrived promptly and is good as gold; he still can't cash it. And, as with an unsigned check, it can take a month or two to spot the error and notify the debtor. In fact, there's a possibility of added delay, because one creditor will invariably take even longer to spot the mix-up than the other, and the debtor can hardly be blamed for waiting until both checks are returned to him. With a triple or quadruple mixup, the possibilities are intriguing.

Creditors, being businessmen, can generally understand the businesslike attitude of not wanting to have two checks outstanding in payment of one bill, but they won't know that this is your concern unless you communicate this fact to them. Here's a suggested form letter:

Gentlemen:

Thank you for your letter and for returning my check #——, which was made out to —— and sent to you in error.

Your consideration has enabled me to forward it to them in payment of my —— (date) bill.

I regret to inform you that in your case, payment will not, unfortunately, be as quick and easy. Upon checking my records, I find that my check #——, made out to your company, must have gone to —— (name of a third creditor), and they have not yet returned it.

Please be assured that as soon as
I get your check back from them,
you will get it from me.

Thank you for your patience.

                    Sincerely,

What is true in the case of complaints to creditors is also
true of any other communication with them; the more
specificity, the more credibility. By including all the details about the "missent" check and its "erroneous" recipient, you make your story sufficiently believable to
forestall both questioning and dunning until a reasonable
period has elapsed for the check to be either "returned"
or declared "lost in the mails."

Another source of common error in checks is social
and geographic mobility. We live in a mobile society,
and nowhere is this mobility more evident than in big
cities, where single people, for example, move on the
average of once every eighteen months. When someone
moves, nothing could be more natural than moving his
checking account with him, to a more conveniently located branch or bank. And, man being the only junk-
collecting animal (even the pack rat leaves one item for
every item he takes), nothing could be more natural
than for him to take his old, unused checks with him
when he moves, even though a change of bank will shortly
render them useless. And, since all checks look alike
(almost all, in fact, regardless of bank, are printed to the
same specifications by Deluxe Check Printing Co. and
one or two similar outfits), it's hardly surprising that from
time to time people inadvertently issue checks on accounts which are no longer open. It's also not surprising
that a simple error like this should take some time to be
detected and sorted out.

It is also interesting to note that you can move your
checking account without having to move anything bulkier
than your body and some pieces of paper. First, you can

open an account at any multi-branch bank in your city (preferably a large one). Then, you can open a second account at another branch, which may have turned out to be more convenient or have shorter lines. When the pre-printed checks from your first account arrive by mail, you can close it, using one of those checks to transfer all your funds to your second account. Of course, since both branches belong to the same bank, their checks will be identical in all but one or two minor details (like the account number, which itself should be enough to keep checks drawn on a closed account from clearing) and therefore easy to confuse for each other. If you do make the perfectly human error of actually confusing them, this is perfectly understandable to your bank and your creditors (if it doesn't happen repeatedly with the same creditor). As is the case with other understandable errors, you should have a cushion of a month or so to have the error noticed and then set everything to rights.

When you can't get checks stopped by error, it's always possible to stop them by design. Just as the law has a double standard of rubber checks, so does the business community.

People who bounce checks are deadbeats. But people who stop payment on checks are shrewd businessmen. Since it costs about as much to stop a check as to have it returned for insufficient funds, you might as well impress your creditors as a shrewd businessman instead of as a deadbeat. This is important, because while deadbeats eventually lose their sources of credit, shrewd businessmen somehow never do.

If you stop a check on an 18 percent-per-year-interest account, and that check is for $200 or more, there's a minor financial advantage as well. The interest on your account works out to 1½ percent per month. The stop-payment charge to the bank is usually three dollars, or one month's interest on a $200 debt. The delays in writing the check, having your creditor process it and send it to the bank, having the bank return it to the creditor, having the creditor obtain and note your records, and then send a form letter to you, can easily consume one month or more. And because the check is stopped, rather than bounced, you are in an excellent position to demand that the creditor's interest charges be rescinded.

A bounced check immediately puts you morally on the defensive, which leaves you in no position to demand anything, no matter how valid your demands may be.

A stopped check, however, leaves you positively reeking with moral rectitude. The check may have been stopped, for example, because of shoddy goods or services, which puts the creditor himself on the defensive. Or you may have been victimized by theft, loss, acts of nature, or banking errors, all of which make the thief, nature, or the bank—but not you—the bad guy.

And stopping payment on a check is as easy and painless as it is inexpensive. According to the Uniform Commercial Code, which is in effect in at least forty-eight of the fifty states, an oral stop order (i.e., one you place by telephone) must be honored by the bank for a period of fourteen days. If, during those fourteen days, you confirm the stop order in writing, the bank must honor it for a period of six months. For your own protection, you should give the bank every relevant detail about the check in question, so they'll know what to look for: the check number, the name of the payee, the amount, the date it was drawn, your name, and your account number.

In addition to transforming deadbeats into shrewd businessmen, and giving exploited debtors bargaining power, stopped checks can also provide the timid with a convenient whipping boy:

CREDITOR: This is the Metropolitan Life Insurance Company. We're calling in reference to this premium check which you stopped payment on . . .

DEBTOR: You must be mistaken. I didn't stop any check I sent your company.

CREDITOR: I'm sorry, sir, but *you're* mistaken. I have the stopped check in my hands.

DEBTOR: Wait a second . . . *(Pause for meditation, shuffling of papers in background)* Did you say you're from Metropolitan *Life* Insurance?

CREDITOR: Yes, sir.

DEBTOR: That confounded secretary of mine! We had a disputed bill from Aetna *Fire* Insurance, and I told her to stop payment on that. You have no idea how hard it is getting competent help these days . . . *(weary sigh)* If it's satisfactory to your employers, you'll receive another check during the next billing cycle.

CREDITOR: That'll be just fine, sir. Thank you.

DEBTOR: Thank *you*. And now, if you'll excuse me, I must call my bank to stop that other check.

A variation on this technique is to stop payment on all your checks and even close your account or have it renumbered, on the basis that your checkbook has been lost or stolen.

In this case, the scapegoat will not be your poor, non-existent secretary, but your rich, existent bank.

When a creditor calls about his stopped check, explain this unfortunate circumstance to him, and he'll be most understanding.

A week or two later, write him that the checkbook has been recovered, there was no evidence of foul play, the account has been reopened, and he can redeposit the check if it's still in his possession. Then, call the bank to make sure they keep the stop order in effect. (This is also a good idea for stop orders placed on checks you issue for disputed bills, because banks tend to get lax about stop orders more than a day or two old.)

When he deposits the check again, it will be stopped again, and he'll call you again. Giving you a chance to rail at "those dummies at the bank! I called them only yesterday about that stop order."

If this sounds like too much expense or bother, instead of stopping your checks, you can post-date them (sign now, pay later). Contrary to popular belief, post-dated checks are not illegal. Post-dating does not affect the negotiability of a check one bit. Post-dated checks are, however, unpopular with creditors, for several understandable reasons.

For large creditors, processing bill payments is as much an assembly-line process as making automobiles. A post-dated check must be pulled off the assembly line, and someone must keep an eye on it until the payment date arrives. This is very inefficient and unbureaucratic. With the kind of clerical people most creditors employ, it's entirely possible that the post-dating won't be noticed, in which event the bank will return it to the creditor uncashed. Or, if the creditor's people catch it themselves, company policy will almost invariably dictate that they prepare a covering letter and send the check back to you (although there are occasions when, by the time they get around to doing this, and the letter reaches you, the check is no longer post-dated).

Although post-dated checks are legal, there's a practical reason why nobody wants to touch them. After you write a post-dated check, but before it can be deposited to your account, there's no guarantee that you won't walk in front of a speeding garbage truck, be assassinated in the bath, or meet with some other untimely end that would cause your bank accounts to be frozen until your executor is well on his way to settling your estate.

There are other ways to write perfectly legal checks that won't be cashed because, like post-dated checks, they don't happen to fit the automated system. Just as the computers that write your bills are designed to handle certain standard-size punch cards, so the banking computers that process checks are designed to handle only certain size pieces of paper, with the necessary information in certain specified locations. If you have your own checks printed up, and if these are of odd size and have things like the coded numbers at, say, the top of the check instead of at the bottom, the computers won't be able to cope with them. You can also write out checks on blank paper in pen and ink, and these, too, will be legal but beyond the abilities of the computer to cope with. Whenever a check can't go through the computer, the computer automatically turns it over to people to process. People invariably take longer—as much as three

190

weeks longer—and that adds time before which your account will be debited.*

Nor can computers cope with handwritten account numbers. The computer generally rejects these checks, and when enough of them accumulate, the pile is turned over to a person who types the coded number on adhesive labels, affixes the labels to the bottom of the checks, and puts the checks in another pile to go back to the computer. This, too, adds time.

You can buy blank checks, without coded numbers, at most stationery stores. Also, if you've forgotten your checkbook and want to write a check on any given day, your bank will be glad to give you blank checks with the bank and branch numbers encoded, but not the account number (provided you don't ask too often). There should be no extra charge for processing the latter, even though there should be extra delay.

Some computers read numbers optically, and others do it by reading impulses from magnetic substances mixed with the ink used for printing the account number. If you have the latter kind and carry it around in your pocket a few weeks instead of keeping it in the check book, the magnetic impulses usually fade. If you fold the check in half, so that both halves of the account number face each other, or if you carry it next to a check with a different magnetic coding, the impulses will get scrambled to the point of illegibility (at least for the computer). Of course, the human eye, which can't see magnetism, will be perfectly able to read the numbers. As a result, if the computer rejects a check with faded or scrambled magnetic coding, the people will see nothing wrong with it and put it into the computer

* It should be noted, however, that most commercial banks have a small charge—usually 25 cents—for processing non-standard checks. If you're writing such checks for any decent sum of money, that's a very reasonable fee to pay for up to three weeks' interest-free credit. Also, if you live in those states where banks have combined savings/checking accounts, where you draw day-to-day interest on the money that you haven't drawn checks against, the three weeks' interest can offset the non-standard check charge.

again. This can go on for some time, until the check gets put in the pile for recoding (see above).

The gentleman from London who cuts extra holes in punch cards (see Chapter 5) has another, diabolical, plan for dealing with magnetic coding. He has a tape-recorder head demagnetizer (cost: under $50), which he uses to literally wipe the magnetic coding away. This, too, adds to the time the check takes to clear, but for him, that's only secondary. His reason for demagnetizing the checks is to ensure the tender, loving, human care that he feels, and quite understandably, the bank should give his checks as a matter of course.

It may seem hard to believe, but in the entire United States there is no one central clearing house for checks. Instead the country is divided into Federal Reserve Districts, each with its own clearing house. At the end of each day, each district clearing house takes all the "foreign" checks (i.e., checks drawn on banks in different districts) and sends them to the appropriate clearing house, often by mail. As a result, checks drawn on out-of-town banks usually take a week to ten days longer to clear than checks drawn on local banks.

Surprisingly, checks drawn on suburban banks can also take this extra time to clear when deposited in a bank in a nearby, big city, and vice versa. This is because many big cities are in self-contained Federal Reserve Districts, which puts suburbs into different districts and therefore makes checks drawn on suburban banks "foreign." This presents some interesting possibilities. For example, if your biggest local creditors are in town, you can pay them with checks drawn on suburban accounts. If your biggest local creditors are in the suburbs, then you can pay with checks drawn against an account at a city bank. If it's fifty-fifty, you can use two accounts. It will take up to two working weeks for the checks to be debited to your account, leaving you with that much time to use the money for other things. Also, you don't hurt your creditor, since his bank usually credits him with the amount of the check as soon as he deposits it. In fact, you don't even hurt the banks, who are left holding the bag in the interim. Your piddling check is just one of many billions of dollars' worth caught in the same situation, known as "cash float." Banks have had many years' experience with cash float, have costed it out, and have surely adjusted their interest pay-outs and service charges to cover it. In other words, if you do business with a bank, you're already paying for cash float, so you might as well get what you've paid for.

In fact, you'll be doing on a small scale what the corporations who are your creditors do to rip off the Federal Reserve System to the tune of an estimated $1 billion a year.*

Here's how it works. The United States is divided into 12 Federal Reserve Districts. One city in each district—specifically Boston, New York, Philadelphia, Richmond, Atlanta, Chicago, St. Louis, Minneapolis, Kansas City, Dallas, Cleveland, and San Francisco—has a Federal Reserve Bank. In addition, 21 cities have Federal Reserve branches, and one—Miami—has a Federal Reserve Bank facility. In short, throughout the entire United States, there are only 34 places where checks can go through central clearing. There is no Federal Reserve facility for this purpose in the states of Maine, Vermont, and New Hampshire. There is no Federal Reserve facility anywhere in the state of Wisconsin. The same is true for the states of South Carolina, Iowa, North and South Dakota, Idaho, Wyoming, New Mexico, and Arizona.

By keeping their money on interest-bearing deposit in cities where the Federal Reserve has facilities, and paying their bills with checking accounts in cities where it doesn't, creditor corporations can earn interest on their huge deposits days longer before having to withdraw some money to cover their outstanding checks. "For the past four years," wrote Business Week," Houston-based Exxon Co. U.S.A. . . . has been using the disbursement float notion to some degree on the $5 million to $6 million it averages each day in payments. The idea works this way: Say that Exxon pays a supplier in Dallas

*Making millions by stretching the float," Business Week, November 23, 1974.

$1 million with a check drawn on a central account in Houston. Once the supplier deposits the check, as few as two days may elapse before the check is presented for payment to Exxon's Houston bank. But if Exxon pays the Dallas supplier with a check drawn on a special 'remote disbursing account' in a small branch of a major regional bank in, say, North Carolina, the check is forced through at least two Federal Reserve Banks, and the float can be extended as much as five days. By special arrangement with the North Carolina bank, Exxon can delay funding the disbursement until the day after the check is presented for collection. Counting mailing time, the time required for the check to be processed through the supplier's books and deposited, and the time the check is floating through the Fed's clearing system, Exxon can hold onto its $1 million in cash for as long as two weeks after it issues the check and thus keep earning interest on the funds . . . In the case of a corporation paying out $5 million a day, the concept can allow it to hold onto an additional $12 million in cash during the year, adding more than $1 million a year to its pretax income . . ." †

Banks throughout the country, including Wachovia Bank & Trust Co., Winston-Salem, N.C.; First National Bank, St. Louis; Seattle-First National Bank; and Citizens & Southern National Bank, Atlanta and Savannah, are helping corporations to cash in on this windfall. And where is all this money they make coming from? Ultimately, your pocket. "If we're getting screwed," said a Federal Reserve spokesman, "then the Federal Treasury —the taxpayer—is getting screwed. Last year, we paid $3.7 billion into the Treasury. If an extensive effort to take advantage of the system's payment policies held that figure down, the taxpayer was the one who lost." ‡

Finally, you can take advantage of a check's magnetic numbers by crossing them out. A bank teller recommends the following procedure for dealing with an obnoxious neighborhood creditor:

† Ibid.
‡ Ibid.

Visit his place of business to tender a check in payment and suddenly discover that you've forgotten your checkbook. (Since American folklore calls for them to do scatterbrained things like that, women can make this claim more convincingly than men.) Explain that everything is fine, however, because you know your account number by memory, and if he'll give you one of his checks, you'll alter it accordingly.

His check in one hand and fountain pen in the other, proceed to line out his bank's name and address and his account number. Substitute yours, and fill out the rest of the check as you would any other.

You have now given your creditor a perfectly legal check. A check which has the five essential elements discussed earlier.

And a check which will be debited to your creditor's account instead of yours. Even though you've lined out his numbers and substituted yours, his are magnetic and yours aren't. So the clearing house computer will ignore yours and read his under the crossing out. And unless he checks his statements very, very carefully, he may never learn that you've used the computer to turn his own checkbook against him.

CHAPTER TEN

What to Do Until the Lawyer Gets There

IN MANY RESPECTS, dealing with a collection lawyer is like dealing with a collection agency, except you get to meet a nicer class of people.

As outside services, lawyers add to the cost of collection, so again, more attrition takes place before a lawyer is called in on the case. Unlike collection agencies, however, lawyers are generally paid not on a flat fee, but according to the amount of work they do, so the more involvement you create for a lawyer, the more costs his client will incur, and the less money he is likely to earn for himself and recover for his client. Unlike the people you've dealt with so far (except for corporate officers, if you've had a complaint), lawyers have the ability to spot the point of diminishing returns, and their training and obligation to their client cause them to recommend disengaging from further action as that point approaches.

The ironic result is that lawyers, as a rule, hate litigation.

Sitting in his office, a lawyer can charge $20 an hour and up for handling many cases. Sitting in a courtroom, he must waste hours handling nothing just to wait for the half-hour or so during which he'll handle his client's case against you. Attorneys charge much more for sitting around waiting in court than they do for sitting around working in their offices, but compared to what they could have made on correspondence and paperwork, they still lose money.

In any jurisdiction, you, the debtor, can act as your own lawyer in personal (not corporate) debt cases. But in many jurisdictions, although corporations are legally persons, the law regards them much in the way the Bible regards idols ("They have eyes but cannot see, ears but cannot hear, legs but cannot walk," and so on), so when a corporation goes into court in those jurisdictions, it must be represented by an attorney.

In other jurisdictions, corporations trying to collect small debts cannot sue in small claims court, but must proceed in civil court, which requires more formality, more time, more paperwork, and therefore more expense. The chart on pages 198 and 199, which covers small claims courts in five big cities, illustrates this.

So when you're being sued by (or suing) a corporation, chances are excellent that you can run up its legal costs while keeping yours down, and thus hasten the arrival of the point of diminishing returns, beyond which it becomes more economical for a creditor corporation to write off your debt than to collect it.*

Of course, even if you do little or nothing to run up your creditor's legal costs, they can be pretty astronomical to begin with. Robert Coulson, executive vice-president of the American Arbitration Association, estimates

---

* An auditor for a major aircraft firm says that creditors generally get paid for bad debts, though not necessarily from the debtor who contracted them. "It's all figured right in there. That's part of their costs. So many debts per thousand—reserve for bad debts. Even when they lose, their loss is not 100 percent, because they write it off on their taxes, and they've already collected a lot of interest." (Jerome I. Meyer, "How to Go Bankrupt and Start Over," *New York*, September 10, 1973.)

197

How the deck is stacked against creditor corporations in small claims court

City	Maximum that can be sued for	Can Corporations sue?	Must corporations be represented by attorneys?	Can defendants have attorneys?	Fee for summons and service	When court is in session (all are Monday–Friday)
Boston	$400*	Yes	No	Yes	$3.53***	Afternoons
Chicago	$300	No	Yes	Yes	$9.50***	3 PM–6 PM
Los Angeles, San Francisco, others in California**	$500	Yes	Attorneys are forbidden for either side. Corporations are represented either by an officer or a designated representative whose name is on file with the state.	No	$2.00 for filing plus mileage charge if served by marshal. No service charge if served by a friend, relative, etc.	8 AM–5 PM for filing. Trials take place from 8:15 AM to 11 AM, and from 3 PM to 4:30 PM.

New York	$500	No	Yes	Yes	$3.24***	9 AM–5 PM for filing. Trials are from 6 PM to conclusion.
Washington, DC	$750	Yes	Yes	Yes	$1.53 by mail** $2.00 by marshal	9 AM–4 PM

NOTES:

* A bill is pending before the legislature to raise this limit.

** Small Claims is a state court, so the information here applies for any town or city in California.

*** Service is by certified or registered mail, return receipt requested. These fees may be raised a few cents as a result of the postal rate increase which took effect on March 2, 1974.

about fifty hours' worth of legal work merely in preparing a relatively simple accident case for trial †:

	HOURS
Taking depositions of three witneses at three hours each	9
Preparing and arguing a motion to compel answers to questions asked	6
Preparing interrogatories (questions)	3
Objecting to opponent's objections to the interrogatories	2
Answering interrogatories (as amended)	10
Arranging for a medical examination	3
Preparing a motion for production of a medical report	2
Resisting the opponent's motion to produce	5
Reviewing all the discovery (i.e., pre-trial information) in order to prepare pre-trial memorandum	10
TOTAL	50

At $20 per hour, that comes to a cool thousand dollars. Of course, some of the time spent on this case would be unnecessary in a case involving a disputed bill. But even eliminating ten hours' work on medical reports, three hours' work for one witness and another ten hours for good measure, we still have a total of twenty-seven hours, or $540. And that doesn't include ancillary expenses, like hiring a stenotyper to take the witnesses' testimony, filing and serving the summons, and the attorney's actual appearance in court.

What lawyers charge varies from city to city and state to state. Every bar association, however, has its schedule of minimum fees for different legal jobs, and this information is available, on request, to the general public. If you don't want to call your bar association, the following table should give you a better idea of some sample charges:

† Robert Coulson, *How to Stay Out of Court* (New York: Crown Publishers, Inc., 1968).

200

Minimum Recommended Lawyers' Fees

SOURCE: ASSORTED BAR ASSOCIATIONS

State	Office work, per hour	Trial work, per day in court
Alabama	$10–20	$120–250
Alaska	—	—
Arizona	25–30	250
Arkansas	12–25	100–250
California	20–30	150–250
Colorado	15–20	100–200
Connecticut	20	200
Florida	20–30	100–250
Georgia	20	150–200
Hawaii	—	—
Idaho	—	200
Illinois	15–30	150–250
Indiana	10–25	100–200
Iowa	15–20	125–200
Kansas	10–25	100–250
Kentucky	20–25	200
Louisiana	30	250
Maine	15	100–150
Maryland	15–20	100–150
Massachusetts	—	125
Michigan	15–25	100–250
Minnesota	15–25	150–200
Mississippi	—	200
Missouri	15–25	100–200
Montana	20	150
Nebraska	18	150–175
Nevada	20–25	200–250
New Hampshire	—	—
New Jersey	20–25	100–250
New Mexico	20	200
New York	15–25	100–250
North Carolina	15–25	100–150
North Dakota	15	150
Ohio	15–25	100–175
Oklahoma	15–25	125–200
Oregon	20	200
Pennsylvania	15–25	100–250

Rhode Island	10	100–150
South Carolina	20–25	150–200
South Dakota	15	150
Tennessee	15–25	150–250
Texas	15–25	100–250
Utah	15–18	100–200
Virginia	20–25	150–250
Washington	15–20	150–200
West Virginia	10	80–150
Wisconsin	20	200
Wyoming	20	150

Notes:
1. These are recommended figures, and the operative word here is "minimum." Many attorneys charge more. Bar Associations frown only on those who charge less.
2. A rule of thumb here seems to be that one day (7 hours or less) in court is worth about the same as ten hours in the office. This is why creditors who threaten court are less anxious than their threats imply to go to court over debts that can't be collected through attorneys' office work.
3. If your debt is for less than the cost of a day in court, all but the most hell-bent creditors will usually drop the matter after trying to scare you with a summons.

As of a June, 1975, United States Supreme Court ruling, these fees will not, in theory at least, be firm minimums. The ruling decided a case that started in 1971, when Lewis and Ruth Goldfarb bought a home in Reston, Virginia, and found that no lawyer would handle their title search for less than $522.50, or 1 percent of the purchase price. They sued the Fairfax County Bar Association for violation of the Sherman Anti-Trust Act, and four years later the Supreme Court upheld them. As a result, the suggested minimums are only suggestions.* But we're still a long way from the day when we'll see lawyers engaging in price wars and cut-rate competition.

Obviously, if your debt costs more to collect than it's worth, your creditor and his attorney are less likely to put up a vigorous fight for it, provided you're willing to fight and you make sure they know it.

*"Discount Lawyers?," *Newsweek*, June 30, 1975.

One way to make sure they know you're just as willing to fight as they are is to drop the role of a refined gentleman (the one you assumed in taking your complaints to the company management) and start acting like an idealistic, fanatical troublemaker.

In fact, if you start doing this in the early stages, chances are excellent that you can get the case dropped or settled before it reaches the later stages.

Though full-blown litigation is expensive, the preliminary efforts aren't. A lawyer's letter costs next to nothing to send, and a summons costs about $4 to file and $5 to serve. Therefore, regardless of how small the sum, lawyers will automatically take one or both of these steps for practically any debt bigger than $10. At relatively little cost, a lawyer's letter or summons brings amazingly good returns, since the sight of either is enough to scare the living daylights out of debtors who either don't know their rights or are unaware of the mechanics of the situation.

For example, when a copywriter quit his job at Young & Rubicam for a better job at another agency, Young & Rubicam suddenly rejected several dozen dinner payments (incurred while working late) on his final month's expense report, came up with several hundred dollars' worth of alleged cash advances whose existence had been hitherto unsuspected and, using these as an excuse, withheld his last paycheck. In retaliation, the copywriter refused to pay several hundred dollars' worth of car rental bills incurred on his company Hertz card.

About three months after his last day there, with much correspondence going back and forth, he received a lawyer's letter demanding payment of the rental bills and threatening a lawsuit if he didn't pay them. His return letter to the lawyer, read, in part:

> I do not owe your client, Young & Rubicam, any money.
>
> They, in fact, owe me money.

The letter went on to list, in very general terms, some of the legal recourses he felt their actions had made them liable to.

> If you'd like to pursue the matter further and cost your client a lot of money on a lost cause in the process, I'll be only too happy to see you in court.

Apparently, the lawyer had little appetite for pursuing the matter, for about two years have gone by since that letter, and he has yet to answer it.

In any correspondence with a lawyer, incidentally, it is useful to indicate your willingness to accept service of a summons, for legal reasons as well as psychological ones.

In most jurisdictions, a summons can legally be served in one of two ways. First, a process server can hand you the summons. This is called personal service, and you have ten days from the date of service (as attested to in an affidavit executed by the process server) to answer. Second, you can be served by substituted service, which is best described by its slang name, "nail and mail." The server may affix one copy of the summons to your door and mail you another copy by certified mail. You then have thirty days from the date of service to answer.

There is a third, and highly illegal, method of service known as "sewer service." It is called this because the server "serves" the summons to you by throwing it down the sewer or into any other handy garbage receptacle.

Sewer service may take place for one of two reasons. First, a process server generally earns from $1.50 to $5.00 for serving a summons. Assuming he serves five a day, and works six days a week (in New York City and other jurisdictions, it's illegal to serve civil summonses on Sundays), he earns a big $150 a week before taxes. With lax enforcement, process servers found they could collect on more summonses by filling out the affidavit of service while neglecting the service itself. One process server made the newspapers by getting arrested for doing this for about 150 summonses a day for several months. And if he hadn't been so greedy, he probably never would have gotten caught at it.

The second reason for sewer service is that it gives dishonest lawyers cheap victories. You can't answer a summons you've never received. And you can't know that the court has an affidavit saying that the summons has been served on you. So when you fail to answer within the prescribed period, the court reads the sworn statement by the process server attesting to the fact that he spoke to you personally and ascertained you were the person named in the summons and were not a member of the armed forces, assumes on the basis of this notarized statement that you knew of the action and chose not to contest it, and awards a default judgement to your opponent. Of course, you don't know about this judgement until your opponent garnishees your salary or sends a marshal around to seize some of your property, and by then it's usually too late.

The problem is, many process servers indulge in sewer service without even going to the trouble of dumping your copy of the summons in the nearest sewer. Instead, they simply sign and notarize the affidavit parts on blank summonses and, when the time comes, fill in the names and addresses of plaintiffs and defendants.

In 1969, according to then U.S. Attorney Robert Morgenthau, half of all default judgements against debtors in New York City—some 138,000 default judgements—were obtained as the result of fraudulent service of summonses, most of which was practiced by some forty process serving agencies.*

When one of them, Attorney's Service Company, was searched by postal inspectors, a total of 6,235 affidavits signed on blank summonses by more than 150 process servers were found. And according to Assistant U.S. Attorney Frank Tuerkheimer, this is typical of a widespread practice.

For example, a collection lawyer doing business for

*Whitney, Craig R. "U.S. Attorney Finds False Process-Serving Widespread Here," *New York Times*, October 14, 1969.

Macy's, Gimbel's, Saks, B. Altman, other department stores, Hertz car rental, and Franklin National Bank employed a process server whose affidavits indicated that he had the superhuman ability to be in several places at once. At 8:30 A.M., March 7, 1968, this process server simultaneously served summonses (and personally spoke to the recipients) in Queens and Manhattan, miles apart. But that was nothing compared to January 5 of that year, when he served papers on defendants on Broad Street (Manhattan), on East 85th Street (five miles north), and in Flushing, Queens (eight miles east)—all at 9 A.M. A search of the process server's files by Mr. Tuerkheimer's office disclosed records of about 100 similar feats of sleight-of-hand and legerdemain.

Another New York process server filed affidavits showing he had served summonses on people in Harlem and the Bronx during one forty-eight-hour period when postal inspectors, who had him under continuous surveillance, never saw him head north of 14th Street in Manhattan.

Of course, there are some forms of service that can achieve the same result, but perfectly legally, if you don't watch out.

There's a borderline tactic of serving you a summons in such a manner as to make you discard it unnoticed, as hidden in a "free sample" magazine or a package. So if you have any long-standing debts and anyone hands you an unsolicited package, be sure to examine it before you throw it out.

In the past, if you could prove sewer service, you could only neutralize the default judgement against you. But now, in New York City and many other jurisdictions, there are anti-sewer-service laws that have teeth in them. In New York, for example, a conviction for sewer service gets the server up to a $5,000 fine and up to five years in prison.

Even without going to the district attorney, there are ways to profit from this law. One day, a customer received a summons from attorneys retained by Macy's. One of the names in the law firm had a familiar ring, and a few minutes' reflection placed it as the name of an attorney who'd just been sent to Sing Sing for sewer service (the one referred to in paragraphs above). A method actor, the customer tore up the summons, threw it in the garbage can, retrieved one coffee-ground-stained fragment, and stared at it long enough to work himself into a healthy state of rage. Fragment in hand, he ran to the phone and called the law firm, demanding to speak to one of the other partners. When the attorney came to the phone, the customer opened the conversation, "I see you want to join your partner ———— up the river."

This was met by a sharp intake of breath and a very polite inquiry as to what was the matter. The customer then proceeded to tell him about the fragment of a summons he "found" in his garbage can, neglecting, of course, to relate how it got there.

The lawyer was only too happy to drop the matter, which was worth a few hundred dollars to his client.

With stringent laws against sewer service in effect, it's not that likely that you'll be a victim of it. But in case someone tries it on you, a copy of a letter from you to the other side's lawyer, stating that you'll be happy to take service on any summons, is a point of evidence in your favor.

Once the summons is served, most attorneys are prepared to do nothing other than sit back and wait for you to either call or send in a check. (In acting this way, they are not being lax, but realistic. More than 90 percent of New York City's bill-collection suits are decided in favor of the creditor simply because the debtor fails to show up in court. Even assuming that the U.S. Attorney's crackdown on sewer service failed, and that half of these default judgements resulted from fraudulent service, that still means that the other half—or more than 45 percent of the total number of bill-collection cases—were lost because the debtors knew of the lawsuit but didn't bother to contest it.) * But when you answer the summons, instead, this creates certain difficulties for them. Now they must either drop the case, meet you in court, or arrange some kind of mutually satisfactory settlement.

* "Doubtful Defaults," *Money*, January 1974.

Which choice they opt for depends in part on the size of the debt and in part on how you answer the lawsuit.

Physically, you answer the summons by going down to the court building and filing an answer with the clerk of the court. The clerks have the necessary forms and, if you're representing yourself, will have them served for you. As a rule, they'll also be very helpful in translating your response into the proper legal-language reply.

When you make your reply, you make the first of your pre-trial maneuvers. In most jurisdictions, when the original summons fails to specify the particulars against you, your reply can demand a full bill of particulars, and it should whenever possible, for several good reasons.

First, a bill of particulars takes time to prepare, and the lawsuit cannot proceed without it. If nothing else, this postpones the trial date.

And there is something else, namely, the time your creditor's attorney must take (and the money that your creditor must consequently spend) for its preparation. In addition to dragging out your case, you're also making it even less profitable to pursue.

In some localities, you can just submit a blanket demand for a bill of particulars. In others, you have to specify which particulars you want, in which event you should try to think of as many as possible.

In jurisdictions where you can't request a bill of particulars, or else when the other side finally supplies it, you can respond with a simple two-word answer: "General denial." You can also be more specific in your defenses, like "defective merchandise," "breach of warranty," and the like. Most of the complaints discussed in Chapter 6 make good legal defenses, and the clerk of the court will help you word your answer properly.

Another way to raise the stakes and communicate your eagerness to fight to the end is to apply for a jury trial. This means that if the case comes to trial, three things will happen: (1) The case will take longer to come up for trial, (2) your creditor's attorney will have to waste an additional day in court empaneling the jury when it does come up, and (3) you'll have a trier of fact that's even more sympathetic to underdogs than some judges are.

Once alerted that you won't give up without an expensive (for his side) fight, your creditor's lawyer will probably call you to arrange a settlement.

A shopper once purchased three suits, at a total price exceeding $400, from Barney's in New York. Even after three fittings, the tailors failed to get the clothing to fit right. On a white Sidney Greenstreet suit, they had ignored his instructions to put cuffs on the trousers, and then said that since the suit was white, the cuffs couldn't be changed without leaving marks on the trouser legs. In the months thereafter, seams opened, linings fell out, and buttons fell off. (Note: this was without any weight gain on the shopper's part.) He spent money to get these defects corrected by a tailor in his neighborhood, and telephoned requests for adjustments to reimburse him for these costs were ignored by Barney's. So the shopper therefore ignored their bills, and about two years later, they sued him.

The customer went to the offices of the New York Civil Court and filed his answer, which consisted of general denial, defective merchandise, and breach of warranty. At that time, he was assigned a trial date. A few days later, Barney's lawyer sent a letter to his home, asking that he telephone.

He did, and the lawyer asked him what the problem was. (Although lawyers can read from your answer what your problem is, they want to see how articulate a witness you'll make in court.) The customer told the lawyer his problems with the clothes, said he had no intention of paying the full purchase price, much less the 18 percent per year interest that Barney's had charged him, nor the 5 percent interest (not only on the purchase price, but on the other interest) claimed in the summons. The lawyer asked him if he had copies of the tailor's receipts and if he'd send them. He had them, and he sent copies. He also demanded a further settlement for the absence of cuffs on the Sidney Greenstreet suit. The lawyer acceded to these demands, which were no worse (and probably much better) than he'd have gotten from a judge, and the customer sent him a much reduced sum of money.

If your creditor's lawyer doesn't contact you before trial, you can show your willingness to fight by contacting him. But before you make your call, plan it thoroughly so that you communicate with everything you say and do your ability to fight the matter out to a drawn-out end in court.

One way to communicate both points is to visit him in the middle of the working day—either in the morning or afternoon, but not at lunch time. This will show him you have plenty of free time for court. It will also take up his time, which is far from free, in both senses of the word.

When you get in to see him, indicate your great devotion to the ideal of justice. "I want justice, and I don't care how much it costs or how long it takes for me to get it."

It also helps for you to show up with a stack of 8″ x 10″ photographs of the defective merchandise or damages caused by it. Some depositions from witnesses to wave in his face don't hurt, either, in showing him what an earnest nut you are.

It helps to indicate in the course of the conversation that you have a source of free legal advice. For example:

LAWYER: Those photographs are very interesting, but they really have nothing to do with the case.
DEBTOR: That's funny. My brother didn't think so.
LAWYER: Who's your brother?
DEBTOR: A lawyer.

Alternatively, you can gain psychological advantages through his knowledge that you have no source of legal advice. Many people regard the phrase "legal ethics" to be a contradiction in terms, but legal ethics do exist, and, among other things, they dictate that a lawyer, even an opposing lawyer, cannot use his expert legal knowledge to take advantage of you (except in court, that is). Therefore, you can demand that he explain every legal phrase and principle he mentions to you, and he is re-

210

quired to put himself in the annoying, to say nothing of time-consuming, position of giving you, his opponent, free legal advice.

At some time during the pre-trial conversations, your creditor's lawyer is likely to say the seven magic words that signify you've won: "You realize you'll have to pay something." If you understand how lawyers work, you'll know how this indicates he's throwing in the towel. First of all, for the reasons we've already discussed, lawyers prefer settlements to trials. Secondly, even if your creditor's case is absolutely without legal merit, the lawyer has a compulsion to try and come back to his client with something. This way, he can keep his client's future business and not have to answer comments like, "I didn't pay you $250 to tell me to forget it."

Once you agree to pay something, the lawyer doesn't have to worry about this kind of client reaction. He can say, "Look, I got you fifty bucks and saved you another three hundred on trial costs." Your agreement assents in principle to his winning a technical victory, with the only remaining issue being how much you're actually going to settle for. The rule of 25 percent is good here, too. Depending on how strong your case is, knock off the interest charges (both the 5 percent demanded in the summons and the 18 percent demanded under the terms of your revolving credit account) and the legal fees, if any; take 25 percent of the remainder as your going-in figure, and be prepared to haggle from there. After all, you said you'd pay something, and 25 percent *is* something. Remember, if his demands get unreasonably high, you can always stop your role as reasonable negotiator and become a fanatic about justice again.

There are many advantages to handling your case without a lawyer, cost being not the least of them. But for pre-trial work, as opposed to appearing at a trial itself, retaining an attorney can give you several different advantages for a relatively nominal cash outlay.

If your creditor's counsel is particularly hard-nosed and obnoxious, your attorney automatically becomes a buffer between you and your opponent's attorney. Once you retain counsel, legal ethics prohibit your creditor's counsel from dealing directly with you under pain of disbarment. (Of course, your creditor can deal directly with you, but his lawyer has to talk to your lawyer.)

In some jurisdictions, a lawyer can do things that a private citizen representing himself can't do. In New York, for example, a civil-suit defendant can't ask for a bill of particulars, but his lawyer can.

Finally, in negotiating a settlement, your attorney can cast you as the bad guy in the good guy–bad guy routine in order to get better terms. ("Look, counselor, I know it's a reasonable settlement, and I've advised my client to accept it, but he refuses. Off the record, the guy is some kind of nut. Keeps running around taking photographs and getting depositions on his own, rants all the time about stuff like justice—you know. But he's paid me a very large fee, so he's obviously not in it for the money, and if he wants to fight this to the end, I'm just going to have to go along with him.")

Of course, none of the foregoing has to be true—especially the part about the large fee. But a good attorney will use this kind of tactic to get you a good settlement.

Regardless of what you decide about using an attorney for pre-trial work, it's usually better to go without one for the trial itself, particularly if your case is a relatively simple one—like unpaid bill vs. shoddy merchandise. Before the trial, an attorney can be well worth the money. During a trial he can be worth the money too, but what you pay him can negate what you save by fighting it. With a lawyer, you go into court at even odds. But when your creditor has to go in with a lawyer, and you can go in without one, the scales of justice tip sharply in your favor.

CHAPTER ELEVEN

Justice Delayed
Is Justice Achieved

IN THE PREVIOUS chapter we saw that lawyers, particularly lawyers retained by your creditors, don't like to go into court. In this chapter, you're going to see why.

Even though creditors constantly threaten to take you to court and constantly imply in their threats that the court is just another in a long string of collection agents of theirs, these threats carry more weight in prospect than in actuality. Because civil courts seem structured, almost by design, to keep plaintiffs from getting what they want, particularly if what they want is justice.

This is because of the Anglo-American system of jurisprudence. In many countries, particularly those on the European continent, courts are set up as fact-finding bodies, and their purpose is to utilize all sides of and parties to a case to arrive at The Truth, regardless of what that Truth might be. In England, and even more so in the States, courts are run on a different principle, known as the adversary system. The adversary system is, to put it simply, a contest or game between the good guys and the bad guys, with the court existing to make sure both sides play by the rules.

The rules of the game seem to be set up under the assumption that you, the individual debtor acting as defendant, are almost always the good guy.

For example, the plaintiff is obliged by law to make a *prima facie* case against you. If he doesn't succeed, or if he makes a mistake in doing so, all you have to do is sit there and move for a dismissal after he finishes trying. You don't even have to open your mouth if you don't want to. (Of course, if the judge rules he's made his *prima facie* case, you do have to make a showing for your side. But in, say, a French court, the very idea of ruling on a case with only one side heard would be considered ridiculous.)

If your creditor is a corporation, the court often imposes a heavier financial burden on him than on you by requiring him to be represented by an attorney (see previous chapter), who, of course, doesn't work for nothing. You, however, don't have to pay for an attorney because you don't have to hire one.

By fighting a case all the way through court and losing it, you have little more to lose than if you'd caved in and paid up at the start. The loser of a court case has to pay court costs, but these run only a few dollars (see page 129). You may also have to pay interest, which many states set at about 6 percent, and in some states, the loser pays a small part of the winner's legal fees. What all this boils down to is that while dunning letters may threaten you with being forced to pay your creditor's legal fees and court costs, the threat seems much bigger than it actually is. (Note: some credit contracts stipulate that you pay a legal fee equal to 20 percent of the debt if litigation is necessary to collect it. Usually, creditors' attorneys will waive this payment to get a settlement, but there's a better protection against this charge than settling and throwing yourself on their mercy: Read the credit contract before you sign it, and if it contains this kind of clause, don't sign it.)

The legal process is fraught with opportunities for delay, and when your creditors are being sued by individuals, they take full advantage of each opportunity to wear down the opposition, until the opposition becomes too worn out to oppose them. As a debtor, with the money still in your pocket, you can profitably turn the tables on them. Each delay keeps the money in your pocket longer, which is good for reasons discussed at the beginning of this book. In addition, not having your money gives your creditor another financial burden, namely, the cost of obtaining additional capital to make up for the sum, however small, he hasn't received from you. In an age of mass production, where unit costs as low as a hundredth of a cent can make the difference between profit and loss, this burden can be heavier than you think.

Finally, each additional delay means an additional appearance in court by your creditor's attorney, with an additional expense to your creditor.

And civil courts seem to be created to encourage delay. To begin with, the caseload is far too great for the number of judges available to cope with it, even by working overtime. Second, many judges don't bother to work full-time, much less overtime. (For civil court judges in many large cities, a four-to-five-hour day seems to be the norm.) In courts whose sessions are slated to start at 9:00 A.M., it's likely for the clerk to start calling the calendar at 10:00, and for the judge to make his appearance sometime around 10:20. During the calling of the calendar, some of the litigants will have indicated their desire to make an application (usually for a postponement), and the first order of business for the judge is ruling on these applications, which usually brings us up to 10:30 or 11:00. Some judges like to take two-hour lunches, and others like to quit early. And often, cases that go unheard one day cannot be heard the next day (because there's already a full calendar for that), but the same day of the week two weeks later. As a rule, judges are generally very courteous in granting litigants (and their attorneys) postponements for valid-sounding reasons, and these postponements add still more delay.

To top it all off, many courts, like schools, have summer recesses. This means that a creditor who sues you in late May may not get you into court until early October. Until recently, New York courts had summer recesses, but the judges eliminated them, at least temporarily, to cut down the backlog of cases. And in many jurisdictions this backlog can be staggering.

In Pittsburgh, for example, in 1968, cases took an average of forty-one months (that's almost three and a half years) just to come to trial. In personal injury cases throughout the country, pre-trial delays average twenty-two months. In more than ten areas, according to a New York University law professor, the delay is more than forty months. And in New York City, obtaining an eviction order can take more than a year.

Of course, a conscientious debtor doesn't have to wait for the courts to start delaying things. He can use pre-trial discovery procedures to add delay first.

By letting both sides in civil cases take testimony by deposition before trial (this is called pre-trial discovery), the laws theoretically eliminate the in-court delays of examination and cross-examination before a judge. But theory isn't always the same as practice. "Time-saving" discovery procedures can be used to really slow things down.

For example, if your creditor's attorney wants to examine you, he can subpoena you to appear in his office (the Fifth Amendment doesn't apply in civil cases) to give testimony. He must also have a licensed court reporter on hand to make a stenotyped record of what you say. He must then have the stenotyped record transcribed into regular English and, in most cases, has to furnish you a copy.

Every time a court reporter is called to his office, the attorney has to shell out some money. Court reporters, like lawyers, don't work for nothing. And the more money he has to shell out, the more attractive a settlement becomes.

It stands to reason that the more times a stenotype reporter reports to the attorney's office, the more money he'll have to be paid. And you can see to it that he has to show up a few more times than is absolutely necessary.

216

For example, suppose you're the one who's going to be examined. It's entirely possible that a few minutes before your appointment, a pressing business or family problem will come up, preventing your appearance. If you telephone the attorney and tell him your problem, he'll have no practical choice but to reschedule the examination, pay the court reporter his minimum fee just for showing up, and send him on his way. The same holds true, incidentally, if you inform him of the emergency a few minutes *after* the scheduled start of the examination.

Theoretically, you run the risk of being held in contempt of court for not answering the subpoena, but no judge would deal harshly with you for one or two delays with plausible excuses. And that's assuming the attorney wanted to press the issue; doing so, of course, means more court appearances, which mean more delay. Since attorneys hate court appearances like the plague, and since the delay in charging you with contempt will probably be longer than the delay in merely rescheduling the examination, few attorneys are likely to press the issue.

Stenotypers, incidentally, are usually paid by the page, and each page has remarkably little room for recording testimony. So the more dragged-out your testimony under examination, the greater the cost to the attorney and the greater the impetus to settle. This example, based on an examination of one debtor by a creditor's attorney, shows how it's done. As you read it, picture the stenotype machine clicking away like a taxi meter:

QUESTION *(holding Xerox copy of letter):* Did you send this letter to my client on July 25, 1970?
ANSWER: May I see the letter, please?
QUESTION: *(handing over photocopy):* Here it is.
ANSWER: Thank you.
(Pause)
QUESTION: Well, did you send this letter?
ANSWER: What?
QUESTION: Did you send this letter?
ANSWER: No.

217

QUESTION: Is that your name and address at the top of the letter?

ANSWER: Yes, that's my name and address at the top.

QUESTION: Is that your name at the bottom of the letter?

ANSWER: Yes, that's my name at the bottom.

QUESTION: Is that your signature over your name at the bottom of the letter?

ANSWER: No, that's not my signature.

QUESTION: Isn't it in your handwriting?

ANSWER: It appears to be my handwriting.

QUESTION: Then isn't it your signature?

ANSWER: No.

QUESTION: Do you mean that someone forged your signature?

ANSWER: No, but someone copied it.

QUESTION: Copied it?

ANSWER: Yes, in a Xerox machine. So it's not my signature, but a reasonable facsimile of my signature. And this piece of paper is not my letter, but a reasonable facsimile of a letter.

QUESTION: All right. Is this a reasonable facsimile of a letter you sent my client on July 25, 1970?

This line of questioning has gotten the attorney nothing. It has taken him approximately two minutes (of time worth more than $20 an hour). In addition to his own time, this exercise has cost the attorney about $5 worth of stenotype pages, which he'll later have to pay to have transcribed. And he has yet to get one useful answer.

If the attorney conducts pre-trial examination of witnesses from your creditor's side, you have the right to cross-examine, and with the other side footing the bill, your cross-examination can be as drawn-out as your testimony.

Just as your creditor has the right to subpoena your testimony, you have the right, before trial, to subpoena testimony, records, and other relevant evidence from your creditor. The clerk of the court will issue the subpoena for free, and you can either pay a process server five bucks or so to serve it, or you can have a friend or relative who isn't a party to the case serve it as a favor. (As a litigant, you're not allowed to serve it yourself.)

With the disadvantages of pre-trial examination, you don't want to actually interrogate witnesses before the trial starts. But through the subpoena(s), you can show that you're ready to fight to the finish and at the same time increase the costs of the case to your opponent. You are perfectly within your rights to subpoena bills, financial records, and correspondence records pertaining to the case. If your case involves a product defect, you're entitled to subpoena records relating to the quality of the product and the existence of similar complaints. And, along with those records, you're entitled to subpoena an officer of the corporation to explain them.

This will necessitate that your creditor go through his files for this material, and searching the files will cost time and money. Moreover, officers of the corporation are high-paid executives and, as such, will cost your creditor a lot of money to have sitting around a court room.

As a result, you raise the stakes to the point where litigation becomes more and more unappealing and settlement, even with a substantial reduction of the amount you pay, becomes increasingly attractive.

If a creditor or his attorney persists in taking the case to trial and forgoing a settlement in spite of your delaying tactics, it's perfectly possible to continue those tactics when the case comes up in court.

For example, many courts will postpone your case if you send the calendar clerk a telegram saying you're too ill to appear and asking an adjournment. (New York City Small Claims Court does this, for example.) They postpone your case and change the calendar, but they generally won't notify your opponent. (New York City Small Claims Court is an example of this, too.)

Picture the result: Your creditor has paid an attorney to come to court. He's searched his files, tied up records that may be important to him, and will have to pay to have the records re-filed when the case is over. His senior executives, who earn high salaries, are along to explain the records, and their unproductiveness is costing the creditor a lot of money. At the beginning of the day, attorney, records, an executives arrive in court, and the attorney suddenly learns that the case is now scheduled two weeks later!

In many jurisdictions, telegrams are not accepted for postponement applications; here, they have to be made either in person or by counsel. If you've hired an attorney for pre-trial work, you can have him get the postponements very cheaply, since getting postponements doesn't involve his going to court. Most attorneys retain answering services, which send representatives to court to answer calendar calls when schedule conflicts or other problems make it impossible for the attorney himself to appear there. The charge for these answers is nominal, and since attorneys are officers of the court, and judges are themselves attorneys, the excuses are universally accepted, and delays are universally granted.

If you don't have an attorney, you can get delays on your own. For example, you can send a relative to court with a handwritten note to the judge that you're sick in bed and request an adjournment.

Or else you can appear yourself, to ask for a delay because of problems created by your mythical attorney. The first time, you can ask for a delay on the grounds that you're having trouble finding an attorney with time to handle your case. As lawyers, judges like to see litigants hire lawyers, so a delay on this basis is very likely to be granted.

Next time in court, ask for another delay on the grounds that your attorney is appearing before another court (preferably a higher one). Lawyers have their answering services use this one all the time, so judges shouldn't have any qualms about accepting it from clients.

Each time, your creditor's lawyer, his evidence, and his witnesses will all show up in court for nothing (except as far as your creditor's money is concerned), and in between adjournments, the attorney may approach you to offer a settlement. If you're a good haggler, there's nothing to prevent you from approaching him with a settlement offer, although this does lessen his conviction that you're going to be the kind of costly fanatic who fights to the end for justice. However, with the trial about to come up anyhow, he already knows you're ready to fight it.

Even if the lawyer doesn't want a settlement, the court may impose one on him. We've talked before about the principle of vested interest, and court clerks (who do the actual legwork that keeps the court moving) and judges have a vested interest, too. And that vested interest is to get cases out of the courtroom as quickly as possible and so stem the onrushing flood tide of cases. In this overall purpose they're about as successful as King Canute, but their never-ending efforts create an important advantage for you, the debtor-defendant. In the interest of moving the cases out, judges are far less concerned with arriving at decisions of Solomonic wisdom than with arriving at settlements that will leave both sides of the case equally dissatisfied. In all but the most open-and-shut cases, they'll exert every effort to get the litigants to split the difference.

Generally, the judge will hold a quick, off-the-record question-and-answer session to find out what the case is all about, and then, before officially trying the case, he'll tell the litigants to go somewhere and settle it. With all the settling that goes on, finding a place to settle in presents a problem in and of itself.

JUDGE: Okay, you two go out into the hall and settle this.
CLERK: Judge, Magruder vs. Zoltan is out in the hall.
JUDGE: Then try the men's room.
CLERK: Chicago Electronics vs. O'Malley is in the men's room.
JUDGE: The steps in front of the courthouse, then.
CLERK: Macy's vs. Catalano.
JUDGE: The coffee shop?
CLERK: Pulaski vs. Mickleberry.
JUDGE (sighing): Well, I don't usually do this, but why don't you use my chambers?
CLERK: Can't, your honor. St. Pierre vs. Columbia Record Club.

Of course, although cases, as a rule, are settled before

221

an official trial starts, yours may be the exception. So before you go into court, you should plan out your defense. And in order to do this, you should know which possible defenses are good ones (assuming you can prove them) and which aren't. Certain arguments are not legally valid defenses, and if you use them, you'll succeed only in losing your case. That's if you're lucky. If you're not lucky, you'll get thrown out of court before you can even get two sentences out. The following defenses are not legally valid, and you should at all costs avoid them. In reading about them, the reasons for avoiding them seem self-evident, but you'd be surprised how many people who should know better attempt to use them:

1. A defective-merchandise defense when you accepted the defective merchandise knowingly. If you knew the merchandise was defective and bought anyhow, it's your problem, not the seller's. When your defense is based on a defect in the merchandise, never blurt out that you saw the defect before buying. The merchandise looked perfect, and it wasn't until you got it home and either examined it, tried it on, or used it that the defect became apparent.

2. Rudeness on the part of the salesman is no excuse for nonpayment. Of course, if the salesman happened to slander you (see Chapter 13) or push you around a bit, you may have a counter-claim.

3. The delivery of the goods or performance of the service was late. Legally speaking, time is not of the essence (as you may notice from the way courts operate). The only exceptions to this rule are when a contract specifies a delivery date (and has no escape clause) or when the urgency was made clear to the seller at the time of the purchase and thus became a condition to the verbal sales contract. This legal doctrine works both ways, because time is also not of the essence when you pay for what you bought, as long as you do eventually pay for it.

4. The merchandise is defective, and the seller is making attempts—however feeble, incompetent, or misguided—to fix the defect. He's off the hook, and you're legally supposed to pay him.

222

5. The defects in, or damages to, the merchandise don't lower its fair market value. According to law, damages equal the difference between original and current fair market value. So if there's no loss of market value, there are no damages, and if there are no damages, there's no case.

6. The goods were damaged while being delivered by you or someone you hired. It's the same principle as the one for knowingly buying defective merchandise; your creditor doesn't have to pay for your stupidity.

7. The packaging was damaged, but not the merchandise inside. Since you're going to throw the package away anyhow, damages to it alone don't cost you anything. One exception to this rule is a package that was gift-wrapped when you were not present. Of course, damaged gift-wrapping isn't likely to create a major calamity, so as a defense, it's pretty trivial.

8. A claim for damages when you've already waived your right to collect them. You can waive these rights by signing a sales ticket with some fine print on it, but the most likely way that people waive their rights is to purchase something that they saw, knew, or should have known to be defective, because at the time of purchase the defects were obvious. If you go into court with a perfectly straightforward defective-merchandise defense, your creditor may try to prove that the defect in, say, the stereo you bought was obvious at the time of purchase (at least to his salesman, who has a degree in electrical engineering). This then becomes a question of fact, and the judge or jury will rule on it.

Now that you know which defenses aren't good legally, you should pick a defense that is. Generally, the simplest defense is that of defective merchandise or incompetent performance of services. If you've made defective-merchandise complaints to creditors (Chapter 6), you should know what to base them on in court.

In considering defective-merchandise complaints, you should look up the Uniform Commercial Code on implied warranties (or see Appendix 2), because this will provide you with possibly unsuspected grounds for defects and will also make your defense sound more legal.

("Breach of warranty" means the same thing as "bad merchandise," but it sounds a lot better.)

Just because you didn't get a piece of paper with the word "warranty" on it, that doesn't mean you don't have a warranty. Under the law, every product sold has implied warranties, which assure you, in essence, that what you've bought will do what you've bought it for, matches the label's description, and so forth. Everything that's sold comes with these implied warranties unless the seller gives you a written warranty which limits his obligations. For example, car warranties limit the manufacturer's liability to certain parts of the car, and the period of time during which he's liable to twelve months or 12,000 miles, whichever comes first. When you buy the product, you agree to the written warranty, when there is one. As a result, you generally get more protection without a written warranty than with one.

One interesting implied warranty is that of fitness of purpose, which means that the product must be effective for the purpose it was sold for. Now, this doesn't mean that an aspirin has to be 100 percent effective at relieving your splitting headache. (Some headaches are more splitting than others, and a few have causes that can't be cured by simple aspirin.) What it does mean is that a pen should be able to write, and a steam iron should be good for ironing clothes, not just for being a paperweight, bookend, or doorstop.

One pitfall in a fitness-of-purpose defense is that if the seller (your creditor) didn't manufacture the unfit merchandise, he can claim that he's entitled to payment from you and you should go and sue the manufacturer.

In many jurisdictions, you can thwart this kind of argument with a principle known as privity of contract. Every sale is an unwritten contract, and privity of contract means that you have a counter-claim or defense against whoever entered into a contract of sale with you. You had no contract with the manufacturer. You had a contract with your creditor, who is therefore responsible for the breach of warranty (and can, if he wants to pass on his costs, sue the manufacturer).

Of course, you can also make privity of contract work

the other way if you need to. For years, manufacturers got off the hook when merchandise failed to live up to claims made in national advertising, simply by arguing that the contract of sale involved the consumer and the seller, but not the manufacturer. (When you make complaints to national companies about franchised "independent" dealers, they also try to use this argument against you.) But courts have held that the seller is responsible for a product's nationally advertised claims (if they didn't think the product lived up to the claims they didn't have to sell it), so if a creditor has sold you some misleadingly advertised product, you have a defense against him for nonpayment, even if he sold you the product in perfect condition.

Your creditor is also responsible for claims and guarantees made by his salesmen. His salesmen is his agent, and he is responsible for words said and deeds done in his name by his agent in the normal course of business. Of course, you will have to prove what the salesman said, and in order to do that, you'll first have to identify him—by name, number, handwriting, or any other means handy. Sales slips usually identify the salesman, so save them.

Whatever defense you choose, it's important to remember that your defense starts not with the beginning of your statement of the case, but with your creditor's statement of his case, which comes first. He must prove by a preponderance of evidence that you bought something from him, didn't pay for it, and have ignored attempts on his part to collect the money owing. You have a right to examine his documentary evidence and cross-examine his witnesses, and you should be alert for every opportunity to refute his case as he states it.

For example, creditors' attorneys sometimes try to prove the existence of your purchase, and hence the validity of the debt, through documents that don't really prove anything. This kind of "proof" shouldn't go unchallenged. One may, for instance, introduce a copy of your bill or of a monthly statement to "prove" you made a purchase. But in fact, it proves nothing of the sort. It proves that you were billed for a purchase, which is not exactly the same as proving you made it.

If you went into a department store, picked out an item, and charged it, there will probably be a sales slip with your signature on it, and this will prove that you bought something. In the absence of this kind of sales slip, however, only direct testimony from the salesperson will prove you made the purchase. Since rules against hearsay require the most direct possible evidence (so that the other side can have the fairest opportunity of refuting it), you are well within your rights to insist that the salesperson be subpoenaed to identify you in court and prove that you actually made the purchase in question.

At worst, this will create delay, and we know what advantages that brings. At best, it may jeopardize your creditor's case against you. Employee turnover being high among department-store salespeople, your creditor may no longer be able to even contact the salesperson. And if he succeeds, with the tremendous number of purchases made every day in large department stores, the salesperson may fail to remember you or what you bought.

If you ordered the merchandise by phone, there will be no sales slip with your signature, so your creditor will have to rely on direct testimony of the telephone order-taker, if you press the issue. Here again, there's a turnover problem. There's also the volume-of-purchases problem. And to complicate matters, the witness has not a person but a disembodied voice to try and identify.

Once he proves you purchased the merchandise, your creditor's attorney is still not out of the woods; he must also prove that you received it. If your signed sales slip shows you took the merchandise with you, he has no problem, but if you had it delivered, it's another story entirely. Documents like the sales slip, the store's delivery records, the truck driver's trip ticket, and the like, merely prove that someone was *supposed to* deliver your purchase. They don't prove that the merchandise was actually delivered or that you actually received it.

As in the case of the signed sales slip, your creditor

must be able to produce either a receipt for the merchandise signed by you (or a member of your family) or the delivery man to testify he handed it to you. Delivery men, too, present turnover and volume-of-delivery problems. Moreover, if the delivery man arrived when you were out and left the package in front of your door, that really doesn't prove you received it.

One customer took advantage of this principle, although not in court, in a dispute with Macy's. He had charged a wine rack, to be delivered to relatives in Princeton, New Jersey. Macy's delivery service, United Parcel, didn't deliver to Princeton so the wine rack was sent by Parcel Post. When the customer later wrote Macy's that the gift had not been delivered and refused to pay unless they could produce a receipt showing him wrong, they were able to do nothing but issue a full credit.

Once you know how to spot this kind of hearsay evidence (and hearsay can include written documents), you can do one of two things about it. You can challenge the "evidence" as the attorney presents it, demand he produce the required witnesses, and cross-examine them to question the accuracy of their testimony. Or you can let your creditor present his case and then move for a dismissal on the ground that the actual purchase and delivery of the merchandise were "proved" by nothing better than hearsay. Or you can do both.

The attitude of the judge should decide the issue, and you can observe his attitude by sitting in the court room with your eyes and ears open while the cases before yours are tried. This will reduce the anxieties that most normal people experience in a court room (even a civil court room) and give you an idea of how much latitude the judge will allow (in simple English, this means how much he'll let either side get away with).

Also observe the judge's prejudices. You can often capitalize on them to make points which are really irrelevant to your case but can help win it.

Once a man who was having his house renovated appeared as defendant before an Italian judge in a case where an architect was suing him for nonpayment of a fee for designs. (Designs done rather poorly, as a matter of fact.)

DEFENDANT: Your honor, I refused to pay this architect his fee because he refused, for reasons of bigotry, to work with my carpenter.

JUDGE: Can you prove that? Did he say or do anything to show this? [Note, he does not ask what this has to do with the case.]

DEFENDANT: Yes, your honor, but what he said was so shameful, I wouldn't want to repeat it in a court of law.

JUDGE (*his interest aroused*): Really, if we're going to get anywhere with this case, I'll have to order you to repeat it.

DEFENDANT (*resignedly*): Well, your honor, he said he'd be damned if he'd work with any guinea. . . I can't go on.

JUDGE (*repeating it so it really sinks in, on his own mind, and on the jury*): Any guinea what?

DEFENDANT: Any guinea wop. . .

JUDGE (*turning purple*): Any guinea wop what?

DEFENDANT: Any guinea wop bastard.

The case was dismissed.

In another case, a man was sued for not paying for a defective electric heater he'd bought from a Jewish merchant "as is." Anyone who buys something "as is" does so completely at his own risk, and if his purchase is defective, he has no legal basis for getting repairs made or his money back. So instead of fighting the case on its merits, he took advantage of a little ethnic prejudice.

Every night for two weeks before the case came to trial, he'd telephone his creditor at some time between two and three in the morning. After identifying himself on the phone, he'd tell his Jewish creditor how it was a shame "Hitler didn't turn all of you into lampshades," and kind words of that nature. By the time he got to court, the creditor was livid. He was so enraged that, to someone unaware of the phone calls, he acted like a lunatic. And the judge, of course, was totally unaware of the phone calls. So when he saw the creditor grab the defendant by the lapels, shake his fist at him, and denounce him as a Nazi swine, he suspected that at least one of the litigants before him was totally unbalanced. In a manner of offended reasonableness, the defendant then proceeded to confirm the judge's suspicion. He told the judge that he was Jewish, that his father was a rabbi ("Do you know him, your honor?" "Yes, of course"), and that he therefore couldn't understand his creditor's reaction and resented it.

This whipped the creditor into still greater frenzy, which, in turn, alienated the judge even more. Eventually, the creditor got so out of hand that he had to be thrown out of court. And his case along with him.

Judges also have some prejudices that are non-ethnic and stem from their being lawyers. Lawyers are trained to deal in specifics, and as a result of this training, judges often tend to equate specificity and detail with honesty. To go a step further, many believe so strongly in facts and figures that they perceive an absence of facts and figures as evasiveness (and evasiveness as a sign of guilt). Any testimony you give should take this bias into account. The more specific details—like date, day of the week, time of day, location of your home or the store, or whatever—you can add to your testimony, no matter how relevant or irrelevant they are, the more likely a judge is to believe it. Since many cases come down to your word against your creditor's, this can be an important edge.

Second, like detail, judges are more impressed with your quantity of documentary evidence than with its relevance. The more letters, photocopies of bills, statements, documents and 8 x 10 photographs of the defects in the goods or services you purchased (or the damages caused by these defects), the better. When the house belonging to the man who beat the architect was under construction, the owner took photos of the walls, floors, and ceilings, and these are his "atrocity photos" to bring into court whenever he alleges that some creditor's product did damage to his home. They usually work. When you gather documentary evidence to take into court as a defense against your creditors, remember that Justice is blind and carries a set of scales.

If you're going into court without an attorney, as, for most cases, you should, you'll have to nullify one bias that judges have about lawyerless litigants and capitalize on another bias.

Some judges tend to resent litigants who represent themselves. This is because judges and lawyers are a clannish lot who frown on amateurs poaching on their livelihood. So if a judge gets upset about your not having a lawyer, the last thing you want to tell him is that you didn't think you needed one. Instead, you must present yourself as a person who tried to retain an attorney, but through no fault of his own, was unable to get one to represent him in court.

One way to do this is to respond to questions from the bench about the whereabouts of your lawyer with a statement that your lawyer was supposed to be here, but he had to try another case in, say, the federal court.

Another way is to tell the judge a heart-rending story, in excruciating detail, of how you tried to get a lawyer but failed in your task: "Well, your honor, first I went to John Doe, and he said he'd take my case for a $250 fee, but it's only a $200 case. So winning the case would cost me more than losing. And then I went to . . ."

Either way, you'll set yourself up to take advantage of another judicial bias. When a judge is convinced that through no fault of his own a defendant was unable to get a lawyer, he will take over many jobs that the defense counsel would normally perform. He will cross-examine your creditor's witnesses. He'll study and challenge documentary evidence. He'll examine you and any of your witnesses. He'll make motions on your behalf. And he'll look for holes in your creditor's legal arguments. This forces the judge to simultaneously work under two conflicting states of mind. First, he must be the impartial trier of fact and law. Second, he must be an advocate for you, the defendant.

Confronted with such a situation, most judges will make a conscientious effort to separate one role from the other, but the effort required is all too often a superhuman one. In most instances, try as he will to avoid letting his role as defense advocate interfere with his role as unbiased jurist, a judge will often unwittingly slant the case in favor of the side he's "representing." Mind you, it doesn't always happen this way, but if you can gain enough of the judge's sympathy to engage his participation on your side, he'll win your case for you.

One thing to remember about all these tactics is that while they've all succeeded before and will probably succeed again at one time or another, no tactic is infallible. The chances are overwhelming that your creditor will settle before going through a full-blown trial, and equally overwhelming that a judge will order a settlement in the middle of the case. But overwhelming odds aren't 100 percent odds.

Nonpayment cases have been known to go all the way, and judges have been known to give creditors everything they went to court for. But even if the judge rules against you, it doesn't mean you've necessarily lost the case. He may find in favor of your creditor but award him a reduced amount. This very often happens and results in a big discount for the debtor, which was one thing we were after to begin with.

And regardless of the amount a judge may award your creditor, there's another important thing to bear in mind: After your creditor is awarded his money, he still has to collect it.

CHAPTER TWELVE

Keeping the Marshal from Your Door

IF YOU FAIL to get a favorable settlement in court, and if the judge then rules against you, he will hand down a judgement in a specified amount in favor of your creditor. But for a creditor, getting the judgement is not the same as getting the money.

When a judgement is issued against you, there's a ten- to thirty-day period (depending on the jurisdiction) for you to pay up. Your creditor is allowed to do nothing but wait for your payment until the grace period expires.

Then, your creditor must engage a marshal or sheriff to seize some of your property to be sold at public auction with the proceeds going to satisfy the judgement, or attempt to seize your bank account, or to garnishee your salary. For a creditor, these procedures are always time consuming, often frustrating, and sometimes completely unsuccessful. And this chapter should show you how to make them more so.

As a debtor, your most immediate problem with a judgement is that it becomes a matter of public record, is noted by credit-rating outfits, and until finished, can prevent you from getting further sources of credit.

This makes it advisable to get credit from as many companies as possible in advance, because they check your credit rating before giving credit, not after. Incidentally, when a judgement is entered against someone with a fairly common name, standard credit-rating company practice is to enter it against all the people in the files with that name, so it would behoove you to visit your local credit bureau(s) periodically or write to the large national credit bureaus, exercise your rights under the Fair Credit Practices Act (see Appendix 2) and make sure you're not down for someone else's judgements.

In many jurisdictions, before your creditor can have a marshal seize property to satisfy a judgement, there must first be a court proceeding to determine exactly what property is seizable. This is called a supplementary proceeding, and in it you are required to come into court and answer, under oath, questions about whether you own different kinds of property (car, house, boat, and the like), whether you have bank accounts and so on. A supplementary proceeding can take up about as much of a lawyer's time as a short trial, and since time is money, especially with lawyers, it may not pay your creditor to conduct one. He may find it more profitable to drop the whole matter instead, at least temporarily.

But if there is a supplementary proceeding, there are ways to make it ineffectual. To begin with, instead of going to testify yourself, you should send a close relative to testify for you. There's a very logical and highly believable reason for doing this. You owe money (or so the court has ruled), and the relevant courts usually sit during working hours. How can you pay back the money you owe if being in court prevents you from earning it? (And this is the answer that your wife, or brother, or whoever, should give when your creditor's attorney asks why someone else is there in your place. Since he doesn't want to throw good time after bad, the attorney will probably allow your surrogate to take the stand, rather than postpone the proceeding and blow another day in court.)

Now that you know the excuse for having someone testify in your stead, you ought to know the reason. When you take the stand, you swear to tell "the truth, the whole truth, and nothing but the truth." When a stand-in testifies, he swears to do the same, but the law recognizes that he can only do so to the best of his knowledge. And as the following example illustrates, the best of his knowledge can be none too good:

QUESTION: Does your brother-in-law own a house?
ANSWER: I don't know, sir.
QUESTION: Well, do you know if he lives in a house or an apartment?
ANSWER: He lives in a house, but I think he rents it. I dunno for sure.
QUESTION: Does he own a car?
ANSWER: Maybe.
QUESTION: Maybe? Does he drive a car?
ANSWER: Yeah, but I think he said the other month he got a company car. Or did he say it was my sister's car?

And so it goes.

The question of who owns what is very important. If it can be established that you own property, then it's the marshal's lawful duty to seize it. But if the property in question is someone else's, any seizure is not an act of law but an act of larceny and, as such, one that a marshal should shy away from.

Many companies, like those you owe money to, set out to confuse the issue deliberately by creating shell corporations. Shell corporations are usually owned by other corporations, which have no debts but all the assets. Since these latter corporations own the shell corporations through the ownership of stock, their liability is limited to their share of the assets of the shell corporation. And zero divided by any number equals zero. New York taxi companies carry this principle to an extreme, having a shell corporation for all the debts and a separate corporation for each of the hundreds of taxicabs in their fleets. (See Chapter 3.)

Another way for companies to avoid the expense of shell corporations but still obtain the same judgement-proofing advantages is to lease all of their seizable property from another corporation, which, of course, is quite innocent of all wrongdoing. The Society of Sky Roamers, Inc. has been repeatedly sued for selling seats on charter flights that somehow never managed to get off the ground. Default judgements have been obtained against them, and marshals have invariably been unable to collect on those judgements.

It seems that the Society of Sky Roamers leases its seizable assets from other companies, whose addresses and identities the Attorney General of the State of New York is still trying to ascertain. And even if the Attorney General knew who and where they were, it still wouldn't make any difference legally, because under the law, those other corporations are separate legal entities, even if they should turn out to be owned by the owners of Sky Roamers.

If you've set up a company for yourself, you can play the same game as your creditors do, by keeping all the assets to yourself and contracting for all the debts in the name of the company.

The offices of record for one particular company are a mile and a half from the place where its business is actually conducted, and these "offices" consist of part of a room shared with other companies. Its property at that office consists of a beat-up desk, chair, and filing cabinet, and just to make things difficult for the marshal, every stick of furniture is tagged with the name of one of the companies it shares the room with.

Of course, even if you don't do business in the name of a corporation, if you do have a salary that can be garnisheed,* and if you have blurted out everything your creditor needs to know at a supplemental proceeding,

_____

* Garnishment is a procedure by which your employer must, under court order, pay part of your salary directly to a creditor in settlement of a judgement.

your creditor still isn't off the hook, because many states have laws that severely crimp what he can take from you.

In Pennsylvania, for example, creditors can't attach your salary unless your debt is for support (e.g., alimony or child support), room, or board. In Florida, a creditor's ability to attach your wages depends on whether or not you support a family; if you're the head of a family, he can't touch a penny of your salary, no matter how high it is, but if you're not a family head, he can attach your salary to the limits of the federal Consumer Credit Protection Act. This is a law that became effective in 1970; it exempts the first $48 a week of your take-home pay from garnishment and limits garnishments of your earnings above $48 to 25 percent of what remains after taxes. This 25 percent is a maximum, and states are permitted to set lower limits. Some states permit only 10 percent of your salary to be garnished. Texas prohibits any garnishments that prevent the employer from paying you your salary, but once the money's in your hands, it's fair game if you don't get rid of it quickly (by spending it, for example).

Since garnishments entail a lot of extra paperwork for your employer, he probably doesn't take a very sanguine view of employees with garnishments. One nice feature of the Consumer Credit Protection Act is that it prohibits your employer from firing you because of a garnishment for "any one indebtedness." But from the second on, you're on your own.

Just as most of your salary is protected from seizure under state and federal law, so is a lot of your property, the theory being that if you lost everything, you'd only go on welfare and cost the state money. The way the states see it, better your creditors should lose some money than the state treasury.

If you're the head of a family, most states exempt your homestead—that is, your house and the grounds immediately surrounding it—from seizure. (This exemption does not include mortgage foreclosures.) Most states also exempt the tools and instruments of your trade, and the court interpretation of just what constitutes a tool or instrument varies from court to court and from state to state. A mechanic's screwdriver definitely qualifies. An attorney's law books almost always do. Sometimes a salesman's car does, but not always.

Household goods and personal effects are usually safe from the sheriff. Again, exactly how much protection you get depends on where you live. In some states, it may be limited to a specific list of items (beds, clothing, toothbrushes). In others, the law sets down lists of categories. Some states exempt "necessary" items of clothing, and some courts have ruled that expensive lace shawls, gold rings, and watches fall into this category.

Some places exempt motor vehicles and livestock. Most states exempt life insurance proceeds and the cash surrender value of policies in effect. Many kinds of pension payments are exempt. Some states exempt any kind of property up to a specified dollar value, usually $1,000.

Where the state laws don't exempt part of your property from being seized to satisfy a judgement, they may permit you to own property in a way that protects all of it. This is called an "estate by the entirety," and it works like this: For any kind of property that you take title to, from your house to your car to your stocks, bonds, and bank accounts, you take title in the name of yourself and your wife (e.g., "John Doe and Jane Doe, his wife"). Once this is done, you and your wife become one legal entity, and in order to seize any property owned by this entity, the creditor must have judgements against both of the people who comprise it. In simple English, this means that in states that allow estates by the entirety, if John Doe incurs debts and Jane Doe doesn't, then a creditor is powerless to attach a bank account held by "John Doe and Jane Doe, his wife."

Alaska, Arkansas, Delaware, the District of Columbia, Florida, Hawaii, Kentucky, Maryland, Massachusetts, Mississippi, Missouri, North Carolina, Oklahoma, Pennsylvania, Rhode Island, Tennessee, Utah, Vermont, Virginia, and Wyoming recognize estates by entireties.

Michigan recognizes estates by entireties only for real estate, bonds, stocks and notes. Indana, New Jersey, New York, Oregon, and West Virginia recognize estates by entireties for real estate only.

The remaining states generally recognize joint ownership, which, in the case of married couples, would protect half of your property from seizure. Under this arrangement, if the Does own something jointly, and if a creditor gets a judgement against John, he can't touch Jane's half of the property. Some states that don't recognize joint ownership do recognize community property. Some of these states protect the spouse's half of the community property from judgements against the other spouse (of course, this raises certain problems for creditors, like how to repossess half a sofa); some of them don't.

Arizona, California, Idaho, Louisiana, Nevada, Texas, and Washington are community-property states.

One final word on joint ownership and estates by entireties. While they're great conveniences in protection from judgements, they can cause problems in other areas, like divorce, death, and taxes. So before you rush out and transfer all your property to joint ownership, you'd do well to check all of your state's laws in these areas (or have a lawyer do it for you); it may be that other forms of ownership, like a corporation, may work better for you.

When a creditor can't use the law to collect on a judgement against you, he may resort to psychology. Specifically, he may send a letter like the one on page 239 to the sheriff or marshal, with a carbon copy going to you.

This letter is ostensibly to the sheriff, but it's really written for your consumption. County sheriffs aren't sitting around with nothing to do, just waiting for the opportunity to seize all your property just for kicks. Moreover, even if they were, the law wouldn't let them do it. They're only allowed to seize property by court order, and then only enough property to satisfy the judgement. And before they seize anything, they must first make sure it's yours.

Sheriff of —— County
(Address)
(City and state)

Re: (Your name)
(Your address)
Case No. ——

Dear Sir,

Please seize, and levy against, all
available assets and property of
the above named defendant, within
seven days after the date of this
letter.

By a copy hereof, we are advising the
defendant of our intentions. If payment is made to us in the meantime,
we will advise you promptly.

Thank you.
Sincerely,
(COMPANY NAME)
By (signature)

copy to:
(Your name)
(Your address)*

Regardless of what the sheriff is actually going to do,
the letter is intended to make you think he's about to
confiscate everything you own. He isn't; the letter's a
bluff. Should you ever receive a letter of this nature,

* E. Siegel, *How to Avoid Lawyers* (New York: Information,
Inc.)

you're advised to treat it exactly as the sheriff treats the original, namely, file it and forget it. Or send a copy, with a letter of complaint, to the Postal Inspection Service and the Federal Trade Commission.

Psychological warfare isn't limited to the creditor's side; debtors have much more leeway for practicing it.

One tactic is to write a letter to your creditor, enumerating the sum total of your assets (but not itemizing them so he can seize them) and itemizing your debts, which by far exceed them. Tell him that you're just keeping your head above water, and that collection of his judgement will be the straw that breaks the camel's back and forces you to file for bankruptcy. Creditors hate bankruptcy (for reasons explained in Chapter 14) and will do almost anything to keep you from filing for it. The mere threat of bankruptcy may be enough to produce a moratorium on the judgement for quite a while.

But since you'll be more likely to deal with a marshal than your creditor at this point, psychological warfare against the marshal might prove more productive.

One debtor once used psychology to reduce a marshal to total inaction. It just happened that when the marshal visited him with a writ of execution of judgement, there was a portable tape recorder sitting on his desk. The recorder was plugged in, there was a blank tape in it, but no microphone was connected. As the marshal started to speak, the debtor turned the tape recorder on. As the tape started winding, the marshal stopped talking. "Go on, go on," the man encouraged him. The marshal looked at the debtor, looked at the tape recorder, swallowed hard, ran from the room, and has never been heard from since.

If you can muddy the issue of who owns which property, and better yet, if you have some documents to prove that all the seizable property in your home or office belongs to someone else, you can threaten the marshal wtih a criminal trial for larceny. In fact, some people with particularly good documentation have been known to call the police to arrest over-zealous marshals, who often disappeared before the police arrived.

A word of explanation is in order here. A sheriff is always a government officer. In many cities, he may be in charge of the police, and in many counties the police force may be made up of deputy sheriffs. In New York and other cities, there are, in addition to sheriffs, marshals, who are not law officers, but licensed private practitioners, much in the way that a private detective, a bail bondsman, or process server is.

While city marshals are associated with the courts, they are not, as a rule, peace officers. They are authorized to seize property in execution of civil judgements, and they are paid a percentage, set by law, of the cash raised through such seizures. City marshals are not to be confused with United States marshals, who are peace officers, can throw people in jail, and have more important things to do than go around collecting on civil court judgements.

Sometimes, the best tactic of all is simply, as was the case with bill collectors, to make your adversary lose his cool. One debtor had dealings with a city marshal who was Jewish, and whose secretary was kind of paranoid about it. The secretary telephoned the debtor because of her employer's inability to gain access to his residence. Once the secretary identified herself and her employer, the conversation went like this:

DEBTOR: Is he the portly Jewish gentleman I saw loitering about my premises?

SECRETARY: Whaddya mean by a smart-aleck remark like that?

DEBTOR: Like what, madam?

SECRETARY: That portly Jewish gentleman stuff.

DEBTOR: Well, you must admit your employer appears to be of more than average girth.

SECRETARY: Yeah.

DEBTOR: And since he hasn't done anything to prove otherwise, I assume he's a gentleman.

SECRETARY: Yeah.

DEBTOR: And from his name, I think it's safe to assume he's Jewish.

SECRETARY: You leave his religion out of this!

241

DEBTOR: I only mention it as an identifying characteristic.

SECRETARY: Identifying characteristic! Jews don't go
around with horns, y'know.

DEBTOR: Look, if you saw a heavy-set gentleman of
Afro-American descent, wouldn't you describe him
as a portly colored gentleman?

SECRETARY: Yeah, but that's a different story.

DEBTOR: How is it different? You've already admitted
that your employer is just what I said he is: a
portly Jewish gentleman.

SECRETARY: Look, you anti-Semitic creep. Mr. ———
and I don't have to deal with garbage like you. As
far as I'm concerned, you can keep your lousy
money. Mr. ——— and I wouldn't touch it with a
ten-foot pole.

Which was just what the debtor (who, incidentally,
is Jewish) wanted all along.

CHAPTER THIRTEEN

Creditors' Prison

DEBTORS' PRISON WENT out with the nineteenth century. Today it exists only in the minds of creditors, collection agents, and debtors who don't know any better.

Creditors will threaten to take you to "court," leave you with a "record," and make you pay their lawyers' fees for the privilege. Yet, anyone who has read the previous chapters, instead of just his creditors' dunning letters, knows that the "court" in question is a civil, not criminal, court; the "record" is simply a trial record and not a criminal record, and the "legal fees" are mostly nominal court costs paid only if the debtor fails either to win or get a settlement.

Just as creditors raise the threat of debtors' prison some hundred years after that threat ceased to carry any weight, they raise a series of additional threats; and just like this one, they pose no real threat at all to the debtor who can see through the creditors' linguistic smoke screen, knows his rights, and is prepared to make a few minor efforts to make sure those rights are respected.

Your creditors can threaten to ruin your credit rating,

cost you your job, harass you day and night, or sic the sheriff on you. But, in contrast to the nineteenth century, today a debtor has the legal power to nullify these threats, cost his creditors money, and possibly put *them* in prison for making them.

At least once in every creditor's dunning cycle, a thinly veiled threat to your credit standing will appear ("Dear Customer, Your credit rating is very important to you, and we're sure you wouldn't want to jeopardize it. . . ."). But most of the time this threat is made, it's more apparent than real.

In the first place, it costs a company money to give out such information on you. The file has to be pulled, a letter has to be written, typed, and sent, the file has to be replaced, and so on. This all takes up man-hours, and man-hours cost money.

Secondly, if a creditor's vindictiveness is strong enough to overcome his avarice, and he does have such a report sent, it should have absolutely no effect on your existing credit. The way most credit-rating bureaus operate, each company using their services must pay a fee for each credit rating supplied. A company you're already doing credit business with can check its own records far more cheaply. It's only when you're after a new source of credit, and when the source company uses the specific rating service that's gotten derogatory information on you, that you'll notice any effect of a bad report from a creditor. Of course, if you followed the advice in Chapter 3 and opened as many accounts as possible *before* starting your deficit spending program, you shouldn't feel the pinch at all.

But even then, there are ways of correcting damaging information that credit rating companies publish about you. And there are ways of collecting cash damages for damaging lies. But first, you have to know whether any derogatory information is being published and, if so, what that information is.

Now, there's no such thing, thank goodness, as a monolithic national credit bureau. Some credit-rating companies are local, some regional, and some national. Some, like the Credit Bureau of Greater New York, work by hand, with index-card files. Some, like TRW Credit Data, are computerized and have 40,000,000 files from debtors all over the country. (According to *Newsweek*, TRW has been adding 50,000 files a week for the last three years, and expects to have a dossier on everyone who's ever applied for credit anywhere by 1975—a touch of 1984 nine years early.)* Some credit-rating outfits deal with particular goods and services. Credit Bureau of Greater New York is used primarily by department stores, for example, and Check-Mate, also a New York outfit, by rent-a-car companies.

Some companies, like Retail Credit Co. in Atlanta, lace their credit reports with such highly colorful and subjective data as the subject's drinking habits and alleged participation in "radical movements and demonstrations."

With a patchwork of organizations and procedures like this, it's impossible to generalize with 100 percent accuracy. But, bearing in mind the caveat of Oliver Wendell Holmes, Sr. ("No generalization is worth a damn, including this one"), it is possible to state that there are several operating features that most have in common.

One such feature is that reports are inclined to be superficial and cursory. Credit-rating companies charge a nominal fee for each report and, if they're to make any profit at all (they *are* profit-making organizations), must rely not on unit price but on volume. The greater the volume of reports churned out per day, the less time and thoroughness can be devoted to each one. Employees of Retail Credit Co., for example, are expected to process some sixteen "investigations" a day, allowing ten to fifteen minutes a file.

A second common feature is that many credit raters rely almost exclusively on items of public record. In every city of any consequence, there is a periodical known as a law journal. The law journal gives, among other pieces of legal news, complete lists of lawsuits filed with the court and of judgements awarded. Since the

* "The Assault on Privacy," *Newsweek*, July 27, 1970.

information is a matter of public record, credit bureaus generally can use these sources with impunity ("We didn't say there was a lawsuit against him. The Law Journal did").

Third, when these records are used, they are never followed up and are rarely used with the benefit of any intelligent thought. For example, let us assume that a creditor goes down to civil court and takes out a summons against you. When the case receives a trial date, news of its existence appears in the law journal.

Unfortunately, it appears with only an index number and the names of the antagonists (e.g., Smith vs. Jones), which leaves something to be desired (e.g., which Smith and which Jones?). Consequently, credit bureaus employ an alternate method of obtaining information. Every day, an employee goes down to the office of the clerk of each big-city court for a look at the day's summonses and complaint forms, and he copies down the names and addresses of all the defendants (and usually slips the clerk a few bucks for his trouble). Meanwhile, down at the credit bureau, a low-paid employee is ready to transfer this information from the law journal or complaint record to your file. As we said, credit bureaus make their money on low cost and high volume, so the employee in question is probably sufficiently skilled to read the law journal or complaint lists, pull files, and make file entries, but no more. So as soon your name appears, this employee will enter in your file the fact that you've been sued. Now, your creditor may never have actually served the papers, but this doesn't show up in the complaint records. He may have served you with the papers to bluff payment out of you but defaulted in court. The complaint records and law journal won't show this, either. Upon hearing a complaint from you about the merchandise, he may have lowered his price and settled with you before trial, but this won't be on the complaint records or law journal. You may have beaten him in court, but this, too, won't be in the complaint records or the law journal. He may have won a judgement against you and received your payment, but while the judgement will be published in the law journal, neither the journal nor the complaint record will show you've paid it.

However, this credit bureau employee is not paid to follow up on what's in the law journal or the complaint records; only to copy it down in your file. Moreover, to prevent any possibility of error in favor of a debtor, and to make allowances for America's mobile society, all files with the same name (e.g., John Smith) for the county in question will usually get the same derogatory entry.

In New York City, at least some local improvement of this situation is in the works. A 1975 ruling of the Civil Court requires credit rating bureaus doing business in New York to follow up on lawsuits they've listed in people's files and record the final determination.

Many times, the results of one-sided and slipshod credit rating procedures would be laughable if the consequences weren't potentially tragic, as witness the case of Sigmund Arywitz, $30,000-a-year executive secretary/treasurer of the Los Angeles County Federation of Labor, AFL-CIO and, before that, California State Labor Commissioner. It seems that in spite of Mr. Arywitz', high income, good credit standing with many companies, and prompt bill-paying habits, he'd been turned down for credit at five department stores and one car-leasing company in the course of one year.*

In dealing with a second car-leasing company, who extended credit in spite of his "bad rating," he learned that the credit bureau had him down as the defendant in a lot of lawsuits. Now, in California, as in many states, you can't sue the state government or any of its departments (e.g., the Labor Commission). You have to sue the man in charge of the department (e.g., Labor Commissioner Arywitz). As State Labor Commissioner for eight years, Arywitz was named as a party to literally hundreds of lawsuits. In each of them, the state of California was the real defendant, but nobody at the credit bureau seemed to know this. Or care one way or the other.

Of course, there's no way to combat falsehoods like

* "The Assault on Privacy," *Newsweek*, July 27, 1970.

this one if you don't know they're being spread, but credit bureaus have traditionally done everything they could to hinder the (to them) unwarranted nuisance of debtors' coming around to take up their time and bother them with irrelevancies like facts. Since 1971, however, they've been obliged to tell you what they have on you, and make grudging corrections, no matter how much of an imposition they regard this to be, because of a federal law called the Fair Credit Reporting Act.

This law gives the debtor a lot of protection he wouldn't otherwise have, but it doesn't require creditors and credit bureaus to extend these protections voluntarily. In other words, you have to know what your rights are and then demand them.

If your application for credit is rejected, for example, a creditor is obliged by law to tell you what information this rejection is based on, and where he got it, but only if you ask him.

The credit bureau that issued a derogatory report is obliged to tell you what's in your dossier, but again, you have to ask them. If you've had credit denied because of a report from them, they must do this on request, at no charge to you. You must either go down to their offices, telephone, or make a written request by mail.

If you haven't had credit refused but want to check up on your file anyhow, they are also obliged to let you do it. Again, you must go down in person, phone, or make the request in writing. But in this case, they are entitled to charge you a "reasonable" fee for this service. We might add in passing that it's a good idea to check your file once a year or so, and well worth the minor investment. When you do this, however, it's important to make sure you cover the right rating service, or, that failing, to make sure you've covered the most probable ones.

The reason this is important is that in a large city with several credit bureaus, any consistency of information from one to the other is often purely coincidental. Last year, while the Credit Bureau of Greater New York was giving out derogatory reports on one man because of a year-old lawsuit that the plaintiff had withdrawn,

248

another rating service (no doubt the more accurate of the two) was putting out such glowing ratings that he was being approached by banks to sign up for Master Charge.

Once you know what they're saying about you, you can then do something about it. Exactly what you do depends on how serious the misstatement is, how you find out about it, and where you live.

In Illinois, for example, state law permits you to delete incorrect information from your credit files. (If you think that's good, in England, companies are required to send you a copy of every report about you they make.)

In the other states, credit bureaus are required by federal law to correct your file and mail out corrected reports, but they will often do so only grudgingly, and the burden of proof is almost invariably on you. If a lawsuit has been withdrawn or settled, you can obtain either a stipulation of withdrawal or a settlement form from your creditor's lawyer (these are furnished on request, as a matter of course, but it's easier if you ask for one while the case is still fresh) and then show it to the people at the credit bureau.

If the papers were never served on you, or you won a default judgement, or your creditor wants to give you a hard time, you can still correct the records, although an extra trip may be necessary. First, go to the credit bureau and get the index number of the lawsuit (if you don't know it already; if you do, you can skip this step) or the date. Then, visit the court in question. The clerk's office maintains records on the disposition of each case, and these are available for the asking. They generally can't be removed from the court building, but in most cases, a coin-operated Xerox machine will be in the same room as the records. The records will show that the case never came to trial, was dismissed, was against a John Smith living at another address, or whatever. Make a copy and show it to the credit bureau. Make them correct their records and send out letters of correction, where applicable. And quote the Fair Credit Reporting Act by name, if you have to.

If you live in Atlanta, or run afoul of another organization like Retail Credit Co., you will have trouble producing a legal document that proves you're not a drunk or a long-haired-pot-smoking-weirdo-communist-hippie-punk, so The Fair Credit Reporting Act obliges a credit-rating company to conduct a re-investigation.

But though the Fair Credit Reporting Act contains some very good protections, its provisions are more often honored in the breach than in the observance, and until recently, nothing but the individual debtor's vigilance and persistence kept unscrupulous credit rating outfits from ignoring the law with impunity.

This state of affairs may be starting to change. On December 18, 1973, some two years after the Fair Credit Reporting Act went on the books, the Federal Trade Commission rushed into the first major lawsuit to enforce its provisions. Appropriately enough, the defendant is none other than the aforementioned Retail Credit Co. of Atlanta. With over 300 so-called Branch Offices, and 1,500 other offices, in every state of the union, and with more than 8,500 paid snoops preparing about 35,000,000 reports each year, Retail Credit certainly makes a big enough target; according to the FTC, Retail Credit can provide information on 98 percent of the population of the United States. And, the suit maintains, the manner in which much of this information is obtained, evaluated, reported, and corrected violates both the Federal Trade Commission Act and the Fair Credit Reporting Act.

In all fairness, it should be pointed out that the following charges made by the FTC are only accusations, but if even some of them are true, it's pretty scary.

First, the FTC charged that Retail Credit Co. employees passed themselves off as agents or employees of the company to which the consumer applied for credit, insurance, and the like. In fact, they were no such thing of the kind.

Second, they claimed that the information that a consumer supplied to them during an interview would be sent only to the insurance company, potential creditor, and so on, in whose name the interview was being conducted. In fact, however, this information also became a part of the consumer's general file and was supplied by Retail Credit to any client of theirs who asked for it.

250

Third, Retail Credit was also hired to investigate the physical condition of people making injury claims to client insurance companies. When they conducted these investigations, they conducted interviews under the guise of "routine credit checks," the theory being that this would lull an injury claimant into walking and moving normally instead of faking a nonexistent injury. In fact, it is alleged that the sole purpose of these interviews was "to observe the consumer's physical appearance, movements, or mental or physical capabilities . . . under false pretenses."

In addition, the FTC accused Retail Credit of providing information gathered by this misleading technique not just to the specific client who asked for it, but as a general datum for any and every client of theirs.

Fifth, Retail Credit is accused of giving information which was represented as coming from face-to-face interviews, when in fact this "information" was culled from telephone conversations. Three typical pieces of information that the FTC culled from Retail Credit reports are (1) the consumer presents a "healthy appearance with no obvious [sic] impairments or apparent tensions" (how this could be determined over the telephone is an interesting question), (2) the consumer's "residence seems small and inadequate," and (3) the consumer "had a white gauze bandage tacked over his eye to shield it from the light." Apparently, not only were data obtained by phone passed off as information from personal interviews and neighborhood observation, but only some of the "sources" listed in the reports were actually consulted, either in person or by telephone. And many people's eligibility for important things like insurance was evaluated on the basis of this "information."

Sixth, Retail Credit solicited the release of medical information, again for specific purposes like life and disability insurance applications. Having obtained this information from doctors and hospitals, the FTC says that Retail Credit then made photocopies, put those copies in the permanent files, and made them available to any customer of theirs who asked for them.

And too often for comfort, supposedly confidential information was sent not only to Retail Credit clients who asked for it, but to many who didn't. One of the many benefits that a creditor enjoys from doing business with Retail Credit is their "Voluntary Follow-Up Service." The "Service" in question consisted of volunteering to creditors who didn't ask for it any derogatory information on debtors which had been gathered in the course of conducting investigations on those debtors for completely different creditors. In other words, if, after opening a charge account with Sears Roebuck, you applied for an Exxon credit card, and Retail Credit conducted an investigation on you for Exxon, any bad information they dug up would go not only to Exxon, who asked for it, but Sears, who didn't. This kind of practice is forbidden by Section 604 of the Fair Credit Reporting Act.

Section 605 specifically prohibits credit rating outfits from supplying information more than seven years old to creditors. According to the FTC, Retail Credit called attention to the existence of this out-of-date, derogatory information by noting on credit and employment reports, "In compliance with the Fair Credit Rating Act no additional information can be reported . . . covering experience prior to seven years ago." In reports on eligibility for auto insurance, seven-year-old driving violations were not eliminated but merely masked out, the size of the masking giving the Retail Credit client an idea of the number of obsolete violations.

The FTC also found fault with a number of anti-consumer biases induced into Retail Credit reports as a result of the company's workload policies. For one thing, Retail Credit was accused of requiring so many completed reports per day from its employees that insufficient time was allowed for making each report as complete and correct as possible. A little arithmetic shows the basis for this contention. As was stated earlier, Retail Credit employs some 8,500 investigative people who are responsible for turning out some 35,000,000 reports per year. This means 4,118 reports per year per investigator. Assuming 242 working days per year (this excludes weekends, two-week vacation, and five legal holidays), each investigator must then average seventeen reports per day, which (assuming a seven-hour work day) works out to one every twenty-five minutes—including research, composing the report, and getting it down on paper.

While this flurry of activity is going on, the 8,500 investigators are also responsible for conducting some 200,000 interviews per year. Of course, the workload here is not so heavy, for it averages out to 23.5 interviews per investigator per year, or slightly less than two a month—a very unimpressive number of sources of information.

On the basis of these figures, the Retail Credit system cannot really be said to foster accuracy. It can, however, be said to foster almost deliberate distortion, for, according to the FTC, the salary/production system requires that a specified proportion of consumer reports contain negative or derogatory information.

If that weren't enough, while the Fair Credit Reporting Act requires that organizations like Retail Credit reinvestigate derogatory information at the request of the consumer, the investigators can count such re-investigations toward their production quotas if, and only if, those re-investigations show that the original reports were accurate. This kind of system does not exactly encourage the admission and correction of previous errors.

Under Section 609 of the Fair Credit Reporting Act, consumers are entitled to know the sources of information reported (except investigative sources) and the names of all companies that have received employment reports on them during the previous two years or credit, insurance, or other reports during the previous six months. Even if no reports have been sent out, the consumer is entitled to know the nature and substance of all information (except medical information) in his dossier. Retail Credit has been accused of withholding such information.

Credit rating companies are required to disclose this information when asked for it by telephone, but Retail Credit has "discouraged such disclosures." In addition, they have "refused and are refusing to make said disclosures at offices designated by [themselves] as "Sub-Offices,' even when some of those offices are staffed by full-time office personnel and a person in a supervisory

253

capacity. Rather, [Retail Credit Co.] makes disclosures only at offices designated by it as 'Branch Offices.' "

Finally, Retail Credit stands accused of refusing to re-investigate disputed information, to record the fact that such information is disputed, to delete unverifiable information, to tell consumers that they may ask that creditors be furnished with notice that information has been corrected, deleted, or disputed, and of failing, even when asked, to send out corrections of previous reports. All this is in violation of Section 611.

At this writing, the case has yet to reach a conclusion. Even if Retail Credit Co. signs a consent order to cease and desist from these practices, nobody knows whether other credit bureaus will cease and desist also. On the basis of personal experience, however, we think it's safe to answer that they probably won't.

The day that news of the FTC action against Retail Credit hit the newspapers, Credit Bureau of Greater New York released a statement in which they dissociated themselves from all the nastiness engaged in by those bad boys down in Atlanta. Some time before that, one of the authors had occasion to visit that organization to have some erroneous information (about a lawsuit that had been withdrawn) corrected. At that time, Credit Bureau of Greater New York

Refused to show him his complete dossier, alleging that it was written in code, so that he wouldn't understand it if he saw it.

Refused to initiate a re-investigation, claiming that the burden of proof rested with the consumer.

Promised to send out letters of correction, but, as far as has been ascertained, never did so.

It is also worthy of note that while legal action has been undertaken by the FTC, nothing more stringent than a consent decree—like monetary fines, for example—has been contemplated, and corporate malefactors are slow to mend their ways when their pocketbooks remain unthreatened.

So if you can't afford to wait a few years for the FTC to act, you need another protection against credit misinformation. Fortunately, you have one: suing for libel.

Naturally, before you sue anyone for libel, you should make sure that the statement you're going to court over is, in fact, libelous. First off, it must be in writing. If it's made in face-to-face conversation or over the phone, it's not libel, but slander.

Second, it must be "published." This doesn't mean it has to be printed in a magazine or book (although either would qualify) but rather made public, to some third party. If a creditor sends you a letter questioning your legitimacy, impunging your ancestry, and accusing you of certain incestuous acts, it's not libel unless he's sent someone a carbon. Of course, the way business letters are generally prepared, such a letter would probably qualify as "published" even if you were the only recipient, simply because few businessmen sit down to write or type their own letters. If the letter was dictated to a stenographer or typed by a secretary (and you can sometimes prove this simply by the presence of the secretary's initials in the lower left-hand corner of the letter), then, in the opinion of many courts, she is a third party to whom the libel has been "published."

Third, the statement must be untrue. If the defendant called you a homosexual and you happen to be a card-carrying member of the Gay Activists' Alliance, your day in court isn't going to be a fruitful one.

Fourth, the untrue statement must be one that would make you the object of scorn, contempt, disrespect, or ridicule with your friends and associates, or cause you other damages.* If someone publishes a statement that

* An interesting British case illustrates this principle. The plaintiff was one Princess Yossoupov, a Russian emigrée whose husband, before the Revolution, had been involved in the assassination of Rasputin. After 1918, she emigrated to Britain, where she seems to have made her living by suing people for libel and slander. This particular case began at a cocktail party, when a journalist walked up to her and said loudly enough to be heard by other people, "How are you today, you bloody old whore?" The Princess sued him for slander. The judge hearing the case

you're six feet tall and you're really 5'8" that's not libelous. However, if someone published a statement that you weigh 195 pounds, and you're really 110, and that statement causes you to be rejected for a job as a jockey, you've got a case.

Although it's not really part of the strict legal definition, there's a fifth consideration to think about, and that is that except in cases where the libel is particularly heinous, e.g., when the defendant accuses you of committing a horrible crime, you need to prove that you've suffered specific financial damages. Otherwise, you could spend hundreds of dollars going to court to win a retraction plus one dollar in damages.

Of course, a court proceeding will be just as costly for your creditor—if not costlier—so the principal usefulness of a libel action is often in the threat, rather than in the actual court trial.

Once, before the Fair Credit Reporting Act was signed into law, a driver learned from a rent-a-car company that Check-Mate had given him a bad report. He asked a lawyer who was in his National Guard unit to write them a letter asking what it was all about and implying that a libel suit would be undertaken if they didn't have some pretty good facts to back their charges with. The letter got a routine acknowledgment, but two weeks later, when he had the same rent-a-car company call Check-Mate again, he got a clean bill of health.

This approach doesn't always work, however. Sometimes it's necessary to take a leaf from your creditors' book and prepare and file the papers, just as they file papers to scare people into paying. Correcting their records is much cheaper than going into court, and once you show you're serious, they may take the attitude that it's no skin off their nose to give you a good rating. But sometimes, if the stakes are high enough, you may have to go to court.

In 1961, Michael Goldgar, chairman of a Southern

---

dismissed it, on the grounds that, in the circles she was known to frequent, being a prostitute was not something that would put one into disrepute with one's friends, colleagues, and associates.

retail store chain called Dejay Stores, Inc., was the victim of incorrect reports put out by Dun and Bradstreet. According to *Newsweek*, "When D&B continued to circulate reports, Goldgar phoned the company president in New York—thereby calling down a vendetta on himself . . . When Goldgar took a Caribbean vacation, Dun and Bradstreet hinted that he would not return. They wrote a false letter to New York University requesting information under the guise of a 'national security' check. Finally they enginered a phony bankruptcy petition against Dejay, in effect ruining the company's reputation so thoroughly that it really did go bankrupt in late 1962. Goldgar and his companies sued and finally won $6,610,000 when the case came to trial" in 1969.*

This chapter is not intended to be a step-by-step course in suing creditors for libel, but there are a few legal principles and developments you ought to know about, since they'll give you some talking points should you decide to threaten a suit. To begin with, as plaintiff, all you basically have to prove is that the statement was made and published, that it did put you into disrepute, and that some damages resulted. Truth is a defense against a libel charge, but the burden is on the defendant to prove his statement true, not on you to prove it false.

Also, some courts have held that in libel cases involving credit ratings, unlike libel cases in general, truth is not an absolute defense. This is because, in addition to an explicit factual statement (for example, you were sued by XYZ Corporation for non-payment of $250 on December 7, 1971), many derogatory credit ratings are worded in such a way as to carry an implicit statement that you're too dishonest to be trusted with money. In order to defend a libel case on the basis of truth, the credit-rating outfit must prove not only that you were actually sued (and not acquitted), but also that you are, in fact, unfit for credit, which is considerably harder.

Finally, credit bureaus have for years been wriggling off the hook with the contention that their false statements are exempt from libel suits because they are what

* "The Assault on Privacy." *Newsweek*, July 27, 1970.

is legally referred to as "privileged publications." The theory here was that information was being given credit man to credit man on a confidential basis, not being made available to the general public, and because of its confidential nature, wasn't public enough for the standards of truth or falsity to apply. In simple words, this means it was okay to spread lies so long as you whispered them. This doctrine is very inconsistent with the purpose and enforcement of libel laws.. It's ridiculous to regard a letter dictated to a secretary as being "published" and awarding damages if it's false and damaging, but to exempt a letter sent to someone else who, unlike a secretary, is in a position to damage the debtor by denying him credit. In 1972, the federal courts agreed and struck down the credit bureaus' privilege to libel. What a credit bureau says to another credit bureau about you now has to be as honest as what they say about you to anyone else.

Now, if you happen to live in Atlanta, where Retail Credit Co.'s reports include such pertinent credit data as how much you drink and when was the last time you took part in a peace march, a libel suit isn't going to help you much, because the statements may be true but not particularly germane to the issue of granting you credit. In this situation, you can sue—or threaten to sue—for invasion of privacy. Your right to privacy includes the right to keep confidential information about yourself confidential, to keep it from being published (in the sense that a libel is published) without a pretty good reason. The advantage to an invasion of privacy complaint is that here truth is no defense. It may be absolutely true that you're a peace marcher, a boot fetishist, or whatever, but a credit bureau has absolutely no right to publish it. Nor has anyone else the right to publish it. In Kentucky, a merchant put up a sign in his window stating that a debtor owed him $9.67. Even though the money was in fact owed, the debtor sued for invasion of privacy and collected more than $6,500 damages. In another Kentucky case, a creditor bought advertising space to proclaim someone's indebtedness in the local newspaper. The debtor sued. The court held that unless the publication was privileged (and, as we mentioned before, the federal courts no longer hold credit matters to fall under this category), or the debtor had consented to its publication, or the publication was only oral, an invasion of privacy had taken place. None of these being the case, both the creditor and the newspaper publisher were required to pay damages.

Your privacy can also be invaded even if a creditor or credit bureau doesn't publish a thing about you. You have a right to be physically left at peace in your own home or office, and if a creditor or bill collector harasses you at either place, either in person, by phone, or by some other means, here again you have an invasion of privacy case.

This means that in addition to a weapon against creditors' first threat—destruction of your credit rating—you now have a weapon against their second major threat, harassment. Moreover, it's a weapon that you can often use without going to court.

In big cities, it's impractical for bill collectors to indulge in face-to-face harassment, so they have to confine their tactics to mail and telephone. A letter is not particularly harassing, since you can always throw it away unopened. (The exception is a special delivery letter or telegram timed to arrive in the middle of the night, and these are relatively expensive.) As a result, the main harassment weapon is usually the phone, and if a bill collector uses it too persistently, he can get himself and his company in trouble.

Toward the end of 1973, a bill collector started telephoning an advertising executive's office and wouldn't take "no" for an answer. No sooner would he or his secretary hang up than he would call again, yelling and heaping abuse on the hapless switchboard operators and anyone else who happened to pick up the phone.

Unfortunately for the bill collector, there were two problems with this approach: (1) it was not only illegal, but contrary to telephone company regulations, and (2) his victim knew it.

Every town, city, and state with telephone service has some kind of regulation against obscene, abusive, or harassing telephone calls, and every telephone company has an abusive-calls bureau to deal with them. Although these bureaus are designed primarily to combat the proverbial obscene call in the middle of a night when the moon is full, bill collectors' telephone harassments also fall under their jurisdiction. Now, this doesn't cover the random call or two from a bill collector who is routinely, and relatively courteously, putting the bite on you. It does, however, cover those bill collectors who go above and beyond the call of duty to tie up your phone, put you into disrepute with your employers and fellow employees, and generally make your life miserable out of sheer vindictiveness. In short, there must be a repeated pattern of these calls, and at least some circumstantial evidence that they are not routine, isolated, normal collection calls. But once you have this, the phone company is almost invariably ready and willing to swing into action, which is precisely what they did for the debtor in question.

After two days of being harassed by phone, he called the New York Telephone Company's abusive-call office. This office, incidentally, is far better equipped to cope with this kind of abusive call than the typical obscene phone call, for three reasons. First, bill collectors, unlike obscene callers, leave their names and numbers, so there's no need to put a trace on their calls. Second, the most immediate threat the phone company can impose on an abusive caller is to cancel his phone service. This threat carries less weight with the amateur phone abuser, who can operate just as well out of a phone booth, than with collection companies, whose ability to do business depends on being able to use the telephone. And finally, abusive bill collectors almost always operate during business hours, and when dealing with the New York Telephone Company's phone-abuse bureau, this is a big help. You see, while more than 99 percent of the obscene and abusive phone calls in New York are made after dark, the New York Telephone Company's abusive phone-call bureau is strictly a 9 AM to 5 PM operation.

If the threat of canceling phone service doesn't carry enough weight, the phone company can, and will, start criminal prosecution, but in this case it wasn't necessary. The mere threat of having the whole collection company's phone service canceled was enough to get their collector out of our debtor's hair.

The telephone company isn't the only communications monopoly that can create difficulties for overenthusiastic creditors. The Postal Service can be pretty good in that department, too. If a creditor sends you a collection post card instead of a collection letter, the possibility of libel or invasion of privacy exists. In some jurisdictions, this may also be the case for a sealed letter opened by another member of your household or company. In addition, the U.S. Criminal Code (18 USCA 335) prohibits creditors (or other people, for that matter) from mailing post cards or envelopes on which there appears matter tending to reflect on the character of the recipient, and for a bill collection company such matter could include just their full company name in the return address. It also includes, according to Postal Service rulings, post cards indicating accounts past due, lawsuit threats, or garnishment threats. The penalty is up to $5,000 fine, up to five years' imprisonment, or any combination thereof.

In most states, merely making a threat against your person or property constitutes the crime of assault, and if a bill collector makes a threat of this nature to you, you can have him arrested and on trial before a criminal court.

Where the threat is not of physical violence, and where it is coupled with a demand for payment, your creditor may be guilty of extortion. A threat to turn your account over to a collection agent or an attorney or to start a lawsuit is not extortion. But a threat to ruin your credit rating, throw you into bankruptcy, cost you your job, or have the bank foreclose on your home, all are—even if the wording in which these threats are made is somewhat veiled. In addition to being a criminal offense, this kind of extortion can be costly, particularly if you can prove in court that it upsets your already frail physical condition, created serious mental stress, and so forth.

Where the bill collector doesn't get abusive enough to warrant an assault or extortion charge, in most states harassment itself is both a civil wrong and a criminal offense. While a lawsuit for damages can be a drawn-out and ultimately unproductive venture, a criminal complaint will come before the judge quickly, will be next to impossible for the defendants to indefinitely postpone, and will scare the living daylights out of them. With the result that most will offer to leave you alone in return for your dropping the charge. If you go for that kind of agreement, make sure you get it in writing. Then, if they break it, you'll have some good evidence to take back to court.

Getting the prosecution rolling is relatively simple. Visit your local criminal court and obtain a criminal summons.* Then get in touch with the police precinct where the harassers in question are working and ask for a policeman to accompany you when you go to serve the summons. As a point of law, you don't need a policeman to accompany you, but as a point of practicality, they're very handy to have along. If necessary, the policeman can testify to the fact that the summons was actually served, and his presence while you're serving it helps to demoralize the people you're serving it against and inhibits the outbreak of violence. After the summons is served, you and the defendant will have to appear at a hearing before a criminal judge, who will decide on the basis of the evidence that both sides present whether to dismiss the complaint, issue a warning, or turn the case over to the District Attorney's office for prosecution. As mentioned before, judges are impressed by names, facts, times, and dates, so our advice about testifying in civil court is equally applicable here. Gather as much specific information as you can to prove that there was, in fact, harassment, and not just normal bill collecting, which is what their defense will claim it was.

* This may be easier in the suburbs, which are less crime-ridden, than in big cities, where minor crimes tend to get shrugged off by prosecutors and judges in charge of granting criminal summonses. By way of analogy, in and around Greenwich, Connecticut, an abandoned car can trigger a State Police investigation. In New York City, less than thirty miles away, so many thousands of cars are abandoned on the streets that they're simply ignored until the Sanitation Department eventually carts them away.

Also, as in civil court, the judge's main interest is to keep things orderly and moving, so he'll more likely issue a warning than have prosecution started. Once the warning is issued, however, it means automatic prosecution if the bill collectors ignore it.

In most states, you have to get at unfair collection practices through the slightly roundabout routes of libel, invasion of privacy, harassment, and where warranted, assault complaints. But for the lucky citizens of the great state of Texas, the line of attack is much shorter and straighter, because under Texas law you can sue creditors and bill collectors just for the act of collecting, if they go about it too vigorously.*

If a creditor or bill collector in Texas goes about his business with malice or the purpose of causing injury or with reckless disregard for your health and welfare (the legal term for this reckless disregard is "negligence"), you, the debtor, are entitled to cash reparations. You don't have to prove that you were hurt or damaged in any specific way, and if you can prove either reckless disregard or malicious intent, you don't even have to prove any specific collection actions (although these are generally evidence from which either malice or negligence is inferred).

Should you be unable to pin a creditor down for what he intends to do, you can also nail him to the wall for what he actually does. Under the Texas statute, unreasonable collection practices—i.e., those means of collection that a person of ordinary prudence, in the exercise of ordinary care, would not have made in the same or similar circumstances—also entitle the victim to a cash award from the court. In addition to proving the unfairness of the collection practices, he must also prove that he was in some way harmed by them. But this is nowhere near as difficult as it sounds. Over the years that this law has been in effect, the Texas courts have been extremely fair and liberal in applying it.

For example, the Texas courts have ruled that "nu-

---

* Hubbard, Paul L. "Recovery for Creditor Harassment," *Texas Law Review*, 1968.

merous telephone calls" to the debtor's home or office constitute an unreasonable collection practice. This is the principal method by which collection agencies operate.

Or "disturbing sleep." Many bill collectors make a point of calling or visiting debtors on weekday evenings, when they're presumed to be at home. If you live in Texas, the bill collector has been running behind schedule, and you have a habit of retiring early, you've got a case.

"Visits at home or office." In most states, the invasion of privacy laws would protect you against unwanted visits to your home. Since your office, however, is a place of business, and as such open to the public, invasion-of-privacy laws generally fail to protect you against bill collectors who hang around your office with the purpose of putting you into disrepute with your company and fellow workers. In Texas, however, you're protected.

Texas bill collectors are similarly prohibited by court rulings from contacting your neighbors or fellow employees about your alleged debt. In many states, you could counter this by suing for libel, but in Texas what is at issue is not the truth or falsity of the statements, but the fact that your creditor stooped to verbal attempts to discredit you. Even if you are, in fact, stiffing him, that's nobody's business but his and yours. In a later case, the Texas courts went so far as to prohibit contacting relatives (in the case in question, a brother-in-law) about uncollected debts.

Unless he comes in armed with a garnishment order, in which event the matter of collection is cut and dried, a Texas creditor may not ask a debtor's employer to help collect the claimed debt.

If all that isn't enough, Texas court decisions have categorized as unfair those collection practices that most bill collectors elsewhere indulge in as a matter of course: "using a harsh, loud voice," "being abusive," "being embarrassing," "being sarcastic," "being foul-mouthed," "being derogatory," "being insulting," calling you "a deadbeat," or even calling you "a liar."

Texas creditors are forbidden to send telegrams and

special delivery letters timed to arrive in the middle of the night.

Finally, they're prohibited from the bullying creditor's last, desperate resort short of taking you to court, where there's at least some respect for your rights. Texas courts impose damages on creditors and collectors who make threats. These can be "general threats" or "specific threats," such as:

    to blacklist you with the local credit bureau
    to cause you to lose your job
    to have your wages garnisheed
    to repossess the merchandise
    to have the sheriff repossess the merchandise
    or to have you arrested

Of course, with all these unreasonable collection practices, you do have to prove you suffered specific damages. But in this connection, specific damages are not confined to monetary loss and include things that even people not being harassed by creditors could prove they suffer from. "Nervousness," for example, or "headaches," "nausea," "vomiting," "loss of weight," "fainting," "numbness," "loss of memory" (like forgetting to pay your bills?), "high blood pressure," "low blood pressure," "crying spells," "chest pains," and "stomach pains." (No mention is made, unfortunately, of "pain in the neck.") In addition, the courts have even gone so far as to award damages for collection-related conditions that most people hear of only in bad television commercials—loss of energy, acid indigestion, and, believe it or not, "that rundown feeling."

If you can prove your creditors or their collectors indulged in unfair collection techniques, and that one of these maladies followed, the Texas courts will set a cash value on it and order your creditors to pay you. If you can prove malice or negligence, the courts will also award extra, or "exemplary," damages.

There are three last collection tactics that Texas residents are not explicitly protected from, but New York State residents are.

First, you may recall Sections 703 and 705 of the General Business Law discussed in Chapter 7. This law specifies time limits in which creditors must acknowledge and answer customer complaints about billing errors, and if creditors fail to meet these deadlines, they may have to pay a penalty. If the bill was correct, but the creditor takes too long to so inform the debtor, he forfeits his right to collection interest on the debt from the time he should have sent his reply to the time he actually sends it. (However, for up to 120 days after the mailing date of the original bill, he can still collect the interest.)

But if the customer was right, the bill was wrong, and the creditor takes too long to correct it, he must pay the customer the cash value of actual damages sustained as a result of the failure to rectify the error, plus twice the amount of the billing error, up to $100. There's a catch to this, however. If the creditor can show by a preponderance of evidence that his excessive delay was unintentional and in good faith, he's off the hook for paying twice the disputed amount. Furthermore, the law requires him to merely answer your complaint, it says nothing about actually correcting it. Thus, a creditor can write you within ninety days of your complaint that he's correcting your records, his computer can churn out statement after statement claiming you still owe the "corrected" amount, and the law will still have been complied with. If you have to take a creditor to court as a result of something like this, though, he has to pay your attorney's fees and court costs. (An addition to the federal Fair Credit Billing Act parallels this law on an interstate level, imposing penalties for creditors who fail to answer complaints about computer errors within 30 days and to resolve them within 90 days.)

A second New York protection has more teeth in it than the first one. It is illegal for New York creditors to threaten you with any action that they have no legal right to take or do not take in the regular course of business. The New York Professional Bureau, a wholly owned subsidiary of the Medical Society of the County of New York, collects bills owing to doctors. According to the state Attorney General's office, one of their collection letters was headed "Telegram." It stated "garnishment or court action is expensive" and informed the debtor that costs of the proceeding would be assessed on commencement of the action. In response to the Attorney General's complaint, the bureau agreed to discontinue the practice and to pay $500 in costs to the state.*

Third, it's also illegal to print and send collection letters designed to look like summonses, judgements, and other legal forms to scare the debtor either into returning the merchandise or paying what may be an unjustified sum. This practice is particularly prevalent in New York real estate circles, where landlords want to force rent-controlled tenants out of buildings in order to take advantage of a state law that permits the apartments to be decontrolled once they're vacated (which means that the only limit on rents is what the traffic will bear). There have been many instances of unscrupulous landlords sending documents that purported to be eviction notices. In one instance, an apparent process server knocked on the doors of the apartments in 56 East 89th Street, Manhattan, and adjacent buildings, and handed each tenant an official-looking form which began, "The landlord of said premises elects to evict you . . . in not less than thirty days . . ." Many tenants, instead of identifying those official-looking papers for what they were, simply packed up and moved out "voluntarily." †

The practice is also indulged in by the more unscrupulous bill collectors, whose collection letters are sent by certified mail and contain such features as "City and County of New York" in Old English type, creditor's name "vs." your name, index numbers, quotations from the Uniform Commercial Code, wordings like "The above named Debtor is hereby officially Summoned" to appear at the offices of [creditor's name] and pay the aforesaid Debt." One collection agent wants so much to appear as an official law-enforcement agent that he calls himself John Marshall.

* "Dun-da-dun-dun," *New York*, August 6, 1973.
† Peter Hellman, "The Landlords' Guerrilla War Against Tenants," *New York*, March 23, 1970.

While these letters may appear to be legal documents they are, in New York at least, exactly the opposite, namely, illegal documents. Under the New York Penal Code,* it is a class B misdemeanor to use any collection document that in language, name and address, format, type face, or general appearance purports to be a court order, summons, or document from any law-enforcement agency.†

So if you live in New York State and receive what appears to be a legal document in the mail, study it thoroughly. If it's not what it purports to be, pick up a Blumberg's law blank, take both down to the complaint section of the local criminal court, show both to the judge (making a point-by-point comparison of similarities), and obtain a criminal summons. Then you'll be able to turn the tables on the bill collector and put him in creditor's prison.

---

* The legal language is as follows: "Sec. 190.50. A person is guilty of unlawful collection practices when with intent to enforce a claim of judgement for money or property, he knowingly sends, mails, or delivers to another person a notice, document, or other instrument which has no judicial or official sanction and which in its format or appearance simulates a summons, complaint, court order or process, or an insignia, seal, or printed form of a federal, state or local government or an instrumentality thereof or is otherwise calculated to induce a belief that such notice, document, or instrument has a judicial or official sanction." At this writing, there's talk of enacting a federal law with similar provisions, but so far this is only talk.

† In the previous chapter, you read that the New York City Parking Violations Bureau, discouraged by city marshals' ineffectuality in collecting on judgements, retained private collection agencies to take over. It was later discovered that, of the three collection agencies the city hired, two had been prosecuted, tried, and convicted of violating this ordinance. Each had been fined $2,500. After wiping the egg off its face, the Parking Violations Bureau had to replace them.

CHAPTER FOURTEEN

Bankruptcy Is
Not Leprosy

ON JUNE 14, 1934, Primo Carnera lost the world heavy-weight championship to Max Baer on an eleventh-round knockout. In the months before the fight, Carnera is reputed to have delivered a knockout blow to a collection of New York's more prominent creditors.

When the fight contract was originally signed, Carnera was guaranteed a minimum purse in the neighborhood of 50,000 Depression dollars. As soon as the ink dried, according to the story, a whole bunch of merchants rushed forward to extend all kinds of credit, which Carnera obliged them by taking advantage of. Shortly before the fight, however, he went into court and filed for bankruptcy.

His case was as follows: He owed his creditors some $50,000. At the moment of filing, he didn't have $50,000. Therefore, since his liabilities so heavily outweighed his assets, he wished to declare himself bankrupt. The creditors claimed that he would be shortly fighting Max Baer and earning a minimum of $50,000. Therefore, he would shortly have the money to pay the debts owed them and should consequently not be allowed to wipe out those debts through bankruptcy.

The judge ruled that there was no absolute guarantee that Carnera would make the fight and collect the $50,-000. He could trip on a curb and break his leg. He could walk in front of a speeding subway train. He could cut himself shaving and bleed to death. Or any of a number of other calamaties could befall him. In any event, his getting the $50,000 guarantee was by no means a sure thing, and he should therefore be allowed to declare himself bankrupt. Which is exactly what the story says he did.

His meager assets were divided among his creditors, averaging out to a fraction of a cent on the dollar. Over the following weeks, he was very careful not to trip on a curb, walk in front of a subway train, or cut himself shaving. He fought, lost, received his $50,000 and promptly left the country to be alive and well in his native Argentina. But even had he stayed in New York, his former creditors would have been powerless to get hold of any of his money. The bankruptcy had wiped out his legal obligations to them.

This story may be apocryphal, but it has a recent, documented counterpart. In February, 1973, racing driver Gordon Johncock found himself $369,000 in the hole and petitioned the courts to file for bankruptcy. Legal proceedings started in the spring. Then, on Memorial Day, Johncock won the Indianapolis 500. The first prize was $238,000 and, under the terms of Johncock's agreement with his sponsor, he got to keep $90,000 (before taxes) as his own share.

Naturally, his creditors wanted to get their mitts on this money, the fact that he earned it after filing for bankruptcy notwithstanding. So far, the money has been placed in an escrow account by the federal bankruptcy referee, who has yet to determine that Johncock's creditors are entitled to it.*

As a bankrupt, Johncock will move in just as fast

---

* Deane McGowen, "People in Sports," *New York Times*, June 9, 1973.

circles as those he moves in as a racer. Eddie Fisher, Mickey Rooney, Betty Hutton, and George Sanders have all declared bankruptcy, as has one of the DuPonts of Wilmington, Delaware, whose debts exceeded $12 million. In the New York metropolitan area (including Long Island and the well-to-do Westchester and Rockland counties), 1,773 personal bankruptcies were filed in 1972; in Buffalo, New York, 1,896 during the same period; 7,966 were filed in Alabama; and 13,997 in Los Angeles.†

Throughout the country, a total of 250,000 people are expected to file for bankruptcy in 1975. As a result there will be more bankruptcy hearings in the federal courts than all other federal cases combined.

The fine old institution of bankruptcy allows a debtor who's in over his head to settle all of his debts with part of his property, wipe out his obligations, and start over again with a clean slate.

For individuals, as opposed to businesses, there are few, if any, assets worth a creditor's while to confiscate; the assets are almost always far, far outweighed by the liabilities, so bankruptcy is usually very one-sided in favor of the debtor.

If a creditor suspects you have a huge hoard of hidden cash or other assets, he can legally petition that you be thrown into involuntary bankruptcy so he can get his hands on those hidden assets. But with the kind of assets most individual debtors have, there's little hope of more than the most meager settlement, so creditors tend to welcome voluntary bankruptcies much as they'd welcome the bubonic plague.

Because it's the creditor, and not the debtor, who loses his shirt in a bankruptcy, even the *threat* that you're going to file for one is enough to merit special consideration from your creditors. The collection manager who was ferocious the day before you mentioned bankruptcy will suddenly become the acme of solicitude, offering extended payments, temporary collection mora-

† Myers Jerome, I., "How to Go Bankrupt and Start Over," *New York*, September 10, 1973.

toria, and the like—anything at all to get some return on the credit his company extended to you.

So if your back is really to the wall, the first step to take is to write your creditors about your imminent bankruptcy and propose a more favorable alternative. You can either ask for a reduction of payments to an amount which you can reasonably handle (Alternative 1) or suggest a debt moratorium for a reasonable amount of time (Alternative 2). The expense of fighting a bankruptcy petition, and the near-certainty of receiving next to nothing from you if your petition is granted, should make most creditors ready to agree to your proposals.

```
American Credit Card Company
Customer Service Division
125A Fifth Avenue
New York, New York 10000

Re: Account Number 5218 307 821
Amount due: $2612.43

Gentlemen:


I have carefully reviewed my fi-
nancial condition, and I find that
it is impossible for me to meet
the scheduled monthly payments
on my indebtedness to you.

(Insert here any special reasons
for your hardship, e.g., lost your
job, large medical bills, other
unexpected emergency expenses.)

After deducting my carefully
budgeted living expenses from my
current monthly income, the bal-
```

ance is simply inadequate to pay
my debts at their present rate.

Alternative 1

Therefore, I propose to you that
my payments be reduced to ($10)
per month for at least the next
year, unless the debt is paid off
sooner. At present, I assure you
that the payments of ($10) a month
are within my means and will be
made regularly.

Alternative 2

Therefore, I propose a (90-day)
(120-day) (6-month) deferrment on
my repayment of my debt. At the end
of that period, I hope to resume
regular monthly payments.

Cooperation on your part will be of
considerable help in avoiding
bankruptcy.

Very truly yours,

The two form letters here are merely suggestions, and
you shouldn't be bound by every detail. But no matter
what style you write it in, your letter should contain some
good excuse for falling behind in payments (see Chapter
7 for a good excuse). It should state that your obligations
far exceed your ability to satisfy them, giving figures
where necessary, and that because of this circumstance
the only way out, short of their leniency, is bankruptcy,
which you like little more than they do since you strongly

believe in paying your bills (try to write this part with a straight face).

If you really want to convince your creditors you mean business, you can do it with one little enclosure in your letter. Like most legal actions, voluntary bankruptcy proceedings call for certain legal forms, and Blumberg's prints blank forms to cover the situation. In this case, you want form #1000, individual bankruptcy forms, containing four copies each of your petition, schedules, oaths, and statement of affairs, all for $1.75. Once you get your set, make photocopies of the blank petition part and enclose the copy wtih your letter, stating that if the creditor can't see his way clear to cooperating, you have the forms, and you and your attorney are prepared to fill them out and use them. A photocopy of a blank form has no legal standing, but it does have its shock value.

In the event that your creditors don't go along with leniency proposals, or that you don't want to take the final plunge, there are two alternatives open to you under the bankruptcy law. With both, you avoid the largely illusory stigma of being officially declared bankrupt, but with both your debts remain intact and undischarged (you still have to pay them, but you can take longer, and the court will protect you from harassment).

Under Chapter XI of the bankruptcy law, you can enter into an "arrangement" with your creditors, and under Chapter XIII, you can set up a "wage-earner's plan." Both proceedings give you either extended payment deadlines, or reduced payments (over a longer period), or some combination. Both are imposed on your creditors by the court. Both fail to wipe out your debts, but they allow you to carry them a bit longer.

There are some differences between the two plans. While Chapter XI is open to both individuals and corporations, Chapter XIII is for wage-earners (individuals) only. Chapter XI is used mainly by corporations and involves a lot of costly paperwork. Because Chapter XIII is for workingmen, it's set up to be a lot simpler. Also, while Chapter XI arrangements cover only unsecured debts, Chapter XIII wage-earners' plans can also cover secured loans like the mortgage on your house or a car loan secured by a chattel mortgage on your car.

Whether you're going to try for an arrangement or go for broke, the mechanics are the same. If liabilities exceed your assets by as little as one dollar, you are insolvent and may file for bankruptcy. You do this by filling out forms listing your debts, the fair market value of your assets, and other pertinent information (these forms are all in the Blumberg's bankruptcy kit mentioned earlier), and filing these documents with the Federal District Court where you live. In listing debts, you can include not only your current debts, but also your contingent liabilities—debts that are expected to become due in the future as the result of present commitments (like the rent due during the unexpired term of your apartment lease or a loan you've co-signed). Your petition is reviewed by a court referee, who ultimately determines which debts can be wiped out and which assets you must surrender to be sold to provide money to distribute among your creditors.

He is also empowered to review your books and financial records, which you're required to provide. The state of these records is required to be consistent with your station in life. A $50,000-a-year stock broker is expected to keep more accurate and complete records than a hod carrier who never finished high school. The absence of records is not in itself a cause for your petition for bankruptcy to be rejected, unless it can be shown that because of your intelligence and the magnitude of your financial affairs, you should have kept financial records. The records you do keep don't have to be in double-entry bookkeeping, or even in conformity with accepted accounting practices. A journal of expenses, or just a checkbook and canceled checks, will usually suffice.

At the discretion of the referee, a trustee may be appointed by the court. The trustee is a lawyer, and his job is to actually take charge of and sell the assets and then distribute the proceeds. He is also empowered to investigate your petition to make sure you're not hiding assets and that the petition is otherwise in order. He will then

275

make a report to the referee, and unless a creditor objects, that will close the case.

The decision of whether or not to appoint a trustee rests with the referee. Some appoint trustees in every case that comes before them; others don't bother with trustees when the petitioner has no assets to declare and a small number of creditors (less than a dozen) is involved.

Once your petition is filed, the court notifies all the creditors you listed, so that they may raise any objections they have to your going bankrupt. Surprisingly, though many creditors probably have objections to having receivables totally wiped out, few bother to come to court to voice these objections. In nine out of ten "no asset" cases, not one creditor appears to object.

From the moment a petition is filed with the court (and until the final adjudication, if the court rejects it), you become safe from creditors' collection efforts. They can't send bill collectors, they can't harass you, they can't sue you, they can't try to garnishee your salary, they can't do anything else to try and get their money back. If they do, the referee will slap them with a restraining order.

So, if you can overcome your conditioned resistance to the very idea of bankruptcy, it can offer you several advantages over the other plans, the major advantage being that most, if not all, of your debts are wiped off the slate.

You can't discharge debts for back taxes. You can't do away with your liability for goods, services, or money you obtained by false pretenses (e.g., overstating your assets on your original credit application). If you owe alimony and child support, you'll still owe them after you're bankrupt. If you owe damages for willful and malicious injury to others (*not* negligence damages), you'll still owe them, as you'll still owe seduction and breach-of-promise judgements (creditors can't sue you for breach of promise). You'll also still owe back wages to employees for the three months preceeding bankruptcy, money deposited by employees as security, and debts you've incurred, if any, through misappropriation of funds entrusted to you as an officer of a business.

You don't get off the hook for secured debts, but this makes little difference, because the bank has probably foreclosed on your house and repossessed your car already.

And finally, you don't get out of existing debts that you fail to list on your bankruptcy petition.

All other debts, however, are fair game.

Moreover, just as there are items of your property that are judgement-proof, there are also assets that are exempt from confiscation in settlement of bankruptcy. By and large, the exceptions are similar to those for judgements (see Chapter 12), and like those exceptions, they vary from state to state. But because of those exemptions, you can come out of bankruptcy with your standard of living largely intact.

Unless you have a mortgage on it, your homestead is the first thing your creditors can't take away. This includes your house and the surrounding grounds, provided they're not too extensive. If your grounds resemble the King Ranch, you'll have to part with most of them, but otherwise you're home free. Your mortgage is still collectable, as are real-estate taxes and debts for labor and materials for the house (which, legally, can be secured by liens on the house).

In New York, the homestead exemption covers land with one or more buildings (this takes account of garages) used as a principal residence for "householders"* or women. If your equity in the property is $2,000 or less, you can keep it. If it's more, the property must be sold, but you get to keep the first $2,000 of the proceeds. If your equity is more than $2,000 but so little more that the costs of appraisal, advertising, and sale will leave just a small amount for your creditors to haggle over, the court will generally let you keep it. It is important to note that you can enjoy a homestead exemption only if you've qualified for it in advance. Either your prop-

* "Householders" are married men with families, widowers, or single men living with dependent parents or relatives.

erty must be designated as a homestead in the deed, or you must file a separate document so designating it. This document runs no longer than one page, a lawyer can prepare it for $25 or less, and you can file it with the clerk of the county where the property is located for a $1 filing fee ($5 in New York City).

Since the idea of bankruptcy is to help the debtor get back on his feet again, your creditors are not allowed to take away the tools of your trade. What, exactly, these tools consist of depends on which state you live in, what your trade is and which tools the courts think are needed to practice it. For an accountant, an expensive color television set would not be a tool of the trade. For a broadcast executive, however, it would be. Your car may be a tool of your trade, and some states exempt it specifically. (In Texas, cars are exempt under a nineteenth-century statute that lets bankrupts keep their horses and cattle.) Some states let you keep your car provided it's not worth too much; in California, for example, bankrupts can keep cars with less than $1,000 of owner equity.

Professional men are generally allowed to keep their equipment, books and instruments. Again, the amount and value of office furniture, instruments, and other tools of the trade that you can keep varies from state to state.

Household effects are generally exempt from being sold to settle bankrupts' debts, as are all but the most opulent parts of your wardrobe. In New York State, "householders" and women, regardless of marital or familial status, can keep "necessary" household furnishings, all wearing apparel, all crockery, tableware, and cooking utensils, one refrigerator, one stove, one radio receiver, and one wedding ring. They can also keep the family Bible, family pictures, books used in the family library not exceeding $50 in value, a watch not exceeding $35 in value, and domestic animals (pets included) worth up to $450.

These values, incidentally, are not the prices paid to buy the books, watches, or animals when they were new, but their fair market value at the time of bankruptcy. Since the fair market value is lower for used property than for brand new property, this works out in the bankrupt's favor.

A New York bachelor can keep his clothing, his watch, and for some strange reason, a wedding ring.

In New Jersey, the personal property exemption allows you to keep all your clothing and $500 worth of selected household articles.

In Connecticut, the court ruled that a color television set was necessary for the care and company of one bankrupt's family. Bankrupts can also keep all clothes, household furniture, military equipment and uniforms, and musical instruments owned and used in an official capacity by members of the militia. You can also keep one cow not exceeding $150 in value, up to ten sheep not exceeding $150 in value, two swine and poultry not exceeding $25 in value, and one boat not exceeding $200 in value, provided that boat is used in the business of taking oysters, shad or clams.

California's Homestead Act allows bankrupts to keep $20,000 equity in their homes, cash on deposit in a savings and loan association or credit union, $2,500 worth of tools of their trade, a cow and her suckling calf, a pig and her suckling piglet, three months' stores, or a three-month supply of food.

Often, proceeds from or the cash surrender value of life insurance policies (provided you're not the beneficiary), accident and disability payments, and pension payments go directly to you, and your creditors can't touch them. If you get such payments, however, you'd better spend the money or hide it in the mattress. In many states, the minute you put it in a bank, it ceases to be an insurance or pension payment and becomes a bank deposit, which your creditors can grab practically at will.

Last but not least, the courts generally allow bankrupts some walking-around money, sometimes as much as $1,000 in cash. New York allows you to keep up to $600 worth of shares of a savings and loan association and another $600 worth of credit union shares.

All of these exemptions can leave a bankrupt in better financial shape than many people who are legally solvent.

A householder living in the Southern District of New York could emerge from a bankruptcy with the following assets intact:

Homestead exemption	$2,000
Savings and loan association shares	600 *(cash)*
Credit union shares	600 *(cash)*
Standard whole life insurance ($30,000) face value, in force 20 years—cash surrender or loan value)	9,540
Household furnishing, tv set, washing machine, china, tableware	5,000 *(estimated value)*
Home library	50 *(market value)*
Tools of trade	600 *(market value)*
Wearing apparel	unlimited
Total value of exemptions	$18,390 *plus all the clothes you can wear*

In addition, he would also be entitled to any state or Veterans Administration disability payments he had been getting. And, if he happened to be a member of the Naval Reserve and had put his prebankruptcy pay into the Navy's servicemen's savings account, that money, too, would be his free and clear.

Before you rush out to declare yourself bankrupt, however, there are pitfalls to watch out for.

First, it's going to cost you money. Bankruptcy proceedings can be very complicated—so much so that you'll need the help of a lawyer. The legal work should run you at least $200 (often as much as $450), and there's a $50 filing fee. (This means, paradoxically enough, that there's such a thing as being too poor to be bankrupt. In many instances, however, the courts will let you pay out the filing fee over a period of time.) Of course, any lawyer you hire will want his money in advance. If any lawyer offers to do the job on credit, he doesn't know enough bankruptcy law to be worth hiring.

Second, you have to be certain to list all your debts. If you omit one, the bankruptcy won't discharge it, unless you can prove that the creditor knew about your petition for bankruptcy in time to make himself a party to the proceedings.

Third, there's probably a fair amount of money at stake, and the court isn't going to let you off just on your say-so. Your financial records for the previous year are important evidence. If you're filing for bankruptcy as a corporation, they're essential.

Fourth, judges pay strict attention to how you've disposed of your assets in the year before filing for bankruptcy. Disposing of assets in such a manner as to specifically avoid their being seized by creditors to settle a bankruptcy is fraud, and judges don't like fraud in their courtrooms. If you've given away your Steinway concert grand piano to your buddy George, or, if you've "sold" your Aubusson carpet to Aunt Gertrude for a dollar, you can expect the court to disallow the validity of the transaction, since you failed to sell for fair market value. Either your bankruptcy petition will be denied, or your creditors will take the piano back from George and the rug back from Aunt Gertrude, or maybe both things will happen.

If, however, you've sold the piano for $1,500 and have a bill of sale to prove it, and in the intervening months you happen to have squandered the money or blown it in the stock market or on the horses, this is perfectly legitimate.

Also, the manner in which you report your assets is as important as the manner in which you've disposed of them. Just as undeclared debts can jeopardize a bankruptcy petition, so can undisclosed, or improperly disclosed, assets. It's impossible to overemphasize the importance of listing both your assets and your liabilities thoroughly, correctly, and in proper form. This is why, although books and articles have been written by the dozen about how you can file for bankruptcy all by yourself, a good attorney is worth the money you have to scrape together to pay him.

The fifth pitfall is your creditors, who have a lot to lose in bankruptcy and can't always be expected to roll over and play dead. One common tactic is to stall the bankruptcy proceedings (much as you'd stall a lawsuit against you) in the hope that they can sue you, win a judgement, and confiscate your property themselves while the others are still bogged down in your bankruptcy proceedings. For people who've read this book, this threat is not as serious as it might be, because the same techniques that are being used to slow down the bankruptcy can be used with even greater effect to slow down creditors' lawsuits. Civil courts are far more overcrowded and backlogged than bankruptcy courts, so each postponement there will produce a greater delay.

However, the chances of creditors actively opposing, or even taking the slightest interest in, a petition to wipe out the debts owed them is slight. The experience of Ron and Arlene Bauman, who went bankrupt to wipe out $60,000 in debts, is indicative. Here is an excerpt from an interview with them televised on *60 Minutes*:

MORLEY SAFER: Which companies got burned?

ARLENE BAUMAN: Union 76, Mobil Oil, Sears, Penney's. Master Charge was the big one, that was the biggest one of all . . .

SAFER: So when you finally appeared in court the other day for the discharge of bankruptcy, did any of them come and challenge? Sears? Penney's? Mobil? Master Charge? Were they there?

RON BAUMAN: No, there wasn't anybody that showed up at all, which was really surprising. I felt that the big companies would at least like to know what's going on. And nobody showed up, nobody challenged anything at all. Which kind of flipped me, because I really thought that somebody would be there, especially with those kinds of amounts.*

*CBS News *60 Minutes*, Vol VII, No. 34, Bankrupt," broadcast September 7, 1975.

Once your bankruptcy petition is granted, your debts will be discharged, but you won't be able to file again for six years. That's if you file under the same status and under the same name. Of course, a bankrupt individual can always form a corporation, the corporation can incur debts, and if the corporation's debts outweigh its assets, the stockholders' past bankruptcies will not prevent the corporation from going bankrupt.

Similarly, if a corporation you own stock in goes bankrupt, there is nothing to prevent its shareholders from forming another corporation, obtaining credit, and if circumstances dictate, going bankrupt again.

In fact, in some industries, continuous reincorporations followed by continuous bankruptcies have become an increasingly fashionable way of doing business. This is one reason why the business bankruptcy rate has skyrocketed.* As noted before, there's a yawning chasm between the standard of morality that creditors demand of you and the standard they observe themselves, and in this example, too, there's no reason short of the corporate fees and taxes why you shouldn't consider making the double standard a single standard by incorporating. But even if you don't do that, you'll still find that bankruptcy is a very rewarding experience.

For one thing, if you play your cards right, you can take a bath without forfeiting your favorite charge accounts. If you've decided, before filing, which charge accounts you want to keep, and if you've paid them off before filing for bankruptcy, they will not be listed on your schedule of creditors, and therefore will not be notified of the bankruptcy proceedings. If you've established yourself as a good credit customer, there should

* According to Dun & Bradstreet, the number of failures among listed firms has gone from a low of 809 companies in 1945 to a high of 17,075 in 1961. For 1972, the latest year for which records have been compiled, the number of business bankruptcies was down to 9,566, but the average liability per failure (i.e., the average amount each company took a bath for) was a record $209,099. (Source: *The Business Failure Record, 1972*, compiled by the Dun & Bradstreet Business Economics Department.)

be little occasion for them to do a new credit check on you, and if they do, the major factor in such a check would be their own credit records, which will show that you've kept your account current. (If you're going to do this, however, it's important that you do it at least four months before you file your bankruptcy petition. Otherwise, your payments will be construed as "preferential," and the trustee, if one is appointed and if he finds out about them, is empowered to recover the money and distribute it evenly among all your creditors.)

And to many creditors who haven't done business with you before, you may appear to be an excellent credit risk. Look at it through their eyes: You have no (or few) outstanding debts, and the law guarantees that it will be a minimum of six years before you can file for bankruptcy again.

Because of this, there are creditors who regularly scan the bankruptcy lists and rush to offer bankrupts credit. Los Angeles attorney Hugh Slate says, "I've had people, more than one, leave the courthouse, their hearing in the bankruptcy court, and they're riding home on the bus and they don't like the way the bus rides. And they get off the bus and go and buy an automobile [on credit] and drive the car home . . . Credit after bankruptcy is easy to obtain. If a person files a bankruptcy here in Los Angeles, he or she will then get letters through the mail from various outfits that want to sell them furniture, sell them anything, sell them cars, or lend them money. Because . . . after bankruptcy he cannot take the cure again for six years. And he's gotten rid of all his old creditors."*

Which means that if you go bankrupt, you get not only a clean slate, but a chance to start your deficit spending program all over again.

*© 1975, CBS Inc. Quoted from CBS News, *60 Minutes*, "Bankrupt."

The Buck Stops Here: Whom to Complain To

Charge Account and Credit Card Companies
GASOLINE AND OIL:

American Oil Company (AMOCO)
910 South Michigan Avenue
Chicago, Illinois 60680
(312) 856-5111
B. J. Yarrington, President

Atlantic Richfield Company (ARCO)
717 Fifth Avenue
New York, New York 10022
(212) PL 8-2345
Thornton F. Bradshaw, President

BP Oil Corporation
See Standard Oil (Ohio)

Cities Service Company
60 Wall Tower
New York, New York 10005
(212) HA 2-1600
Charles J. Waidelich, President

Exxon Company
Bell Avenue and Travis
Houston, Texas 77001
(713) 221-3636
Randall Mayer, President

Gulf Oil Corporation
Gulf Building
Pittsburgh, Pennsylvania 15230
(412) 391-4200
James Lee, President

Marathon Oil Company
539 South Main
Findlay, Ohio 45840

(419) 422-2121
Harold Hoopman, President

Mobil Oil Corporation
150 East 42nd Street
New York, New York 10017
(212) 883-4242
William Tavoulareas,
  President

Phillips Petroleum Company
Bartlesville, Oklahoma 74014
(918) FE 6-6600
W. F. Martin, President

Shell Oil Company
One Shell Plaza
New York, New York 10020
(212) 263-3000
H. Bridges, President

Skelly Oil Company
605 West 47th Street
Kansas City, Missouri
  64141
(816) 561-3575
Ernest B. Miller, Jr.,
  President

Standard Oil Company of
  California (Chevron)
225 Bush
San Francisco, California
  94104
(415) 894-7700
H. E . Haynes, President

Standard Oil Company
  (Indiana)
910 South Michigan Avenue
Chicago, Illinois 60605
(312) 856-6111
Robert C. Gunness, President

Standard Oil Company
  (Kentucky)
Starks Building

Louisville, Kentucky 40202
(502) 587-7531
W. J. Price, President

Standard Oil Company (Ohio)
Midland Building
Cleveland, Ohio 44115
(216) 575-4141
Alton W. Whitehouse,
  President

Sun Oil Company (Sunoco)
1608 Walnut Street
Philadelphia, Pennsylvania
  19103
(215) 985-1600
H. Robert Sharbaugh,
  President

Texaco, Inc.
135 East 42nd Street
New York, New York 10017
(212) 953-6000
John K. McKinley, President

DEPARTMENT STORES:

Aldens, Inc.
5000 Roosevelt Road
Chicago, Illinois 60607
(312) 854-4141
C. R. Wunderlich, President

Arlan's Department Stores,
  Inc.
393 Seventh Avenue
New York, New York 10001
(212) 790-2282
Edward Spector, President

Bloomingdale's
Lexington Avenue and East
  59th Street
New York, New York 10022
(212) EL 5-5900
Marvin Traub, President

Boston Store
331 West Wisconsin Avenue
Milwaukee, Wisconsin 53203
(414) 271-5060
Orren Bradley, President

Burdine's
22 East Flagler
Miami, Florida 33131
(305) 835-5151
Melvin Jacobs, President

Marshall Field and Company
111 North State Street
Chicago, Illinois 60690
(312) ST 1-1050
Gerald A. Sivage, President

Gimbels
Broadway at 33rd Street
New York, New York 10001
(212) PE 6-5100
Paul A. Salamone, President

R. H. Macy & Company, Inc.
151 West 34th Street
New York, New York 10001
(212) OX 5-4400
Herbert Seegal, President

J. C. Penney Company, Inc.
1301 Avenue of the Americas
New York, New York 10019
(212) 957-4321
Jack Jackson, President

Sears Roebuck and Company
925 South Homan Avenue
Chicago, Illinois 60607
(312) 265-2500
A. D. Swift, President

Zale Corporation
3000 Diamond Park
Dallas, Texas 75247
(214) 634-4011
Donald Zale, President

INSURANCE:

Aetna Life and Casualty
151 Farmington Avenue
Hartford, Connecticut 06115
(203) 273-2603
Donald Johnson, President

Allstate Insurance Companies
Allstate Plaza
Northbrook, Illinois 60062
(312) 291-5000
Boyd Christensen, President

American Family Mutual
Madison, Wisconsin 53701
(608) 249-2111
J. O. Miller, President

CUNA Mutual Insurance
   Society
P.O. Box 391
Madison, Wisconsin 53701
(608) 238-5851
Robert Curry, President

Farmers Insurance Group
4680 Wilshire Boulevard
Los Angeles, California 90054
(213) WE 1-1961
Robert E. Early, President

The Hartford Life Insurance
   Group
Hartford Plaza
Hartford, Connecticut 06115
(203) 547-5000
Herbert Schoen, President

John Hancock Mutual Life
   Insurance Company
200 Berkeley Street
Boston, Massachusetts 02117
(617) 421-6000
Frank B. Maher, President

Lutheran Brotherhood Life
and Health Insurance
Society
701 Second Avenue South
Minneapolis, Minnesota
55402
(612) 332-0211
W. P. Langhaug, President

Metropolitan Life Insurance
Company
One Madison Avenue
New York, New York 10010
(212) 578-2211
Richard R. Shinn, President

Mutual of Omaha Insurance
Company
Dodge at 33rd Street
Omaha, Nebraska 68131
(402) 342-7600
J. D. Minton, President

The National Life & Accident
Insurance Company
National Life Center
Nashville, Tennessee 37203
(615) 747-9000
R. L. Wagner, President

Nationwide Insurance
Company
246 North High
Columbus, Ohio 43216
(614) 228-4711
John Fisher, President

New York Life Insurance
Company
51 Madison Avenue
New York, New York 10010
(212) 576-7000
Marshall Bissell, President

North American Life and
Casualty Company

1750 Hennepin Avenue
Minneapolis, Minnesota
55403
(612) 377-5511
Howard Barnhill, President

Preferred Risk Mutual
Insurance Company
1111 Ashworth Road
West Des Moines, Iowa
50265
(515) 279-9751
Bernard Mercer, President

Prudential Insurance Com-
pany of America
Prudential Plaza
Newark, New Jersey 07101
(201) 336-1234
K. C. Foster, President

Reliance Insurance Company
4 Penn Center Plaza
Philadelphia, Pennsylvania
19103
(215) 864-4000
A. Addison Roberts, President

Sentry Insurance
Strongs Avenue
Stevens Point, Wisconsin
54481
(715) 344-2345
John W. Joanis, President

State Farm Mutual Automo-
bile Insurance Company
112 East Washington
Bloomington, Illinois 61701
(309) 967-612?
E. B. Rust, President

The Travelers Corporation
One Tower Square
Hartford, Connecticut 06116
Morrison Beach, President

CAR RENTALS:

Avis Rent A Car System, Inc.
900 Old Country Road
Garden City, New York
    11530
(516) 222-3000
W. V. Morrow, Jr., President

Hertz Corporation
600 Madison Avenue
New York, New York 10021
(212) PL 2-2000
Gerald Shapiro, President

National Car Rental System,
    Inc.
5501 Green Valley Drive
Minneapolis, Minnesota
    55437
(612) 944-1100
R. L. Thorfinnson, President

TRAVEL AND ENTERTAINMENT CARDS:

American Express Company
65 Broadway
New York, New York 10006
(212) WH 4-4000
William Morton, President

Carte Blanche Corporation
3460 Wilshire Boulevard
Los Angeles, California
    90054
(213) 381-7111
James E. Hawthorne,
    President

Diners Club
10 Columbus Circle
New York, New York 10019
(212) CI 5-1500
R. Newell Lusby, President

AIRLINE CREDIT CARDS:

American Airlines, Inc.
    (Vacation Card)
633 Third Avenue
New York, New York 10017
(212) 867-1234
George Warde, President

Eastern Air Lines, Inc.
10 Rockefeller Plaza
New York, New York 10020
(212) 956-4000
S. C. Higginbottom, President

Pan American World Airways
    (Takeoff Card)
200 Park Avenue
New York, New York 10017
(212) 973-7700
William Seawell, President

Trans World Airlines, Inc.
    (Getaway Card)
605 Third Avenue
New York, New York 10016
(212) 557-3000
F. C. Wiser, Jr., President

United Air Lines (Travel
    Card)
P.O. Box 66100
Chicago, Illinois 60666
(312) 952-4000
Edward Carlson, President

Source: Credit Union
    National Association, Inc.

State Consumer Offices

ALASKA

Honorable John Havelock
Attorney General of Alaska
Pouch "K," State Capitol
Juneau, Alaska 99801
(907) 586-5391

ARIZONA

Honorable Gary K. Nelson
Attorney General of Arizona
159 State Capitol Building
Phoenix, Arizona 85007
(602) 271-4266

John W. Keogh
Assistant Attorney General in
    Charge Consumer Fraud
    Division
(602) 271-4266

ARKANSAS

Honorable Ray Thornton
Attorney General of Arkansas
Justice Building
Little Rock, Arkansas 72201
(501) 376-3871

Robert Moorehead
Assistant Attorney General in
    Charge Consumer
    Protection
(501) 376-3871

CALIFORNIA

Honorable Evelle Younger
Attorney General of
    California

500 Wells Fargo Bank
    Building
Sacramento, California 95814
(916) 445-4334 (Sacramento)
(213) 620-2600 (Los
    Angeles)

Robert O'Brien
Senior Assistant Attorney
    General
Consumer Protection Office
600 State Building
Los Angeles, California
    90012
(213) 620-2494

Donald Livingston, Director
Consumer Affairs Department
1020 N Street
Sacramento, California 95814
(916) 445-4465

COLORADO

Honorable Duke W. Dunbar
Attorney General of Colorado
104 State Capitol
Denver, Colorado 80203
(303) 892-2542

C. Patrick Carrico
Assistant Attorney General
Office of Consumer Affairs
503 Farmers Union Building
1575 Sherman Street
Denver, Colorado 80203
(303) 892-3501

CONNECTICUT

Honorable Barbara Dunn,
    Commissioner
Department of Consumer
    Protection
State Office Building
Hartford, Connecticut 06115
(203) 566-4999

Arthur James
Director, Consumer Frauds
   Division
(203) 566-3822

DELAWARE

Honorable W. Laird Stabler
   Jr.
Attorney General of Delaware
Public Building
Wilmington, Delaware 19801
(302) 658-6641

Mason E. Turner
Deputy Attorney General,
   Consumer Protection
   Division
1206 King Street
Wilmington, Delaware 19801
(302) 658-6641

Robert Halbrook, Secretary
Department of Community
   Affairs and Economic
   Development
Old State House
Dover, Delaware 19901
(302) 678-4000

Frances West, Director
Division of Consumer Affairs
704 Delaware Avenue
Wilmington, Delaware 19801
(302) 658-9251

FLORIDA

Honorable Robert L. Shevin
Attorney General of Florida
State Capitol
Tallahassee, Florida 32304
(904) 222-3440

Louie Wainwright Jr.
Executive Assistant to

the Attorney General
(904) 222-3440

Honorable Doyle Conner
Commissioner of Agriculture
State Capitol
Tallahassee, Florida 32304
(904) 599-7345

Robert Bishop, Director
Division of Consumer Affairs
Florida Department of Agri-
   culture and Consumer
   Services
State Capitol
Tallahassee, Florida 32304
(904) 599-7284

GEORGIA

Bob Longenecker, Program
   Director
Georgia Consumer Services
   Program
15 Peachtree Street, Room 909
Atlanta, Georgia 30303
(404) 656-2141

HAWAII

Honorable Jann L. Yuen
Director of Consumer
   Protection
Office of the Governor
P.O. Box 3767
Honolulu, Hawaii 96811
(808) 531-5995

IDAHO

Honorable W. Anthony Park
Attorney General of Idaho
State Capitol
Boise, Idaho 83707
(208) 384-2400

Richard Greener
Assistant Attorney General in
   Charge, Consumer Protection Division
(208) 384-2400

ILLINOIS

Honorable William J. Scott
Attorney General of Illinois
160 North LaSalle Street
Chicago, Illinois 60601
(312) 793-2500

Howard Kaufman
Assistant Attorney General
   and Chief, Consumer
   Fraud Section
134 North LaSalle Street,
   Room 204
Chicago, Illinois 60602
(312) 793-3580

INDIANA

Honorable Theodore L.
   Sendak
Attorney General of Indiana
219 State House
Indianapolis, Indiana 46204
(317) 633-5512

Robert Smith, Director
Office of Consumer Protection
(317) 633-5512

Sonya Saunders, Director
Consumer Advisory Council
c/o Indiana Department of
   Commerce
336 State House
Indianapolis, Indiana 46204
(317) 633-4228

IOWA

Honorable Richard C. Turner

Attorney General of Iowa
State Capitol
Des Moines, Iowa 50319
(515) 281-5164

Julian B. Garrett
Assistant Attorney General
   and Chief Consumer
   Protection Division
20 E. 13th Court
Des Moines, Iowa 50319
(515) 281-5926

Douglas R. Carlson
Assistant Attorney General
Consumer Protection Division
(515) 281-5926

KANSAS

Honorable Vern Miller
Attorney General of Kansas
State House
Topeka, Kansas 66612
(913) 296-2215

Lance Burr
Assistant Attorney General in
   Charge of Customer
   Protection
(913) 296-2215

KENTUCKY

Honorable John B.
   Breckinridge
Attorney General of Kentucky
State Capitol
Frankfort, Kentucky 40601
(502) 564-4513

Robert V. Bullock
Assistant Attorney General
Consumer Protection Division
(502) 564-3235

Mrs. Oscar Sowards,

Chairman
Citizen's Commission for
   Consumer Protection
State Capitol
Frankfort, Kentucky 40601
(502) 564-6607

Robert L. Caummisar
Executive Director
(502) 564-6607

MAINE

Honorable James S. Erwin
Attorney General of Maine
State House
Augusta, Maine 04330
(207) 289-3661

John E. Quinn
Assistant Attorney General
Consumer Protection Division
(207) 289-3716

P. J. Perrino, Jr.
Assistant Attorney General
Consumer Protection Division
(207) 289-3716

MARYLAND

Honorable Francis B. Burch
Attorney General of Maryland
1200 One Charles Center
Baltimore, Maryland 21201
(301) 383-3722

John Ruth
Assistant Attorney General
   and Chief, Consumer
   Protection Division
(301) 383-3713

MASSACHUSETTS

Honorable Robert H. Quinn

Attorney General of
   Massachusetts
State House
Boston, Massachusetts 02133
(617) 727-2200

Laurence R. Buxbaum
Acting Chief, Consumer
   Protection Division
(617) 727-5520

Dermot P. Shea
Executive Secretary
Massachusetts Consumers'
   Council
State Office Building
100 Cambridge Street
Boston, Massachusetts 02202
(617) 727-2605

MICHIGAN

Honorable Frank J. Kelley
Attorney General of Michigan
Law Building
Lansing, Michigan 48902
(517) 373-1110

Edwin M. Bladen
Assistant Attorney General in
   Charge of Consumer
   Protection
(517) 373-1152

Charles Harmon
Special Assistant to the
   Governor for Consumer
   Affairs
1033 S. Washington Street
Lansing, Michigan 48910
(517) 373-1870

Professor William Morrison,
   Chairman
Michigan Consumer Council
525 Hollister Building

293

Lansing, Michigan 48933
(517) 373-0947

Dianne McKaig
Executive Director
(517) 373-0947

MINNESOTA

Honorable Warren Spannaus
Attorney General of
    Minnesota
102 State Capitol
St. Paul, Minnesota 55101
(612) 221-6196

Theodore N. May
Special Assistant Attorney
    General for Consumer
    Protection
(612) 221-3854

Sherry Chenoweth, Director
Office of Consumer Services
Dept. of Commerce,
    Room 230
State Office Building
St. Paul, Minnesota 55101
(612) 221-2162

MISSISSIPPI

Honorable A. F. Summer
Attorney General of
    Mississippi
State Capitol
Jackson, Mississippi 39201
(601) 354-7130

Marshall G. Bennett
Assistant Attorney General in
    Charge of Consumer
    Protection
(601) 354-7134

Linda Gray Dickey

Consumer Protection Division
Dept. of Agriculture &
    Commerce
Jackson, Mississippi 39205
(601) 354-6586

MISSOURI

Honorable John C. Danforth
Attorney General of Missouri
Supreme Court Building
Jefferson City, Missouri 65101
(314) 636-7131

Harvey Tettlebaum
Assistant Attorney General
Consumer Protection Division
(314) 636-7131

NEW HAMPSHIRE

Honorable Warren B. Rudmen
Attorney General of New
    Hampshire
State House Annex
Concord, New Hampshire
    03301
(603) 271-3656

Richard A. Hampe
Assistant Attorney General
(603) 271-3641

NEW JERSEY

Honorable George F.
    Kugler Jr.
Attorney General of New
    Jersey
State House Annex
Trenton, New Jersey 08625
(609) 292-4925

Charles J. Irwin, Director
Office of Consumer
    Protection

1100 Raymond Boulevard
Newark, New Jersey 07102
(201) 648-2012

NEW MEXICO

Honorable David Norvell
Attorney General
Supreme Court Building,
  Box 2246
Santa Fe, New Mexico 87501
(505) 827-2844

Charmaine Crown, Director
Consumer Protection Division
(505) 827-5237

NEW YORK

Honorable Louis J. Lefkowitz
Attorney General
The Capitol
Albany, New York 12225
(518) 474-2121 (Albany)
(212) 488-4141 (New York
  City)

Frank Pantalone
Assistant Attorney General
The Capitol
Albany, New York 12225
(518) 474-2121

Barnett Levy
Assistant Attorney General in
  Charge, Consumer Frauds
  and Protection Bureau
80 Centre Street
New York, New York 10013
(212) 488-7450

Lewis B. Stone, Acting
  Director
Consumer Protection Board
380 Madison Avenue
New York, New York 10017

(212) 488-5320

NORTH CAROLINA

Honorable Robert B. Morgan
Attorney General of North
  Carolina
P.O. Box 629
Raleigh, North Carolina
  27602
(919) 829-3377

Gene Benoy
Deputy Attorney General
Consumer Protection Division
(919) 829-7214

Eugene Hafer
Assistant Attorney General
Consumer Protection Division
(919) 829-7741

NORTH DAKOTA

Honorable Helgi Johanneson
Attorney General
The Capitol
Bismarck, North Dakota
  58501
(701) 224-2211

Robert P. Brady
Assistant Attorney General
  Consumer Protection
  Division
(701) 224-2217

OHIO

Honorable William Brown
Attorney General of Ohio
State House Annex
Columbus, Ohio 43215
(614) 469-3376

Henry E. Helling III

Assistant Attorney General
and Chief, Consumer
Frauds and Crimes Section
(614) 469-4986

OKLAHOMA

Richard L. Wheatley Jr.
Administrator
Department of Consumer
Affairs
Lincoln Office Plaza, Suite 74
4545 Lincoln Boulevard
Oklahoma City, Oklahoma
73105
(405) 521-3653

OREGON

Honorable Lee Johnson
Attorney General of Oregon
322 State Office Building
Salem, Oregon 97310
(503) 378-6368

Edward A. Nugent, Special
Assistant Attorney General
for Antitrust and Consumer
Protection
(503) 378-4733

James R. Faulstich
Assistant to the Governor for
Economic Development
and Consumer Services
State Capitol Building
Salem, Oregon 97301
(503) 378-3015

PENNSYLVANIA

Honorable Shane Creamer
Attorney General of
Pennsylvania
238 Capitol Building

Harrisburg, Pennsylvania
17120
(717) 787-3391

Joel Weisberg, Director
Bureau of Consumer
Protection
Pennsylvania Dept. of Justice
2-4 N. Market Square
Harrisburg, Pennsylvania
17101
(717) 787-7109

RHODE ISLAND

Honorable Richard Israel
Attorney General of Rhode
Island
Providence County Court
House
Providence, Rhode Island
02903
(401) 831-6850

S. A. Alessandro, Chief
Assistant of Consumer
Affairs, Consumer Affairs
Section
(401) 831-6850

Edwin P. Palumbo
Executive Director
Rhode Island Consumers'
Council
365 Broadway
Providence, Rhode Island
02902
(401) 277-2764

SOUTH DAKOTA

Honorable George Mydland
Attorney General of South
Dakota
State Capitol
Pierre, South Dakota 57501

(605) 224-3215
John S. DeVany
Commissioner
Office of Consumer Affairs
(605) 224-3215

TEXAS

Honorable Crawford C.
  Martin
Attorney General of Texas
Supreme Court Building
Austin, Texas 78711
'512) 475-2501

Robert E. Owen
Assistant Attorney General
  and Chief, Antitrust and
  Consumer Protection
  Division
Capitol Station, P.O. Box
  12548
Austin, Texas 78711
(512) 475-3288

Honorable Sam Kelly,
  Commissioner
Office of Consumer Credit
1011 San Jacinto Boulevard
P.O. Box 2107
Austin, Texas 78767
(512) 475-2111

UTAH

Honorable Vernon B.
  Romney
Attorney General of Utah
State Capitol
Salt Lake City, Utah 84114
(801) 328-5261

Bernard Tanner
Assistant Attorney General
  for Consumer Protection
(801) 328-5261

W. S. Brimhall
Administrator of Consumer
  Credit
403 State Capitol
Salt Lake City, Utah 84114
(801) 328-5461

VERMONT

Honorable James M. Jeffords
Attorney General of Vermont
State Library Building
Montpelier, Vermont 05602
(802) 223-2311

William A. Gilbert
Assistant Attorney General in
  Charge, Consumer
  Protection Bureau
94 Church Street
Burlington, Vermont 05401
(802) 864-0111

Faith Pryor
Family Economics and Home
  Management Specialist
Room 210, Terrill Hall
University of Vermont
Burlington, Vermont 05401
(802) 656-3280

VIRGINIA

Honorable Andrew P. Miller
Attorney General of Virginia
Supreme Court-Library
  Building
Richmond, Virginia 23219
(703) 770-2071

William T. Lehner
Assistant Attorney General
(703) 770-3518

William B. Robertson
Special Assistant to the

Governor on Minority
Groups and Consumer
Affairs
Office of the Governor
Richmond, Virginia 23219
(703) 770-2211

Roy L. Farmer
Administrator, Consumer
Affairs
Department of Agriculture
and Commerce
8th Street Office Building
Richmond, Virginia 23219
(703) 770-2042

WASHINGTON

Honorable Slade Gorton
Attorney General of
Washington
Temple of Justice
Olympia, Washington 98501
(206) 753-6200

William H. Clarke
Deputy Attorney General and
Chief, Consumer Protection
and Antitrust Division
1266 Dexter Horton Building
Seattle, Washington 98104
(206) 464-7744

WEST VIRGINIA

Honorable Chauncey H.
Browning
Attorney General of West
Virginia
The Capitol
Charleston, West Virginia
25305
(304) 348-2021

James G. Anderson III
Assistant Attorney General

(304) 348-3377

David Griffith, Director
Consumer Protection Division
West Virginia Dept. of Labor
1900 Washington Street, East
Charleston, West Virginia
25305
(304) 348-2195

WISCONSIN

Honorable Robert W. Warren
Attorney General of
Wisconsin
Department of Justice
Madison, Wisconsin 53702
(608) 266-1221

Camille Haney
Consumer Affairs Coordinator
(608) 266-7340

Claire L. Jackson
Administrator, Trade Division
Department of Agriculture
801 W. Badger Road
Madison, Wisconsin 53713
(608) 266-2225

Dan Milan, Director
Bureau of Consumer
Protection
(608) 266-7228

WYOMING

Dwight D. Bonham
State Examiner and Adminis-
trator Consumer Credit
Code
State Supreme Court Building
Cheyenne, Wyoming 82001
(307) 777-7797

County Consumer Offices

SANTA CLARA COUNTY, CALIFORNIA

Robert Horger, Director
Santa Clara County Department of Weights and
    Measures and Consumer
    Affairs
Division of Consumer Affairs
409 Matthew Street
Santa Clara, California 95050
(408) 299-2105

VENTURA COUNTY, CALIFORNIA

Everett H. Black, Director
Division of Consumer Affairs
Department of Weights and
    Measures
608 El Rio Drive
Oxnard, California 93030
(805) 487-5511

DADE COUNTY, FLORIDA

John C. Mays, Director
Consumer Protection Division
1351 North West 12th Street
Miami, Florida 33125
(305) 377-5111

Herbert Klein
Assistant State Attorney and
Chief, Consumer Fraud
    Division
Metropolitan Dade County
    Justice Building
1351 North West 12th Street
Miami, Florida 33125
(305) 371-7671

SEDGWICK COUNTY, KANSAS

David P. Calvert
Deputy County Attorney and
    Director, Consumer
    Protection Division
Courthouse
Wichita, Kansas 67203
(316) 268-7405

PRINCE GEORGES COUNTY, MARYLAND

Eileen Brandenberg, Executive
    Secretary
Consumer Protection Division
Prince Georges County Court
    House
Upper Marlboro, Maryland
    20870
(301) 627-3000

CAMDEN COUNTY, NEW JERSEY

Carol J. Brooks, Director
Camden County Office of
    Consumer Affairs,
    Room 606
Commerce Building, #1
    Broadway
Camden, New Jersey 08101
(609) 964-8700

NASSAU COUNTY. NEW YORK

James Picken, Commissioner
Office of Consumer Affairs
160 Old Country Road
Mineola, New York 11501
(516) 535-3286

ORANGE COUNTY, NEW YORK

James A. Van Zetta, Director
Department of Weights and
     Measures and Office of
     Consumer Affairs
County of Orange
Goshen, New York 10924
(914) 294-5822

MULTNOMAH COUNTY, OREGON

Scott W. Bennett II, Director
Metropolitan Consumer
     Protection Agency
Multnomah County Court
     House
Portland, Oregon 97204
(503) 224-8840

ALLEGHENY COUNTY, PENNSYLVANIA

Donna Deaner, Director
Allegheny County Bureau of
     Consumer Protection
209 Jones Law Building
     Annex
Pittsburgh, Pennsylvania
     15219
(412) 355-5402

City Consumer Offices

BOSTON

Marian Ego, Chairman
Boston Consumer's Council
218 Weld Avenue
West Roxbury, Massachusetts
     02119
(617) 323-5291

CHICAGO

Jane Byrne, Commissioner
Department of Consumer
     Sales and Weights and
     Measures
City Hall, 121 North LaSalle
     Street
Chicago, Illinois 60602
(312) 744-4091

COLUMBUS, OHIO

Richard Mercurio
City Scaler of Weights and
     Measures
City Hall
Columbus, Ohio 43215
(614) 461-7397

DETROIT

Joseph Vitt, Director
Interagency Consumer
     Commission
Office of the Mayor
City Hall
Detroit, Michigan 48226
(313) 224-3440

JACKSONVILLE, FLORIDA

Thatcher Walt, Consumer
    Affairs Officer
Division of Consumer Affairs
Department of Public Safety
220 East Bay Street
Jacksonville, Florida 32202
(904) 356-5432

LONG BEACH, NEW YORK

Sylvia Rosenberg, Director
Consumer Affairs
City Hall
Long Beach, Long Island,
    New York 11561
(516) 431-1000

LOS ANGELES

Robert E. O'Brien, Chairman
Consumer Protection Commit-
    tee of the City of Los
    Angeles
City Hall, Room 303
Los Angeles, California 90013
(213) 485-3304

LOUISVILLE

James Oslin, Supervisor
Division of Weights and
    Measures and Consumer
    Affairs
Metropolitan Sewer District
    Building, 2nd Floor
Louisville, Kentucky 40202
(502) 582-2206

NEW YORK

Honorable Elinor Guggen-
    heimer, Commissioner
Department of Consumer
    Affairs
80 Lafayette Street
New York, New York 10013
(212) 566-5456

PHILADELPHIA

Faye Forman, Director
Consumer Services
City Hall, Room 210
Philadelphia, Pennsylvania
    19106
(215) 686-2797

ST. LOUIS

Brick Storts, Chairman
Citizens Consumer Advisory
    Committee
7701 Forsyth Boulevard
Clayton, Missouri 63104
(314) 863-4654

ST. PETERSBURG

William M. Bateman Jr.
Director of Consumer Affairs
264 First Avenue, North
St. Petersburg, Florida 33701
(813) 894-1392

VIRGINIA BEACH

Robert Loher
Consumer Protection Officer
Bureau of Consumer
    Protection
Inspections Division, City
    Hall

Virginia Beach, Virginia
  23456
(703) 427-4421

Consumer Protection Coordinating Committees

BOSTON

John F. McCarty, Chairman
Boston Metropolitan
  Consumer Protection
  Committee
c/o Federal Trade
  Commission
J. F. Kennedy Federal
  Building
Government Center
Boston, Massachusetts 02203
(617) 223-6621

CHICAGO

Nathan P. Owen, Secretary
Chicago Consumer Protection
  Committee
Room 486, U.S. Courthouse
  & Federal Office Building
219 South Dearborn Street
Chicago, Illinois 60604
(312) 353-4423

DETROIT

Honorable Frank J. Kelly,
  Chairman
Detroit Consumer Protection
  Coordinating Committee
c/o Law Building
Lansing, Michigan 48902
(517) 373-1110

LOS ANGELES

Donald Hauptman, Chairman
Los Angeles Consumer
  Protection Committee
107 South Broadway
Los Angeles, California
  90012
(213) 620-4360

NEW ORLEANS

Patrick D. Breeden, Chairman
New Orleans Consumer
  Protection Committee
1000 Masonic Temple
  Building
333 St. Charles Street
New Orleans, Louisiana 70130
(504) 527-2041

PHILADELPHIA

Charles J. Taggert, Secretary
Philadelphia Consumer
  Protection Committee
53 Long Lane
Upper Darby, Pennsylvania
  19082
(215) 852-9365

SAN FRANCISCO

L. Neil Gendel, Chairman
Bay Area Consumer
  Protection Coordinating
  Committee
c/o Department of Justice
6000 State Building
San Francisco, California
  94102
(415) 557-2544

Some Laws You Should Know About

EXPRESS AND IMPLIED WARRANTIES ON GOODS THAT YOU BUY: The Uniform Commercial Code, which almost every state has adopted, has several sections on warranties that every consumer should be aware of.

UCC Section 2–313 Express Warranties

(1) Express warranties by the seller are created as follows:
(a) Any affirmation of fact or promise made by the seller to the buyer which relates to the goods and becomes part of the basis of the bargain creates an express warranty that the goods shall conform to the affirmation or promise.
(h) Any description of the goods which is made part of the basis of the bargain creates an express warranty that the goods shall conform to the description.
(c) Any sample or model which is made part of the basis of the bargain creates an express warranty that the whole of the goods shall conform to the sample or model.
(2) It is not necesary to the creation of an express warranty that the seller use formal words such as "warrant" or "guar-

antee" or that he have a specific intention to make a warranty, but an affirmation merely of the value of the goods or a statement purporting to be merely the seller's opinion or commendation of the goods does not create a warranty.

UCC Section 2–314
Implied Warranty of Merchantability

(1) Unless excluded or modified (see UCC Section 2–316), a warranty that the goods shall be merchantable is implied in a contract for their sale if the seller is a merchant with respect to goods of that kind. . . .

(2) Goods to be merchantable must be at least such as

(a) Pass without objection in the trade under the contract description; and

(b) In the case of fungible goods are of fair average quality within the description; and

(c) Are fit for the ordinary purposes for which such goods are used; and

(d) Run, within the variations permitted by the agreement, of even kind, quality and quantity . . .; and

(e) Are adequately contained, packaged and labeled as the agreement may require; and

(f) Conform to the promises or affirmations of fact made on the container or label if any.

UCC Section 2–315
Implied Warranty of Fitness for Purpose

Where the seller at the time of contract has reason to know any particular purpose for which the goods are required and that the buyer is relying on the seller's skill or judgement to select or furnish suitable goods, there is unless excluded or modified under Section 2–316 an implied warranty that the goods shall be fit for such purposes.

UCC Section 2–316
Exclusion or Modification of Warranties

(1) Words or conduct relevant to the creation of an express warranty and words or conduct tending to negate or limit such warranties shall be construed wherever reasonable

as consistent with each other; but subject to UCC Section 2–207 negation or limitation is inoperative to the extent that such construction is unreasonable.

(2) Subject to subsection (3), to exclude or modify the implied warranty of merchantability or any part of it, the language must mention merchantability and in case of a writing must be conspicuous, and to exclude or modify any implied warranty of fitness the exclusion must be by a writing and conspicuous. Language to exclude all implied warranties of fitness is sufficient if it states, for example, that "There are no warranties which extend beyond the description on the face hereof."

(3) Notwithstanding subsection (2), (a) unless the circumstances indicate otherwise, all implied warranties are excluded by expressions like "as is," "with all faults" or other language which in common understanding calls the buyer's attention to the exclusion of warranties and makes plain that there is no implied warranty; and (b) when the buyer before entering into the contract has examined the goods or the sample or model as fully as he desired or has refused to examine the goods, there is no implied warranty with regard to defects which an examination ought, in the circumstances, to have revealed to him.

FEDERAL FAIR CREDIT REPORTING ACT, enacted in 1971, was passed by Congress to protect consumers against the circulation of inaccurate or obsolete information and to insure that credit bureaus exercise their responsibilites in a manner that is fair and equitable to consumers.

The Act means that you can take steps to protect yourself if you have been denied credit, insurance, or employment, or if you believe you have had other difficulties because of a credit report on you.

You Have the Right

1. To be told the name and address of the credit agency responsible for the report that was used to deny you credit, insurance, or employment or to increase your cost of credit or insurance.

2. To be told by a credit agency the nature, substance,

305

and sources (except investigative-type sources) of the information (except medical) collected about you.

3. To take anyone of your choice with you when you visit the credit bureau to check on your file.

4. To obtain all information to which you are entitled, free of charge, when you have been denied credit, insurance, or employment, within thirty days of your interview. Otherwise, the credit bureau is permitted to charge a reasonable fee for giving you the information.

5. To be told who has received a report on you within the preceding six months, or within the preceding two years if the report was furnished for employment purposes.

6. To have incomplete or incorrect information re-investigated, unless the request is frivolous, and, if the information is found to be inaccurate or cannot be verified, to have such information removed from your file.

7. To have the agency notify those you name (at no cost to you), who have previously received the incorrect or incomplete information, that this information has been deleted from your file.

8. When a dispute between you and the reporting agency about information in your file cannot be resolved, you have the right to have your version of such dispute placed in the file and included in future credit reports.

9. To request the credit bureau to send your version of the dispute to certain businesess for a reasonable fee.

10. To have a credit report withheld from anyone who under the law does not have a legitimate business need for the new information.

11. To sue a credit bureau for damages if it willfully or negligently violates the law and, if you are successful, you can collect attorney's fees and court costs.

12. Not to have adverse information reported after seven years. One major exception is bankruptcy, which may be reported for fourteen years.

13. To be notified by a business that it is seeking a credit report about you which would include interviews with third persons about your character, reputation, or manner of living. Also, to request from such business that it disclose to you the nature and scope of the investigation into your character, reputation, or manner of living and to discover the nature and substance (but not the sources) of the information collected about you from third persons.

You Do Not Have the Right

1. To request a report on yourself from the credit bureau.
2. When you visit the credit bureau, to receive a copy of or to physically handle your file.
3. To compel a lender or insurance company or any other type of business or employer to do business with you.
4. To apply the Fair Credit Reporting Act when you seek commercial (as distinguished from consumer) credit or business insurance.
5. To request the intervention of any federal agency on your behalf.

How to Exercise Your Rights with Credit Bureaus

If you want to know what information a credit agency has collected about you, either arrange for a personal interview at the agency's office during normal business hours or call in advance for an interview by telephone.

The credit bureaus in your community can be located by consulting the Yellow Pages under "Credit" or "Credit Rating or Reporting Agencies."

If you decide to visit a credit bureau to check on your file, the following check list may be of help.

1. Learn the nature and substance of all the information in your file.
2. Find out the names of each of the businesses (or other sources) that supplied information on you to the reporting agency.
3. Learn the names of everyone who received reports on you within the past six months (or the last two years if the reports were for employment purposes).
4. Request the agency to re-evaluate and correct or delete information that was found to be inaccurate, incomplete, or obsolete.
5. Follow up to determine the results of the re-investigation.
6. Ask the bureau, at no cost to you, to notify those you name who received reports within the past six months (two years if for employment purposes) that certain information was deleted.

7. Follow up to make sure that those named by you did in fact receive notices from the credit bureau.

8. Demand that your version of the facts be placed in your file if the re-investigation did not settle the dispute.

9. Request the agency (if you are willing to pay a reasonable fee) to send your statement of the dispute to those you name who received reports containing the disputed information within the past six months (two years if received for employment purposes).

Index

310

About The Authors

Bruce Goldman, graduate of Columbia University, copy chief at a New York advertising agency, and race car enthusiast, has developed his expertise in the art of deficit spending throughout a long history of redressing grievances. A consumer in the know, he fights a never-ending battle for truth, justice, and his rights with such adversaries as the telephone company, various oil concerns, and American Express. He maintains an uneasy alliance with his landlord, whom he frequently and happily meets in court.

Robert Franklin is proprietor of a New York recording and production firm. While renovating and equipping his opulent studio and townhouse, he perfected many of the skills described in this book.

Ken Pepper is an attorney who often finds himself on the debtor's side in collection cases.

THE BEST OF THE BESTSELLERS FROM WARNER BOOKS

REELING
by Pauline Kael (83-420, $2.95)
Rich, varied, 720 pages containing 74 brilliant pieces covering the period between 1972-75, this is the fifth collection of movie criticism by the film critic *Newsday* calls "the most accomplished practitioner of film criticism in America today, and possibly the most important film critic this country has ever produced."

P.S. YOUR CAT IS DEAD
by James Kirkwood (82-934, $2.25)
It's New Year's Eve. Your best friend died in September. You've been robbed twice. Your girlfriend is leaving you. You've just lost your job. And the only one left to talk to is a gay burglar you've got tied up in the kitchen.

ELVIS
by Jerry Hopkins (81-665, $2.50)
More than 2 million copies sold! It's Elvis as he really was, from his humble beginnings to fame and fortune. It's Elvis the man and Elvis the performer, with a complete listing of his records, his films, a thorough astrological profile, and 32 pages of rare, early photographs!

A STRANGER IN THE MIRROR
by Sidney Sheldon (81-940, $2.50)
Toby Temple is a lonely, desperate superstar. Jill Castle is a disillusioned girl, still dreaming of stardom and carrying a terrible secret. This is their love story. A brilliant, compulsive tale of emotions, ambitions, and machinations in that vast underworld called Hollywood.

STAINED GLASS
by William F. Buckley, Jr. (82-323, $2.25)
The United States must stop a war with one man and one man alone. His name: Blackford Oakes, super agent. His mission: Kill his friend for the good of the world. This is Buckley at his spy thriller best, with the most daring, seductive, and charming hero since 007.

THE BEST OF BESTSELLERS
FROM WARNER BOOKS

BLOODLINE
by Sidney Sheldon (85-205, $2.75)
The Number One Bestseller by the author of THE OTHER SIDE OF
MIDNIGHT and A STRANGER IN THE MIRROR. "Exotic, confident,
knowledgeable, mysterious, romantic . . . a story to be quickly
and robustly told and pleasurably consumed."—Los Angeles
Times.

SCRUPLES
by Judith Krantz (85-641, $2.75)
The most titillating, name-dropping, gossipy, can't-put-it-down #1
bestseller of the decade. The fascinating story of one woman
who went after everything she wanted—fame, wealth, power,
love—and got it all!

ALIEN
by Alan Dean Foster (82-977, $2.25)
Astronauts encounter an awesome galactic horror on a distant
planet. But it is only when they take off again that the real horror
begins. For the Alien is now within the ship, within the crew itself.
And a classic deathtrap suspense begins.